iLife® '11 FOR DUMMIES

by Tony Bove

WILEY

Wiley Publishing, Inc.

iLife® '11 For Dummies®

Published by
Wiley Publishing, Inc.
111 River Street
Hoboken, NJ 07030-5774

www.wiley.com

For general information on our other products and services, please contact our Customer Care Department within the U.S. at 877-762-2974, outside the U.S. at 317-572-3993, or fax 317-572-4002.

For technical support, please visit www.wiley.com/techsupport.

Wiley also publishes its books in a variety of electronic formats. Some content that appears in print may not be available in electronic books.

Library of Congress Control Number: 2010943063

ISBN: 978-0-470-58172-8

Manufactured in the United States of America

10 9 8 7 6 5 4 3 2 1

WILEY

About the Author

Tony Bove loves the iLife and provides free tips on his Web site (www.
tonybove.com). He has written more than two dozen books on comput-
ing, desktop publishing, and multimedia, including *iPod touch For Dummies,
iPod & iTunes For Dummies, The GarageBand Book, The iLife Book* (all
from Wiley), *Just Say No to Microsoft* (No Starch Press), *The Art of Desktop
Publishing* (Bantam), and a series of books about Macromedia Director,
Adobe Illustrator, and PageMaker. In addition to developing an iPhone
application *(Tony's Tips for iPhone Users),* he founded *Desktop Publishing/
Publish* magazine and the *Inside Report on New Media* newsletter, and wrote
the weekly Macintosh column for *Computer Currents* for a decade, as well as
articles for *NeXTWORLD,* the *Chicago Tribune* Sunday Technology Section,
and *NewMedia*. Tracing the personal computer revolution back to the 1960s
counterculture, Tony produced a CD-ROM interactive documentary in 1996,
Haight-Ashbury in the Sixties (featuring music from the Grateful Dead, Janis
Joplin, and Jefferson Airplane). He also developed the Rockument music
site, www.rockument.com, with commentary and podcasts focused on rock
music history. As a founding member of the Flying Other Brothers, which
toured professionally and released three commercial CDs (*52-Week High, San
Francisco Sounds,* and *Estimated Charges*), Tony performed with Hall of Fame
rock musicians. He has also worked as a director of enterprise marketing for
leading-edge software companies, as a marketing messaging consultant, and
as a communications director and technical publications manager.

Dedication

This book is dedicated to my sons, and my nieces, nephews, their cousins, and all their children . . . the iLife generation.

Author's Acknowledgments

I want to thank my Wilcy project editor, Rebecca Huehls, for having the patience of a saint while pulling this project through the process on time. I also thank Wiley copy editor Rebecca Whitney for work that made my job so much easier. Many thanks to my technical editor Dennis Cohen for helping to make this book useful and more accurate. I also thank Rich Tennant for his sidesplitting cartoons. A book of this size places a considerable burden on a publisher's production team, and I thank Production crew at Wiley for diligence beyond the call of reason.

I owe thanks and a happy hour or two to Carole Jelen at Waterside, my agent. And I have editors Bob Woerner and Kyle Looper at Wiley to thank for coming up with the idea for this book and helping me to become a professional dummy — that is, a *For Dummies* author.

Finally, my heartfelt thanks to Jay Blakesberg for his photos, Kathy Pennington for support, and members of my band, the Flying Other Brothers (Pete Sears, Barry Sless, Jimmy Sanchez, TBone Tony Bove, Bill Bennett, Bert Keely, and Roger and Ann McNamee) as well as Stacy Parrish, Howard Danchik, Vickie Garwacki, Chris Flum, Paul Dulany, and DuCharme for letting me use their photographs of the band.

Publisher's Acknowledgments

We're proud of this book; please send us your comments at http://dummies.custhelp.com. For other comments, please contact our Customer Care Department within the U.S. at 877-762-2974, outside the U.S. at 317-572-3993, or fax 317-572-4002.

Some of the people who helped bring this book to market include the following:

Acquisitions and Editorial

Project Editor: Rebecca Huehls

Acquisitions Editor: Kyle Looper

Copy Editor: Rebecca Whitney

Technical Editor: Dennis Cohen

Editorial Manager: Leah P. Cameron

Editorial Assistant: Amanda Graham

Sr. Editorial Assistant: Cherie Case

Cartoons: Rich Tennant
(www.the5thwave.com)

Composition Services

Project Coordinator: Sheree Montgomery

Layout and Graphics: Timothy C. Detrick

Proofreader: The Well-Chosen Word

Indexer: Sharon Shock

Special Art: Corbis Digital Stock, page 419

Publishing and Editorial for Technology Dummies

    Richard Swadley, Vice President and Executive Group Publisher

    Andy Cummings, Vice President and Publisher

    Mary Bednarek, Executive Acquisitions Director

    Mary C. Corder, Editorial Director

Publishing for Consumer Dummies

    Diane Graves Steele, Vice President and Publisher

Composition Services

    Debbie Stailey, Director of Composition Services

Table of Contents

Introduction

· ·

*R*emember the Nowhere Man from the Beatles' classic animated movie *Yellow Submarine?* He was the nerdy little fellow always going round in circles, writing books, making music, taking pictures, directing plays, and making movies, always so very busy. But he was also very sad because no one could see his work; the Blue Meanies had taken art away from the people. Nowhere Man just sat in his nowhere land, making nowhere plans for nobody. But as John Lennon pointed out, "Isn't he a bit like you and me?"

With this suite of software tools, the world is at your command. All your digital assets — your photos, your songs, your videos, everything — are at your fingertips. The iLife software brings together all your digital assets so that you can use them for creative projects and manage them for the rest of your real life.

A day in the iLife might include shooting photos and video clips and transferring them from your digital camera or iPhone into your iPhoto library to share with friends by e-mail. You might want to assemble a slideshow of the photos in iPhoto and set it to music in the iTunes library you created in GarageBand and post it on your new Web page designed with iWeb. You can then bring video footage from your DV camcorder into iMovie and make a music video with all these elements. Finally, you can use iDVD to assemble the music video and the slideshow, along with eye-popping menus to navigate them, and burn a disc that your friends can play on an everyday DVD player. You can find all this and more in this book.

Now you're getting somewhere, man.

About This Book

The publishers are wise about book matters, and they helped me design this book as a reference. You can easily find the information you need when you need it. I wrote it so that you can read from beginning to end to find out how to use the iLife applications from scratch. But this book is also organized so that you can dive in anywhere and begin reading the information you need to know for each task.

I didn't have enough pages to cover every detail of every function, and I intentionally left out some detail so that you won't be befuddled with techno-speak when it isn't necessary. I wrote brief but comprehensive descriptions and included lots of cool tips on how to get the best results from iLife.

At the time I wrote this book, I covered the latest version of each iLife application. Although I did my best to keep up for this print edition, Apple occasionally slips in a new version between book editions. If your version of the iLife applications looks a little different, be sure to check out the book's companion Web site for updates on the latest releases from Apple, as well as the Tips section of my Web site (www.tonybove.com) for free tips.

Conventions Used in This Book

Like any book about computers, this book uses certain conventions.

When I write "Choose iPhoto⇨Preferences," you should open the iPhoto menu from the toolbar (in iPhoto) and then select the Preferences menu item. Some menus have selections that are submenus with more choices. Okay, that's fairly simple, but some commands are long and complicated, such as View⇨Sort Photos⇨By Keyword. If I wrote out every command, this book would be much longer. In an effort to save paper, ink, and your money, I use the command arrows.

It's a relief that we're mostly beyond having to type commands into a computer, even if we have to use some kind of pointing device that may be rodent-like in appearance as well as in name. You can use a one-button mouse or touchpad to do just about everything on a Mac. When I write "Click the Edit tool on the toolbar," you should move the pointer on the screen to the Edit icon on the toolbar and click the button.

Clicking once isn't the only way to use a pointing device such as a mouse or touchpad. When I write "Drag the photo over the name of the album," you move the pointer over the photo, hold down the mouse or touchpad button, and drag the pointer over to the name of the album before lifting your finger off the button.

Sometimes I abbreviate the instruction "click the thumbnail of a picture" to "select the picture." For example, when I write "Select a picture," I mean click the thumbnail so that it's selected. When I write "select the photo album in the Source pane," you click the name of the photo album in the Source pane. At other times, I combine the click-and-drag function — I write "scroll the list in the Source pane" to indicate clicking and dragging the scroll bar for the Source pane window to scroll the list.

Foolish Assumptions

Contrary to popular belief (and rumors circulated by the Blue Meanies), you *don't* need the following to use any of the applications (or this book):

- **A pile of cash for extra equipment and software:** Yes, you need a digital camera for iPhoto, a digital camcorder for iMovie, and a DVD-R drive for iDVD, but you can get all of this, including an iMac with a SuperDrive for DVD-R, for less than $1,200, which is about one-twentieth of what it cost to do the same in 1999. And you don't need any extra software — every important piece of software we describe in this book is either already on your Mac or available for free from the Apple Web site, www. apple.com.

- **A better education:** Courses in film, photography, and music can't hurt, but iLife is designed for the rest of us air-guitar players who barely know the difference between a video clip and a still image. You don't need any specialized knowledge to have a lot of fun with this software while building your digital assets.

- **A tech support hotline:** Never do I feel the need to contact the Apple technical support team. Everything works as it should. I pinch myself daily for this apparent miracle. I never have to wade through inscrutable documentation, either — the built-in help is informative and useful (which you certainly don't need if you have this book).

The iLife software is free, supplied with every Mac. That's really all the software you need.

However, I do make some honest assumptions about your computer skills:

- **How to use the Mac Finder:** You should already know how to use the Finder to locate files and folders, and how to copy files and folders from one disk to another.

- **How to select menus and applications on a Mac:** You should already know how to choose an option from a Mac menu, how to find the Dock to launch a Dock application, and how to launch an application in the Application folder.

For more information on either topic, see that excellent book by Mark L. Chambers, *Mac OS X Snow Leopard All-in-One For Dummies*.

How This Book Is Organized

This book is organized into five parts, with each part covering a different application: iPhoto, iMovie, iDVD, iWeb, or GarageBand. Here's a quick preview of what you can find in each part.

Part 1: Getting to Know iPhoto

This part provides all you need to know about transferring pictures from a digital camera or iPhone, browsing your pictures, and organizing them to produce prints, photo albums, calendars, cards, and even professional-looking photo books. It shows you how to improve and retouch digital photos, create slideshows, and share photos online and by e-mail.

Part II: Winning an Oscar with iMovie

This part introduces digital video and tells you everything you need to know about using digital camcorders with your Mac to create videos of all kinds, even professional videos. It shows you how to manage video clips, create movies with photos and clips, and even edit soundtracks and special effects. It also covers sharing movies online and saving movies in professional formats.

Part III: Burning Your Releases with iDVD

This part describes how to bring all your digital assets together to create exciting DVD discs that can play in DVD players as well as in computers. You find out how to create interactive menus and buttons and special effects, such as video backgrounds. Burn DVDs like the pros and save all your precious digital assets — photos, music, movies, slideshows — at their highest quality on DVD.

Part IV: Getting Out-a-Site with iWeb

This part explains how to quickly design Web pages; add customizable widgets, maps, blogs, and site navigation; and manage and publish the entire Web site using MobileMe. You learn how to experiment with page templates and make changes to your site while maintaining site security.

Part V: Playing in the GarageBand

This part rocks out with GarageBand, which offers some basic functions of an audio recording studio combined with the magic of synthesized instruments and prerecorded loops. It shows how to use Real Instruments as well as Software Instruments to record musical performances, and the best methods for recording vocals and creating podcasts. I describe the audio effects and simulated amplifiers to improve the sound, and how to use the GarageBand track-mixing functions to produce high-quality music.

Part VI: The Part of Tens

A staple of the *For Dummies* series, the Part of Tens offers top-ten lists sure to ease your path through iLife. In Chapter 23, you find tips I couldn't fit elsewhere in the book on topics including installing iLife applications, sharing photos over a network, shooting video, and more. The focus in Chapter 24 is online resources. Find links and a quick introduction to sources such as Apple support sites and great sites for buying cameras, camcorders, and music gear. The Web is also wonderful resource for troubleshooting tips, and I point you to the best online resources for iLife help.

Icons Used in This Book

The icons in this book are important visual cues for information you need.

The Remember icons highlight important information you should remember.

The Technical Stuff icons highlight technical details you can skip unless you want to bring out the technical geek in you.

Tips highlight tips and techniques that save you time and energy, and maybe money.

Warnings save your butt by preventing disasters. Don't bypass a warning without reading it. This is your only warning!

Where to Go from Here

Feel free to begin reading anywhere or skip particular sections or chapters (or go wild, start on page 1 and continue reading to the index). If you want to know how to tackle a particular task, look it up in the index or table of contents and flip to the page you need. Or, if you want to start finding out about an iLife application, start with that part. This is your book; dive right in.

Part I
Getting to Know iPhoto

The 5th Wave   By Rich Tennant

"I've got some new image editing software, so I took the liberty of erasing some of the smudges that kept showing up around the clouds. No need to thank me."

*P*art I is all about using iPhoto to organize your pictures and produce prints, photo albums, and even professional-looking books. It shows you how to improve and retouch digital photos, create slideshows, and share pictures online and by e-mail.

- Chapter 1 gets you started with iPhoto. You find out what it can do, how to bring in pictures from digital cameras or an iPod touch or iPhone, and import images from scanners and other sources.

- Chapter 2 describes how to browse pictures by event, location, and face, and add dates, location information, and face names to your iPhoto library. You also see how to search and sort your library and add information such as titles and keywords.

- Chapter 3 shows how to organize your pictures into photo albums, make a backup of your library, and burn CDs and DVDs with your pictures.

- Chapter 4 describes the best methods of improving your photos, such as cropping and rotating them, retouching and removing the red-eye effect of flashbulbs, and setting brightness and contrast.

- Chapter 5 gets you started assembling slideshows with your pictures for fun (and profit). It shows you how to set up slide transitions and make timing adjustments as well as set your slideshow to music and share it online and on DVD.

- Chapter 6 is all about sharing pictures online, including sending pictures as e-mail attachments, and sharing pictures on MobileMe and on Web sites.

- Chapter 7 focuses on print, including making prints and greeting cards, and ordering professionally-printed cards, calendars, and photo books.

Gathering All Your Shots

In This Chapter

▶ Finding out which features to look for in digital cameras

▶ Checking out what iPhoto can do for you

▶ Importing pictures into iPhoto

*T*oday, John Lennon might have sung, "Instant camera's gonna get you." Everybody's taking pictures — of each other, of places and things, of items for sale, of events as they happen. Digital cameras come in all sizes and are incorporated into cellphones, iPods, and iPhones. But what happens to all these pictures?

Using iPhoto, you can browse them; improve and retouch them; add the information you need in order to organize them and then print them; use them to make photo prints and professionally printed photo books; and share them over the Internet by e-mail, Facebook, MobileMe, and Flickr. And, you can do much more: iPhoto turns your Mac into a digital darkroom for enhancing the pictures — no need for a real-life darkroom with smelly chemicals and film processing equipment.

This chapter tells you all you need to know about importing photos from digital cameras and the cameras built into iPod and iPhone models, as well as from other sources, such as memory card readers, photo services, and scanners. It also provides an overview of what you can do with iPhoto. You find out how to get around in iPhoto and look at your pictures in detail.

Photography in the Digital World

Everything about digital photography is easier and costs less than traditional film photography. Digital photography is truly instant gratification — you see the results immediately and can then take more pictures based on what happened an instant earlier. Delete bad shots and reshoot them instantly. Copy what you like, delete what you don't like, and above all, keep on shooting.

But the features of digital cameras can be intimidating. Camera buffs speak a different language of f-stops, optical zoom, and fish-eye lenses. If you're an amateur photographer (like I am), you probably don't need to be picky about which camera to buy. You can get excellent results from just about any digital camera, or from the built-in camera of an iPhone or iPod touch. You may want one that also captures video clips — you can bring those video clips right into iPhoto.

Connecting a camera to your Mac

To connect a digital camera to your Mac, the camera must be compatible with the Mac USB (Universal Serial Bus) or FireWire (IEEE 1394) connectors. For example, both my Canon PowerShot SD550 (I know, a relic) and my iPhone connect to USB.

USB is used to connect hundreds of nifty devices to your computer, such as keyboards, pointing devices, external hard drives, keychain-size flash drives, printers, scanners, iPods, and iPhones. USB connectors are plug-and-play: You can plug them in at any time while your computer is on or off. Many of these devices get their power directly from the Mac, through the USB connection.

Like USB, FireWire also supplies power to a device, such as a camera, through the same cable that connects it to the computer. FireWire devices are also plug-and-play.

Many Mac models sport both FireWire and USB 2.0 connectors, but not all cameras support USB 2.0 — the camera still works with the USB 2.0 port, but you get only the slower USB 1.1 transfer rate. USB is the connection of choice for most digital cameras (though some very high-quality cameras may offer FireWire) because digital camera manufacturers need to make cameras that work with all types of computers; most PCs and certain new Mac models, for example, come with USB ports, but they don't have FireWire ports.

TECHNICAL STUFF

More pixels mean higher quality

When digital cameras take a picture, they divide the image in the lens into many tiny squares, or *pixels,* to represent the image. Two characteristics of pixels affect image quality. The first, controlled by the digital camera or scanner, is the *spatial resolution* — the number of pixels in the image (horizontally and vertically). With a pixel dimension of 300 x 300, for example, an image has a total of 90,000 pixels. With a pixel dimension of 1,000 x 1,000, the image has 1 million pixels, or a *megapixel.* The more pixels, or specific points of information in a picture, the more detail is represented.

The second characteristic is the *color resolution* of your display. Macs offer more than 16 million colors (on some Macs, this number is controlled by the Display setting in System Preferences — you can set the Display setting to the Millions option). You see more than 16 million colors because a pixel in a typical image can represent 256 levels of red, green, and blue, which gives a possible tonal range of more than 16 million colors (256 x 256 x 256). A color resolution of lower than Millions can cause the image to appear with splotches of the same color rather than a subtle tonal range of color.

You say you want more resolution?

Image quality is measured by the pixel resolution of the digital camera. For example, the iPhone 4 includes a 5-megapixel camera on the back and a 3-megapixel camera on the front, and the Canon PowerShot SD550 is a 7.1-megapixel camera. You may want to base your choice of digital cameras on features such as higher image resolution or optical zoom.

Resolution defines the number of pixels — specific points of information in a picture. Digital cameras are often described as having a resolution of millions of pixels, or *megapixels.* Higher megapixel counts usually result in better images. A 2-megapixel camera produces acceptable 4-x-6-inch prints. A 3-megapixel camera produces very good 4-x-6-inch prints and near-magazine-quality 8-x-10-inch prints. A 5-megapixel camera produces good quality 10-x-14-inch prints. And so on.

Optical zoom uses the optics (lens) of the camera to bring the subject closer — the full resolution of the camera is still available for the image in the lens. *Digital* zoom, on the other hand, enlarges a portion of the image by cropping a portion of the image and then enlarging it back to size at a lower resolution, losing image quality. Many digital cameras offer both optical and digital zoom, but you don't truly need digital zoom — you can create a digitally zoomed-in version in iPhoto from the original shot by cropping in iPhoto, as I describe in Chapter 4, and get at least as good a result.

Got an iPhone or iPod touch? You can shoot photos and videos with a fourth-generation iPod touch, an iPhone 3GS, or an iPhone 4, and you can shoot photos with older iPhone models. You can shoot in portrait or landscape orientation, and the results are suitable for sharing by e-mail or YouTube. See Table 1-1 for details.

Table 1-1	iPhone and iPod Touch Camera Features		
Model	*Camera*	*Video/Audio*	*Other Digital Imaging Features*
iPod touch (fourth generation)	A camera on the back shoots photos at 960 x 720 pixel resolution. A camera on the front can record VGA-quality (640 x 480) photos.	A camera on the back records HD (720p) video with audio. A camera on the front records standard video with audio. Both record at 30 frames per second.	On the back, it has 5x digital zoom, and you can tap the picture to adjust the exposure for lighting conditions.
iPhone 4	Has a 5-megapixel camera on the back and a camera for shooting VGA-quality photos on the front.	A camera on the back records HD (720p) video with audio. A camera on the front records VGA video with audio. Both record at 30 frames per second.	The back has autofocus, auto-exposure, auto white balance, 5x digital zoom, and LED flash for still images. You can just tap the picture to focus.
iPhone 3GS	Has a 3-megapixel camera	The camera records VGA video with audio at 30 frames per second.	Has autofocus, autoexposure, auto white balance, and 5x digital zoom. You can tap the picture to focus.
iPhone 3G	Has a 2-megapixel camera on the back.	n/a	n/a
Original iPhone	Has a 2-megapixel camera on the back.	n/a	n/a

Backing up your photos

Maybe your vacation photos bore other people (at least, if you show them in a long slideshow), but you believe that they're priceless, preserving special memories. Family pictures, vacations, weddings — these events don't happen every day and you want to preserve your photos of these events. You *don't* want your photos trapped on film or on prints that deteriorate due to age, weather, or environmental factors such as kids with peanut-butter fingers. You want your photos to last forever — and in digital form, they can.

But digital information can be destroyed, too. You might accidentally erase the photos on your camera. Your computer or your hard drive can fail. A virus can take over your computer and wreak havoc, destroying files in the process. Your laptop can be stolen. You may drop the computer while moving. Stuff happens, even in the digital world.

You can protect information in a number of ways:

✔ Using iPhoto, you can create CD and DVD archives, as I describe in Chapter 3.

✔ Upload your photos to the Internet (for example, to a MobileMe, Flickr, or Facebook album, or to a Web site), as I describe in Chapter 6.

✔ You can also copy your entire photo library to another hard drive, as I describe in Chapter 3, or include it in your Time Machine backups (if you use Apple's Time Machine software for backing up your Mac over a network).

What You Can Do with iPhoto

iPhoto acts as your own processing lab and photo service inside your Mac to manage the pictures you import from digital cameras, including video clips from digital cameras. (For managing clips recorded with digital camcorders, see Chapter 8.) You can also use iPhoto to manage graphic images (such as business charts and graphs, images from the Web, or computer screen shots) and scanned images. In this chapter, I refer to everything you can bring into iPhoto as a *picture* — whether it's a photo, graphic image, shot of a computer screen, or video clip (a moving picture).

You can browse all your pictures by events, places, or even faces in the photos, as I describe in Chapter 2, and quickly display them onscreen, in any size ranging from thumbnail to full-screen. You can also keep track of pictures by adding titles, descriptions, keywords, locations, and comments.

The iPhoto photo library holds any number of photos, images, and video clips — limited only by how much space you have on your hard drive. Even if you store thousands and thousands of pictures in your library, you can find the one you want quickly and easily.

Even better, you can organize your pictures by combining sets into photo albums to make them easier to find. In each album, you can arrange the pictures exactly in the sequence you want for slideshows and photo books. iPhoto even offers "smart" albums that, like the "smart" playlists in iTunes, update themselves with new pictures automatically based on the criteria that you set.

Even with professional photographers, the chances that your pictures come out perfect every time are quite slim. Some pictures may not be as vivid as you first thought. That *almost* postcard-perfect view from the highway may show a bit of road litter and guardrail that you want to remove. Or maybe the light was too bright or too dim or the camera's flash put red spots in your subject's eyes (the dreaded red-eye effect).

Fixing these problems is easy in iPhoto, which offers a number of ways to improve and enhance your photos, such as

- **You can instantly correct any photo that's too dark or overexposed.** iPhoto provides editing tools for automatically correcting these problems as well as the red-eye effect.

- **You can crop any image.** *Cropping* is the process in which you draw a smaller rectangle inside the image and omit everything outside the rectangle. You can improve a postcard-perfect view of a scenic stop along a highway by removing, for example, the road litter and guardrail from the bottom edge of the photo.

- **You can change color photos to black-and-white (or, more accurately, *grayscale*) or sepia tone.** Changing the color to grayscale is handy for printing in books, newspapers, newsletters, or documents that don't use color. You can also change a color photo to sepia tone to make the picture look old-timey.

- **You can make blemishes disappear like magic.** You can enhance the entire image, retouch portions of the image, and adjust the colors and saturation levels to make anyone look better.

  You don't have to load any special software to make the kind of improvements to your pictures that make them more effective as photographs. Chapter 4 explains how to make improvements.

- **You can share photos in different ways.** Produce slideshows, photo portfolios, and even nicely bound coffee-table photo books and school yearbooks from iPhoto. All you have to do is organize the pictures in an album, select a theme and a layout, and — bingo — iPhoto creates the book in electronic format. You can then print the pages on your own printer, or order professionally printed and bound books from a service directly from iPhoto. (The service is available not only in the United States but also in Japan and Europe.) In the case of a school yearbook, you can place last-minute pictures into it and still make the graduation-day deadline.

If you're on Facebook, you can change your profile picture and publish photos directly to your wall or to one of your Facebook albums. If your friends leave comments on them, you see the comments in iPhoto. You can even keep track of which photos you shared.

You can also e-mail pictures directly from iPhoto. You can even share entire slideshows with others on the Internet using MobileMe or post photos on Web pages. Essentially, everyone can have a copy of your photos.

I describe slideshows in detail in Chapter 5, and you can read all about printing photos and photo books and sharing photos online in Chapter 6.

Pictures are just the beginning of the iLife experience. iPhoto connects to the other iLife applications, and if you explore them, you'll find uses for your pictures you hadn't thought of, such as creating a DVD of a slideshow using music from your iTunes library or using still images in an iMovie project along with video clips and music.

Saving pictures has never been easier. You can copy your entire iPhoto library to another hard drive or burn CDs or DVDs with your images to keep archives, as I describe in Chapter 3. Archiving saves all the information you have about each picture, including date, album, film roll, keywords, and comments. After you archive your pictures on CD or DVD, you can still view them in iPhoto directly from the disc: When you insert the disc, the archived library on the disc appears automatically in iPhoto with its titles, keywords, and photo albums.

Opening the iPhoto Window

This section provides a tour of iPhoto. If you're using iPhoto for the first time, you won't have pictures in your iPhoto library until you import them, which I cover later in this chapter.

The iPhoto icon is available in the Dock, which appears typically at the bottom of the desktop. To start iPhoto, click the iPhoto icon in the Dock or double-click the iPhoto application in the Applications folder.

When you start iPhoto the first time, iPhoto asks the question `Do you want to use iPhoto when you connect your digital camera?` Click Yes to have iPhoto start up automatically whenever you connect your digital camera. If you click No, iPhoto doesn't start up automatically — you have to explicitly launch iPhoto (or another application) to import photos from your digital camera.

Changing your display settings

When you start iPhoto, you may see the message Caution: The current screen resolution is not optimal for iPhoto. Whether accidentally or intentionally, your color display setting is set to fewer colors than the display can handle, or your display's resolution is set to a lower number than possible. Either one of these settings, if not set to its highest value, causes this message to appear.

If you're unlucky enough to see this message, don't panic. All you need to do is change your display settings. Choose ⌘⇨System Preferences from the Apple menu, click the Displays icon, and then click the Displays tab. Choose the highest pixel-resolution setting in the Resolutions list. You can then close the System Preferences window by choosing System Preferences⇨Quit System Preferences. Your display changes automatically to the new settings.

Opening your iPhoto libraries

If you have more than one iPhoto library on your computer, iPhoto first presents a dialog asking which photo library you want to use, with the list of the ones it found. Select an iPhoto library to see where it resides on your hard drive. (The path appears underneath the list.) After selecting a library, click Choose to use it. If you have no iPhoto library file, click Create New to create a new one.

If your iPhoto library file doesn't appear in the list, click Other Library and browse your folders to find it. It may not appear if it has been moved to an external hard drive or outside your user folder.

You can organize multiple iPhoto libraries, as I show in Chapter 3. To choose which one you want to use while launching iPhoto, hold down the Option key to show the same dialog so that you can choose which library to use.

Getting around in iPhoto

The iPhoto window is split into several panes and a toolbar, as shown in Figure 1-1:

- **The Viewer pane:** The largest pane (as in windowpane) — the Viewer — displays event tiles, face tiles, or thumbnails when browsing or the full picture after selecting one for viewing or editing.

- **The Info pane:** The Info pane displays the title, the date, the description, faces, places (including a minimap), and other information about the item or items you've selected. The Info pane appears only after clicking the Info (i) button on the toolbar.

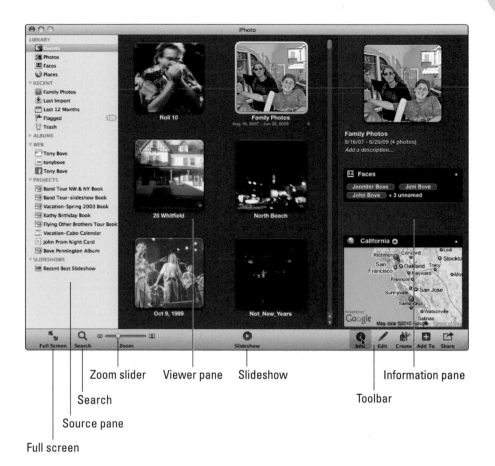

Figure 1-1: The iPhoto window.

Full screen

Source pane

Search

Zoom slider   Viewer pane   Slideshow

Information pane

Toolbar

✔ **The Source pane:** The entire library, the most recent pictures imported from cameras, and the list of photo albums and other sources of images appear in a pane on the left side of the window. You use the Source pane to select the source of your pictures for viewing or other operations — for example, you select a photo album in the Source pane to do something with that photo album (play a slideshow or make a book, for example). The Source pane is divided into these sections:

- *Library:* Browse your entire library by event, photos, face, or place, as I show in Chapter 2.

- *Recent:* Browse the most recent activities, such as the previously selected event, Last Import (the pictures most recently imported), Last 12 Months (the pictures imported in the last 12 months), Flagged (any pictures you've flagged), or the Trash (pictures you've deleted). All these are described in Chapter 2.

- *Albums:* Browse your photo albums — see Chapter 3 for details on creating and using photo albums.

- *Web:* Browse your online Facebook, Flickr, and MobileMe photo albums, add to them, and manage them — see Chapter 6 for more info.

- *Projects:* Browse projects you've created in iPhoto, such as photo books, calendars, or cards. I cover all those items in Chapter 6.

- *Slideshows:* Browse slideshows you created with your photos, which I describe in Chapter 5.

✔ **The toolbar:** The toolbar offers one-click access to the iPhoto tools:

- *Full Screen:* Show full-screen iPhoto and pictures.

- *Search:* Search pictures by title, description, keyword, or rating — see Chapter 2 for details.

- *Zoom slider:* Increase or decrease the size of thumbnail images or zoom into or out of pictures, as I describe in Chapter 2.

- *Slideshow:* Start a slideshow, as I show in Chapter 5.

- *Info:* Make the Info pane appear or disappear.

- *Edit:* Edit a picture, as I describe in Chapter 4.

- *Create:* Start a new photo album, book, card, calendar, or slideshow and add it to the Source pane.

- *Add To:* Add selected photos to a photo album, book, card, calendar, or slideshow.

- *Share:* Order prints of selected photos as I describe in Chapter 7, or post them to Facebook, Flickr, or MobileMe albums as I show in Chapter 6.

When you start iPhoto, the item you selected in the Source pane the last time you used iPhoto appears again. For example, if you selected Events the last time (to browse by event), Events is selected again when you start iPhoto again.

If you have a MobileMe account, it shows up in the Source pane in the Web section — the icon with the cloud next to my name (refer to Figure 1-1). You can select it to view and share the pictures in your MobileMe albums, as I describe in Chapter 6. The Web section also shows your Flickr and Facebook accounts after you've logged in to them (see Chapter 6).

When you start iPhoto, its window takes up a good portion of your desktop, but you may want to make the Viewer pane as large as possible to see all your thumbnails and view individual pictures with as large a viewing area as possible. To do this, click the Full Screen button in the lower left corner to fill

the entire screen with the iPhoto window, as shown in Figure 1-2. The entire
toolbar is still available along the bottom of the Viewer pane. To make the
iPhoto window smaller, click the Full Screen button on the toolbar.

To make the window invisible but accessible from the Dock, choose Window⇨
Minimize. (If you do this and then can't find iPhoto, click either the iPhoto icon
or the newly created minimized document icon in the Dock, and the window
reappears.) iPhoto works like all the other "i-applications" in Mac OS X.

Figure 1-2: The iPhoto Viewer pane, set to full-screen.

Importing Pictures

Using iPhoto, you can import pictures directly from your digital camera. All you
need to do is open iPhoto, connect your digital camera to the USB port, and
click the Import button. Your photographs appear in the iPhoto library ready
for browsing, editing, printing, archiving, or whatever else you want to do.

Don't have a digital camera? You still like to use that old Brownie film camera
your grandmother gave you? Don't worry. In this section you also find out
how to import your photos — even those musty photos of Grandma's that
you found in the attic — into iPhoto.

You can use a scanner to scan photographic prints, or you can send your film rolls to a photo service that can convert your film to digital images on a CD or the Web. (Odds are good that the photo service you already use offers this service. Next time you're there, ask about it.) iPhoto has no problem importing images from a CD or hard drive.

Importing picture files from your hard drive

If you already have picture files on your hard drive (such as scanned images or files from a digital photo service), you can drag the files directly over the Viewer pane of the iPhoto window after starting iPhoto to add them to your iPhoto library, as shown in Figure 1-3. You can also drag an entire folder of picture files, or even a folder that contains folders of picture files.

Don't want to drag? Choose File⇨Import to Library, browse your hard drive to select the folder or files you want to import, and then click the Import button.

Figure 1-3: Drag a picture file over the iPhoto window to import it.

The files are imported into the iPhoto library, leaving the original files intact. You can see the imported files by selecting Last Import in the Source pane, as shown in Figure 1-4 — which is already selected if you just dragged the folders or files.

Because iPhoto copies your photos into its own library file, you don't need the original copies any more — you can delete the original files from your hard drive to free up space.

If you drag a folder that contains picture files, iPhoto adds event titles to the pictures using the folder name. iPhoto also adds a date to the pictures according to when you imported them. To change the event title, click inside the title and then retype its title, as shown in Figure 1-5.

For details about browsing your imported pictures and adding information to them, see Chapter 2.

Figure 1-4: Find the most recently imported pictures by selecting Last Import.

Editing the event title

Figure 1-5: Edit the event title for the imported pictures.

Importing from a digital camera, iPad, iPhone, or iPod touch

After snapping photos, capturing screen shots, saving images from the Web, or recording video clips, you can connect an iPhone, an iPod touch, an iPad, or a digital camera to your Mac to import them into iPhoto automatically. The iPad, iPhone, and iPod touch models are supplied with the appropriate Universal Serial Bus (USB) cable. Digital cameras typically come with either a special USB cable or a FireWire cable that has a tiny connector on one end for the camera and a larger connector on the other end for the computer's USB or FireWire port. (If both ends are the same on the cable you're using, it doesn't matter which end is plugged into the camera or the computer.)

To import pictures from a digital camera or an iPad, iPhone, or iPod touch, follow these steps:

1. **Connect the device to the Mac.**

   • *Digital camera:* Turn off the power first and connect it to the Mac, and then turn the digital camera's power back on. Most cameras have a power-on switch to save battery life. (Even some as smart as myself have sat waiting for the photos to appear, only to find that the camera was off.) Connect your camera *before* you turn it on, because the Mac may not recognize some camera models unless they're turned on while connected. If the Mac doesn't recognize your camera, try turning off the camera and then turning it on again.

   • iPad, iPhone, or iPod touch: Connect your iPad, iPhone, or iPod touch to your Mac.

2. **Click the iPhoto icon to start iPhoto (if it hasn't already started).**

   After you connect and power on a digital camera or connect an iPad, iPhone, or iPod touch, iPhoto comes alive if photos are on the device — like Bruce Springsteen, the iPhoto icon is just "dancing in the Dock" as it starts up.

   iPhoto opens, displaying the iPhoto window (as shown in Figure 1-6 for an iPhone). Your camera's model, or iPad, iPhone, or iPod touch name, appears below Devices in the Source pane. Thumbnails of the pictures in your camera appear in the Viewer pane.

   Depending on how you configure your Mac, iPhoto may or may not automatically start when the computer detects the camera. (See Chapter 23 for iLife installation details.) If you're running iPhoto for the first time, a dialog opens and asks whether you want to always run iPhoto when you connect a camera. Click the Yes button.

3. **(Optional) Click inside the Event Name field to add the event title for the imported pictures.**

   After clicking inside the Event Name field, you can type a title (refer to Figure 1-6), which is useful for sorting and browsing pictures by event title (as I describe in Chapter 2).

4. **(Optional) Click to deselect the Split Events option at the bottom of the Viewer pane to combine the pictures into one event.**

   If you turn off Split Events, you can combine all pictures into one event; leave it on to split them by date and time.

Figure 1-6: Thumbnails appear for the pictures to import.

5. **Click the Import All button to import all pictures, or select thumbnails of pictures to import, and click the Import Selected button.**

   You can import either all pictures or selected pictures. After you click either Import All or Import Selected, the import operation begins and the button changes to Stop Import. Click Stop Import if you want to stop the import operation. After the importing finishes, a dialog appears, asking whether you want to delete the photos in your camera, iPad, iPhone, or iPod touch.

6. **Click Delete Photos to delete the photos in your camera, iPhone, or iPod touch.**

   You can either delete the photos in your camera, iPad, iPhone, or iPod touch to make room for more or keep them to use for another purpose (such as transferring them to another computer or uploading them from your iPhone to Facebook).

7. **Right-click (Control-click) the camera, iPad, iPhone, or iPod touch in the Source pane and choose Unmount before disconnecting the device from your computer.**

Control-click or right-click the device name in the Devices section of the Source pane, as shown in Figure 1-7, and choose Unmount. You can then disconnect the iPad, iPhone, or iPod touch or turn off the digital camera's power and disconnect it.

The photos from the device are imported into the iPhoto library. You can see them by selecting Last Import in the Source pane.

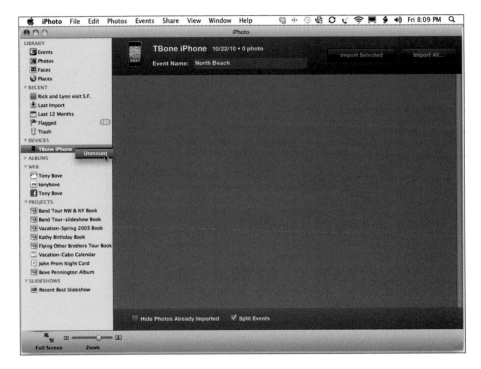

Figure 1-7: Right-click to unmount the camera, iPad, iPhone, or iPod touch before disconnecting it.

Importing from memory card readers

Additional memory cards are like extra rolls of film. A memory card reader is useful if you take lots of pictures and use additional cards. Rather than connect your camera to your Mac every time you want to transfer pictures, leave the card reader connected to the USB port of your Mac and put the camera's memory card in the card reader. If you use multiple memory cards, this method is especially convenient.

Many cameras come with relatively small memory cards — 16MB or less, enough to hold about 24 pictures. Memory card formats include Compact Flash, SmartMedia, and Memory Stick. They all function in a similar manner, but they have different physical sizes and shapes.

If you want to buy more memory cards for your camera, be sure to ask for the right kind of card because the wrong type won't work with your camera. Generally, a sample memory card is provided with your new digital camera, along with information about which type of cards to buy.

To import photos from a card reader, connect the card reader to your Mac. Standard USB cables generally work with card readers, so either end of the cable can be plugged into the card reader and the computer. Power up your card reader — use the Power button on your card reader if you have one; many card readers power themselves on by sensing power from the USB cable. Then insert a memory card — iPhoto doesn't sense the memory card reader until a card is inserted.

iPhoto imports photos from a card reader just as it does from a camera, using basically the same steps. Follow Steps 2 through 7 in the earlier section "Importing from a digital camera, iPad, iPhone, or iPod touch." Your memory card name appears below Devices in the Source pane just like a digital camera or an iPad, iPhone, or iPod touch (refer to Step 2), and after importing, unmount the memory card the same way (Step 7).

Importing files from a photo service

Most photo services offer photos on CDs or DVDs, which can be mailed to you or picked up at your convenience. Typically, the service offers either the Kodak Picture CD or Photo CD format. After inserting the CD or DVD into your computer, you can drag the entire CD or DVD, or open the CDs or DVDs just like hard drives and drag files or folders, directly to the iPhoto window as I describe in the earlier section, "Importing picture files from your hard drive."

If a service offers a format that is not a Photo CD or Picture CD, it most likely offers software you can download that extracts the images from the CD and saves them as image files on your hard drive. Although having every service use the same or similar format would be convenient, some services offer proprietary formats. When a service offers a proprietary format with special software, make sure that the software can save the images to a folder on your hard drive in one of the formats TIFF, PICT, PNG, JPG (or JPEG), or EPS. You don't need to know anything about these formats to import them from your hard drive into iPhoto, except that TIFF and PNG are the preferred formats for photos because they guarantee the highest quality. iPhoto can import images in any of these formats automatically.

Importing scanned image files

A scanner optically scans a photographic print, slide, or negative, and creates a digital image. Most modern scanners can be controlled directly by a Mac using the Image Capture application.

Unless you have a consistent need for scanning, you might get by with using a scanning service at a local copy shop. Many shops offer self-service scanning with instructions, and others do the scanning for you. All you need to know to order scans of photographic prints is described in this list:

- ✔ **Ask for the highest color depth.** The Mac can handle millions of colors, which is also known as 32-bit color in the world of PCs.

- ✔ **Ask for the highest affordable resolution.** Many services offer scanning at 600 dots-per-inch (dpi), which is acceptable for most personal uses.

- ✔ **Select the TIFF or PNG file format.** TIFF or PNG files (uncompressed or compressed with a lossless method, such as LZW) are higher in quality than other compressed file formats (such as JPEG), and should be used for images that you still want to edit or retouch, as I describe in Chapter 4.

If your scanner is connected to your Mac (most likely with a USB cable), install the Mac OS X software that came with your scanner. If you don't have the software, check whether the scanner works with Mac OS X (by checking the manual or the manufacturer's Web site). If your scanner works with OS X, you can use the Image Capture application, located in the Applications folder, to scan photos:

1. **Open Image Capture and click the Full Screen button to see the whole image.**

2. **Use the selection tool in the toolbar to zoom in and define the image scan area.**

   You can select either a portion of the image to scan or select the entire image.

3. **When you're satisfied with the results, click the Scan button to create a TIFF file and save the file on your hard drive.**

   Image Capture provides a dialog box for saving the TIFF file in a folder on your hard drive.

Use the Options button in the toolbar to change the scanner settings to set image-related options, such as resolution if you don't like the outcome of the file. Check the documentation that came with your scanner for more information about its capabilities.

If you want Image Capture to open automatically when you press a button on your scanner, choose the Preferences option from the Image Capture menu. In the Preferences dialog box, select the Image Capture option from the When a Scanner Button Is Pressed, Open menu.

After saving the scanned image in a file on your computer, drag the image directly to the iPhoto window as I describe in the earlier section "Importing picture files from your hard drive."

Now that you see how easy it is to import pictures into your computer, and how you can save thousands of photos in iPhoto without spending money on film, you should realize that you can experiment at will. Go ahead — take hundreds of shots. If you run out of space in your digital camera's memory card, connect your camera to your Mac, download the photos to the iPhoto library, and delete them from the camera. Then go back and take more!

2

Every Picture Tells a Story

In This Chapter

▶ Browsing by event, face, or location

▶ Searching and sorting your library

▶ Viewing pictures

▶ Modifying picture information

An old Chinese proverb, often misquoted, says, "One picture is worth more than ten thousand words." However, a few words may help identify elements in the picture. Other bits of information that can help are dates and places.

Using iPhoto, you can browse even massive quantities of pictures by event or date, by location, and even by recognizable faces in the pictures. You can also add titles, descriptions, ratings, and keywords to pictures, to make them easier to identify. This chapter shows you not only how to browse and view your pictures but also how to add information to make searching for a specific picture even easier.

Browsing Events

Browsing by event is probably the fastest way to find a group of pictures taken on a particular date. And, on many digital cameras and the iPhone and iPod touch cameras, you don't have to enter the date for each picture — the date and time are recorded automatically when you shoot the picture (if you set the date and time on your digital camera). Though you don't see the date on the actual picture, the information is stored with the picture file. When you import the pictures, iPhoto groups the pictures taken on the same date as one event; if the imported pictures span several days, an event is created for each day.

When you perform other import operations, such as files from your hard drive or from a photo CD or data DVD, iPhoto groups them as an event according to the date of the import operation.

You can change the date and time for any picture. You can also merge or split events identified by iPhoto, to keep your pictures organized the way you want.

Selecting an event in your life

Click Events in the Source pane to browse your entire library by event. Event tiles appear with names according to how they were imported — if you entered an Event Name while importing, for example (as I describe in Chapter 1), that name is used for the title of the event; otherwise, the date is used.

You can edit the title by clicking inside the Title field underneath the event tile and typing a new title. See the later section "Creating, merging, and splitting events."

As you browse photos by event, you can move around and check out your photos as described in this list:

- ✔ **Skim by event tile:** As you move the pointer over an event tile (or *skim* it), thumbnail images of pictures for that event rotate into view in succession on the event tile.

- ✔ **Select an event:** To select an event, click the event tile; a yellow border appears around the tile to show that it's selected.

- ✔ **Resize event tiles:** Do you want to see more tiles, or more of each tile? You can change the size of the event tiles — shrink them to see more of them, or make them larger to see more detail in each tile — by dragging the Zoom slider (beneath the Viewer pane) to the right, as shown in Figure 2-1. The Zoom slider has an icon of a large photo on one side and a smaller one on the other.

- ✔ **Sort event tiles:** If you don't like the order the event tiles are in, sort your view of the tiles by date, keyword, title, or rating in ascending or descending order. To sort by date, choose View➪Sort Events➪By Date and choose View➪Sort Events➪Ascending to show earliest dates first or View➪Sort Events➪Descending to show latest dates first. To sort by title, choose View➪Sort Events➪By Title, and then choose View➪Sort Events➪Ascending for normal alphabetical order or View➪Sort Events➪ Descending for reverse alphabetical order. You can also choose to sort the tiles manually by dragging them — choose View➪Sort Events➪ Manually, and then drag the tiles to different positions.

✔ **Scroll the Viewer pane:** Use the Viewer pane scroll bar to move up and down the event tiles. If you're sorting event tiles by date or title, the scroll bar guide appears in the middle of the window as you scroll, showing you the date or the first letter of the title of each event.

✔ **Open an event's pictures:** To open all pictures for an event, double-click the event tile. Thumbnail versions of the event's pictures appear in the Viewer pane, as shown in Figure 2-2. You can scroll the Viewer pane to see all thumbnails for the event. You can then double-click a thumbnail to see an enlarged version of the picture. (See "Viewing Pictures," later in this chapter, for details.)

Zoom slider

Figure 2-1: Drag the Zoom slider to make tiles larger or smaller.

Figure 2-2: Thumbnails of the pictures for an event.

✔ **Use the picture's pop-up menu:** Click the pop-up menu for a picture (refer to Figure 2-2) to

- *Rotate:* Click Rotate once to rotate the picture 90 degrees; click it again to continue rotating the picture.

- *Hide:* Click Hide to hide a picture in an event; choose View⇨Hidden Photos and then click Show in the picture's pop-up menu to show it again.

- *Trash:* Delete the picture.

- *Rating stars:* Give the picture a rating by dragging across the stars.

- *Cut or Copy:* You can use Cut or Copy to cut (remove) or copy a picture from one event and then open another event's pictures and use the pop-up menu of any picture to Paste the picture into the event.

- *Edit in iPhoto* and *Edit in External Editor:* These options appear if you specified a different editing program (such as Adobe Photoshop) in your preferences, as I describe in Chapter 4.

- *Make Key Photo:* Make the picture the *key photo* for the event — the one whose thumbnail appears in the event tile.

✔ **Move back and forth with the Viewer pane arrows:** To jump to the next event from the thumbnails of an event (refer to Figure 2-2), click the right-arrow button in the upper right corner of the Viewer pane. You can then jump back and forth from event to event by clicking the left-arrow button to move backward or the right-arrow button to move forward. Click the All Events button in the upper left corner of the Viewer pane (refer to Figure 2-2) to view all events again.

✔ **Sort event thumbnails:** You can also sort the picture thumbnails for an event. Choose View⇨Sort Photos, and then choose By Date, By Keyword, By Title, or By Rating — the same way as described in the fourth bullet in this list, about sorting event tiles. To find out how to add titles, keywords, and ratings, see "Modifying Picture Information," later in this chapter.

Creating, merging, and splitting events

The dates may be correct, but an event such as a festival can stretch over several days. On the other hand, one vacation day can include several events, if your vacations are like mine. No matter — iPhoto lets you create new events, merge existing events, or split events into two after you've imported the pictures. Events are different from albums and projects: You can copy the same picture to different albums and projects, but a picture can be part of only one event, even though you can move a picture from one event to another.

Creating an event

To create an event using one or more selected pictures, select the pictures first and then choose Events⇨Create Event. You can then see the new event by clicking Events in the Source pane.

You can flag a bunch of pictures first and choose Events⇨Create Event from Flagged Photos. (See "Modifying Picture Information," later in this chapter, to find out how to flag pictures.)

Merging events

Merging two events is easy: Simply drag one event's tile over the other, as shown in Figure 2-3. A message appears, as shown in Figure 2-4, asking whether you want to merge them. Click Merge to merge the events into one, or click Cancel.

Figure 2-3: Drag one event tile over another to merge them.

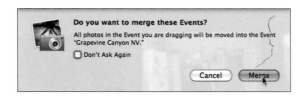

Do you want to merge these Events?

All photos in the Event you are dragging will be moved into the Event "Grapevine Canyon NV."

☐ Don't Ask Again

Cancel   Merge

Figure 2-4: Click Merge to merge the events.

Splitting events

To split an event into two events, follow these steps:

1. **Browse the existing event to show its thumbnails as described in the earlier section "Selecting an event in your life" (refer to Figure 2-2).**

2. **Select the pictures you want to move to the new event.**

3. **Choose Events⇨Split Event.**

   iPhoto creates a new event with the selected photos, leaving the unselected photos in the existing event. Both events are displayed under their titles, with the new event titled `untitled event`.

4. **Retitle the event by clicking its title and typing a more descriptive one.**

You can automatically split one or more events that include merged events from other days by selecting the event tiles and choosing Events⇨Autosplit Selected Events. iPhoto separates the pictures into separate event tiles for each day.

Adjusting dates and times for pictures

You can change the date and time for each picture in your iPhoto library. Changing the date for a picture doesn't move it to another event — it simply changes the picture's information. If you sort the picture thumbnails for an event by date (as I describe in "Selecting an event in your life," earlier in this chapter), changing the date also changes the way the picture sorts.

To change the date and time for a picture, follow these steps:

1. **Browse your library by event, photo, face, or place and select the picture's thumbnail.**

2. **Choose Photos⇨Adjust Date and Time.**

   A dialog appears, as shown in Figure 2-5, which displays the picture and its original time and date, along with an Adjusted field to change them.

3. **Click part of the date (such as the day) or time in the Adjusted field, and then click the up or down arrow to the right of the Adjusted field to change that part.**

   For example, in Figure 2-5, I'm changing the minutes in the time field.

4. **Select the Modify Original Files option to change the tag information within the picture's file to the new date and time.**

   Leave this option deselected if you want to change the date and time for a duplicate or edited copy of a picture but not the original picture.

Figure 2-5: Change the date and time for a picture.

You can change the date and time for multiple selected picture thumbnails all at one time, as a batch operation. Select the thumbnails, and then choose Photos⇨Batch Change. The Batch Change dialog appears. Select Date from the Set pop-up menu in the Batch Change dialog to display the date and time. You can then change the date and time in the same manner as for a single picture, and you can also select the option to add one or more seconds, minutes, hours, or days between selected pictures.

Browsing Faces

With your help, iPhoto can identify faces in your pictures so that you can browse pictures by faces. No, the process isn't as sophisticated as the face recognition technology you see on *CSI: Crime Scene Investigation,* but it's close to perfect for everyday picture browsing. When you need to find all pictures of your favorite relative or friend, just click Faces in the Source pane.

Saving a face you can't forget

First, faces need names: You introduce iPhoto to some faces and give them names. Follow these steps:

1. **Select a picture that has one or more faces that appear often in your library.**

   You can browse by event, photo, or place, as described in this section, and then select a picture.

2. **Click the Info tool on the right side of the toolbar.**

   The Info pane appears and the picture you selected is enlarged in the Viewer pane.

3. **Click the down arrow next to Faces to open the Faces information, and click *n* unnamed in the Faces information. (*n* is the number of unnamed faces.)**

   Faces are marked with *unnamed* labels, as shown in Figure 2-6.

4. **Click inside the label to add a name for a face.**

   As you type the name, suggestions from your Address Book entries appear below, and you can select one to complete entering the name.

5. **(Optional) To add a face, click Add a face in the Faces information, and adjust the face rectangle. Then repeat Step 4.**

   After you click Add a face in the Faces information, a rectangle appears in the picture. You can then drag the rectangle into position on a face and drag the corners of the rectangle to adjust its size. After adjusting the rectangle, repeat Step 4 (add a name for the face).

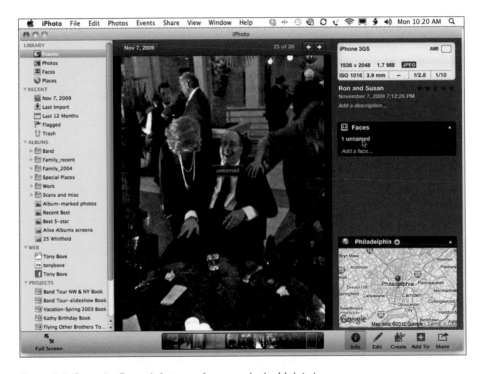

Figure 2-6: Open the Faces info to see faces marked with labels.

As you define faces in a picture, their names show up in the Faces information as shown in Figure 2-7, and arrows appear in the labels — click an arrow in the label for a name (as I do for Rick Bove in Figure 2-7) to see all pictures associated with that face, as shown in Figure 2-8. You can then add the full name, e-mail address, and other information for that person in the Info pane (refer to Figure 2-8).

Figure 2-7: Click a face's label arrow to see all pictures with that face.

Figure 2-8: All the pictures with that face.

Of course, iPhoto isn't intelligent enough to find all pictures that contain versions of a particular face. You have to help it along, as you see in the next section.

Matching faces in your library

To match other pictures in your library with a face and name in the Faces browser, follow these steps:

1. **Select Faces in the Source pane.**

   A corkboard image fills the Viewer pane with any faces you have already named.

2. **Double-click a named face to see more pictures that contain the same face.**

   The Viewer pane shows the pictures you identified as having that face, as shown in Figure 2-9. If iPhoto found more pictures that may also contain the same person, it displays a message at the bottom of the Viewer pane along with the Confirm Additional Faces button. If there are no additional pictures to confirm, you need to define more versions of the face. (See the earlier section "Saving a face you can't forget.")

3. **Click the Confirm Additional Faces button.**

   This button probably should be named Confirm Additional Pictures — it lets you confirm pictures that contain the same face. It displays confirmed pictures in the Viewer pane on top (with a green bar along the bottom) and unconfirmed pictures with the same (or similar) face below, as shown in Figure 2-10.

4. **Click a face to confirm it, or Option-click the face to reject it (refer to Figure 2-10).**

   To confirm that a face is correct, click the face — the banner underneath the face changes to include the person's name. If the match isn't correct, Option-click the face — the banner turns red and says that it isn't the person. This feedback gives iPhoto some information to search more pictures for the face and not include pictures that obviously are incorrect matches.

   You can also click a previously confirmed picture to reject it.

5. **Click Done when finished confirming and rejecting faces.**

   After you click Done, iPhoto looks for more pictures that may include the same face. You can continue confirming and rejecting more pictures and click Done each time, and iPhoto continues until it can't find another match.

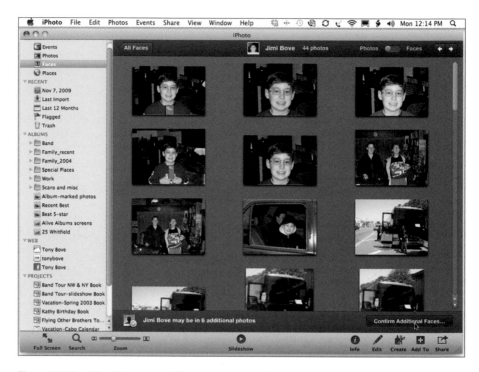

Figure 2-9: Double-click a named face to see more pictures with that face; click Confirm Additional Faces to confirm.

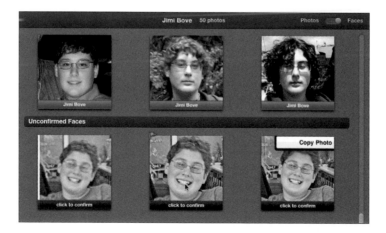

Figure 2-10: Click to confirm (or reject) pictures that have the same face.

Browsing Places

iPhoto puts your pictures on a Google-powered map so that you can find all pictures related to a specific location, such as your home or work or school and all your vacation spots.

Many digital cameras and mobile devices with cameras, such as the iPhone, include support for the global positioning system (GPS), which uses satellites to track your physical location. For example, after turning on Location Services on your iPhone, every photo you shoot is stamped automatically with the GPS location information. (Lewis and Clark would have made quite a convincing presentation of their explorations to Thomas Jefferson if they had owned these cameras or iPhones.)

If you don't have a GPS-equipped camera or iPhone, you're not lost in the wilderness — you can add location information to one or more pictures in iPhoto and they show up on the map, just like GPS-stamped pictures do.

Finding pictures by their locations

Ready to explore? Click Places in the Source pane to browse pictures by location. A map appears with markers for your pictures, as shown in Figure 2-11. The following tips can help you navigate around this view:

- ✓ **Switch between Terrain, Satellite, and Hybrid views:** Just as you can in Google Maps, you can click Terrain in the upper right corner to view the terrain (shown in Figure 2-11), click Satellite to view a satellite image, or click Hybrid to view a hybrid of both.

- ✓ **View the pictures at a location:** Move the pointer over the location marker (in Figure 2-11, I move the pointer over the marker for Haines, Alaska), and then click the right arrow in the marker's heading to see the pictures for that location (displayed as thumbnails). You can then select thumbnails to perform an operation or double-click a thumbnail to see the full picture. Click Map in the upper left corner to return to the map.

- ✓ **Zoom in and out of the map:** To zoom into the map for more detail, or zoom out to see more of the world, drag the Zoom slider in the lower left corner of the Viewer pane (refer to Figure 2-11). Sliding to the right (+) increases detail as you zoom in, and sliding to the left (–) reduces detail as you zoom out.

- ✓ **Pick locations from a menu:** Use the menus to find a specific location. For example, click the Cities menu to go directly to a city. The map shows the area of the city where pictures were taken. You can then use the Places menu to pick a place within the city, as shown in Figure 2-12.

TIP

✔ **Show photos:** Show thumbnails for *all* pictures in the section of the map visible in the Viewer pane — click the Show Photos button in the lower right corner of the Viewer pane (refer to Figure 2-11). The thumbnails appear, as shown in Figure 2-13; above them are both the number of places you're viewing and number of photos in all these places.

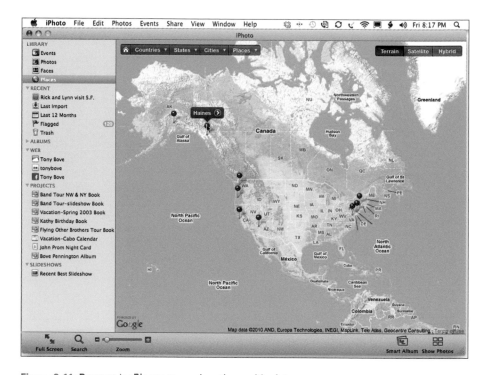

Figure 2-11: Browse by Places to see locations with pictures.

Figure 2-12: Pick places in the viewable area of the map.

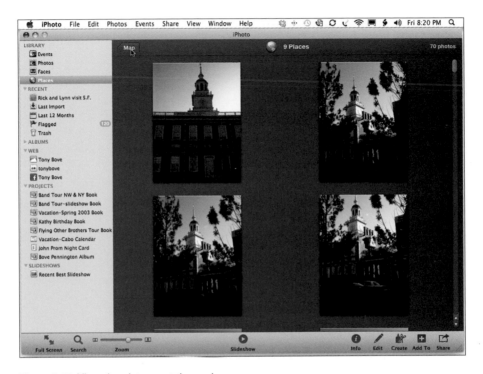

Figure 2-13: View the pictures at these places.

Adding locations to events and pictures

In iPhoto, the entire world is at your command, whether or not your camera is GPS-enabled. You can add the name of any location quickly and easily to one picture or to a set of pictures, such as an event.

To add a location to a selected picture or event, follow these steps:

1. **Browse your library by event, photo, or face, and select the picture's thumbnail.**

2. **Click the Info button to show the Info pane.**

   The Info pane appears, as shown in Figure 2-14.

3. **Click the Assign a Place button and then start typing the name of the location, and iPhoto displays a list of suggestions on a pop-up menu as you type. You can continue typing the location or choose a selection by clicking it.**

   For example, in Figure 2-15, I started typing *Santa Cruz* and the pop-up menu included my exact choice, Santa Cruz in California; I simply clicked it to complete the location information.

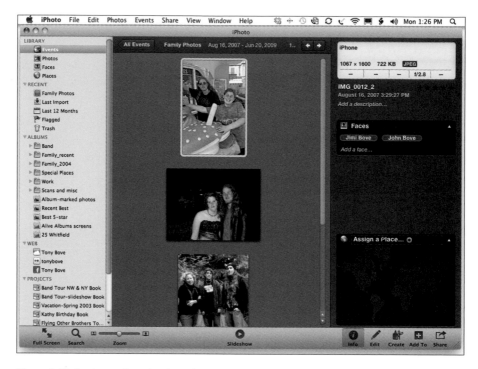

Figure 2-14: Assign a place for the selected picture.

Figure 2-15: Start typing a location and iPhoto makes suggestions.

If you prefer to use a map to add a location to an event, click the arrow to the right of the Assign a Place button (refer to Figure 2-14), and iPhoto displays the map for browsing by Places. Browse the map as described in the earlier section "Finding pictures by their locations," and click the map to set a marker for the selected picture or event. After you click a location on the map, a yellow pin appears, which you can drag to an exact position on the map.

Browsing and Searching Photos

For a basic view of thumbnails of all pictures in your iPhoto library, click Photos in the Source pane. Thumbnails appear for all pictures (photos, images, and video clips) in your library, sorted by date in ascending order (earliest date first), as shown in Figure 2-16. You can scroll the Viewer pane to see all thumbnails, and open and close events by clicking the triangle next to the event title. (For example, I just opened the North Beach event shown in Figure 2-16.)

Figure 2-16: Thumbnails of every picture in your iPhoto library.

You may want to include or remove visual elements in the Viewer pane. Normally, event titles are included, but you can remove them by choosing View➪Event Titles so that the check mark next to the menu option disappears. (Choose the command again to make the check mark reappear and bring back event titles.) You can also turn on the view of titles, ratings, and keywords in the same way: Choose View➪Titles, View➪Ratings, and/or View➪Keywords. You can turn on all these visual elements or just some of them or none.

Sorting the entire library

The Photos view helps you easily sort all your photos at one time. To sort your library by date in descending order (latest date first), choose View➪ Sort Photos➪Descending. To set your library back to ascending order, choose View➪Sort Photos➪Ascending.

To sort all your pictures by keyword or by rating, choose View➪Sort Photos➪ By Keyword or View➪Sort Photos➪By Rating. You can also sort by title by choosing View➪Sort Photos➪By Title. To see how to add titles, keywords, and ratings, see "Modifying Picture Information," later in this chapter.

Searching for pictures

You can zip to the photo you're looking for by using one of several search methods in iPhoto:

- **To use the search field:** Click the Search button (with a Magnifying Glass icon) on the left side of the toolbar at the bottom of the Viewer pane (refer to Figure 2-16). The button changes into a Search field — you can enter characters in this field to search for pictures. iPhoto looks for the characters in titles, descriptions, and keywords. iPhoto assembles the thumbnails of located pictures in the Viewer pane as you enter characters. To delete the entry in the Search field, click the circled *x* on the right side of the Search field.

- **To search for a date:** Click the Magnifying Glass icon within the Search field to see a pop-up menu, and choose Date. A pop-up dialog appears with buttons for each month of the earliest year for which you have pictures — just click a month name to see the pictures for that month. To switch to Calendar view in the pop-up dialog, click the circled right arrow in the upper left corner; you can then click a specific date. To switch years, click the right (forward) or left (backward) arrows in the upper right corner of the pop-up dialog. To clear the search, click outside the pop-up menu and then click the circled *x* on the right side of the search field.

- **To search by keyword:** Click the Magnifying Glass icon for the pop-up menu and choose Keyword. (To see how to add keywords to pictures, see "Adding keywords," later in this chapter.) A pop-up dialog appears with buttons for each keyword — just click a keyword to see the pictures with that keyword. To refine your search to pictures that also have other keywords, click those keywords. (You can click multiple keywords and iPhoto looks for pictures that contain all of them.) For example, if you assigned Vacation and Kids as keywords to pictures that show the kids on vacation, you can search for either *Vacation* or *Kids* to locate pictures including the ones you're looking for or quickly narrow your search by clicking Vacation *and* Kids so that only pictures of the kids on vacation show up.

✔ **To search by rating:** Click the Magnifying Glass icon for the pop-up menu and choose Ratings. (To see how to add ratings to pictures, see "Adding keywords," later in this chapter.) Click inside the Search field, which now offers stars for ratings — you can click or drag to refine the number of stars. iPhoto searches for pictures that are rated as high (or higher) than the number of stars you specify.

Viewing Pictures

To look at a single picture, browse by any method I describe in this chapter (events, places, faces, or photos). Then double-click the thumbnail. The picture fills the Viewer pane. Double-click the picture again to return to the thumbnails.

If the picture is a video clip, after double-clicking it the video-player controls (Previous/Rewind, Play/Pause, and Next/Fast-Forward) appear, as shown in Figure 2-17, and you can drag the scrubber bar under the controls to move to any part of the video. You can also drag the Volume slider under the controls to set the audio volume, and click the gear icon to display the Actions pop-up menu that offers the Actual Size or Fit in Window options. Actual Size displays the video in its actual size (which may cut off the sides of an HD video), and Fit in Window displays the entire video picture inside the window.

Whether you're viewing still photos or video clips, the Viewer pane shows along the bottom a row of thumbnails of other pictures you're browsing. Move the pointer over the row to make the thumbnails larger, and click any thumbnail to move directly to that picture.

To return to the thumbnails of pictures, click Photos in the upper left corner of the Viewer pane.

To fill the screen with your picture or to browse pictures at full-screen size, click the Full Screen button in the left corner of the toolbar at the bottom of the iPhoto window, or choose View⇨Full Screen.

To return to the iPhoto window, press the Escape key or click the Full Screen button in the lower left corner of the full-screen display.

Figure 2-17: Video controls for viewing video clips in your library.

Modifying Picture Information

After taking lots and lots of pictures, you will want iPhoto to help you keep track of them. iPhoto already knows the date the pictures were taken (if the camera records that information) or the date they were imported into the iPhoto library. iPhoto may already know the location of the shots, if you captured them with a camera that offers GPS (such as an iPhone). See "Browsing Places," earlier in this chapter, to find out and to see how to add location information.

However, the date and location may not be enough. You may want to add more information, such as a title, a description, some keywords, and possibly even ratings, to make it far easier to search for or browse your pictures.

Editing titles and descriptions

A *title* is the name of a picture. Titles are the most convenient way to identify pictures. Every picture has a title when imported — iPhoto simply uses the filename as its title (such as `IMG_0147` for the picture file named `IMG_0147.jpg`).

Of course, IMG_0147 isn't descriptive. You can edit the title of each picture by typing directly into the text field at the top of the Info pane, as shown in Figure 2-18. If the Info pane isn't visible, click the Info (the *i*) button on the right side of the toolbar at the bottom of the iPhoto window. The Info pane shows information about the selected picture at the top, including the camera type, shutter speed, aperture, focal length, exposure data, flash status (on or off), and image resolution.

Typing into the text field

Figure 2-18: Type a title for a picture in the Info pane.

Editing a picture's title changes it in the photo library and in all albums and projects where the title appears.

Titles can be useful for sorting purposes. You can arrange your pictures alphabetically by title, which can be quite useful if your titles are Beach 1, Beach 2, Beach 3, Trail A, or Trail B, for example, but not quite as useful if your titles resemble the Pink Floyd song title "Several Species of Small Furry Animals Gathered Together in a Cave and Grooving with a Pict." (Your titles can be quite long, if you want.)

To see titles under each thumbnail image in the Viewer pane when browsing, choose View⇨Titles to turn on the viewing of titles. (Choose it again to turn it off.) Titles appear under the thumbnails while browsing by photo, after choosing an event when browsing by event, after choosing a location when browsing by place, and after choosing a face when browsing by face.

To see titles properly in the Viewer pane, you may want to increase the size of the thumbnails in the pane by dragging the Size slider on the left side of the toolbar.

You don't necessarily have to painstakingly type a title for every picture. You can automatically assign to a batch of selected pictures the same title, such as the date and time, the event name (which you already set for the event when importing the pictures, as I describe in Chapter 1), the filename, or some identifying text. Just follow these steps:

1. **Select the thumbnails of the pictures you want to assign titles to.**

   You can browse by any method described in this chapter and then select the thumbnails.

2. **Choose Photos⇨Batch Change.**

   A tiny dialog box appears with the Set and To pop-up menus.

3. **Select Title from the Set pop-up menu, and choose an option for the Title from the To pop-up menu: Text, Event Name, Filename, or Date/Time (or Empty to leave the title blank).**

4. **Click OK.**

Here's what the options do:

   ✔ **Text** lets you type any text, and if you click the Append a Number to Each Photo option, the text ends with a number that increments for each picture — Sample1, Sample2, Sample3, and so on.

   ✔ **Event Name** sets the titles of all selected pictures to the event name.

- **Filename** sets the titles to their respective filenames — which iPhoto already does when importing, so this option lets you restore the titles to their original names.

- **Date/Time** gives you a number of choices for your title: You can include the date in short, abbreviated, or long formats, or specify the time in a 12-hour or 24-hour clock format, with or without seconds.

Descriptions are also useful for identifying pictures and what they contain. To add a description, click inside the field below the title in the Info pane (in which the Add a Description line appears) and type the description.

You may want to use the description field for captions, as in magazines and books. The descriptions can be included, if you want, in the e-mail messages for the pictures you send by e-mail as well as on Web pages. You can even search for photos by your descriptions, as I describe in "Searching for pictures," earlier in this chapter.

You can quickly add the same description to a batch of selected pictures or append the same description to the batch without deleting the description that's already entered. Choose Photos⇨Batch Change and choose Description from the Set pop-up menu. You can then type a description for all pictures and click the Append to Existing Description option to preserve the original description. (If the descriptions are blank, this option simply adds the batch description.) Finally, click OK.

Adding keywords

Keywords give you the power to organize pictures by topic or other characteristics that likely appear throughout your library — pictures of your kids, holidays, or vacations, for example. The larger your iPhoto library, the more useful keywords can be. After you assign keywords, you can quickly search and locate photos using the keywords.

For example, you can assign the keyword Birthday to photos related to birthdays and find all birthday shots in one search. All photos related to vacations can have the keyword Vacation assigned to them. And, what if a birthday occurred during a vacation? You can assign both keywords to those special pictures so that a search on either Vacation or Birthday finds them — indeed, a search on Vacation *and* Birthday finds only those pictures that have both keywords.

To add keywords, follow these steps:

1. **Choose View⇨ Keywords to turn on the viewing of keywords in the Info pane.**

Choose the option again to make keywords not visible when you're done with these steps, if you like. When this option is on, keywords also appear under the thumbnails while browsing by photo, after choosing an event when browsing by event, after choosing a location when browsing by place, and after choosing a face when browsing by face.

At first, you have no keywords and the Add a Keyword line appears in the Keywords section of the Info pane (refer to Figure 2-18).

2. Click the Add a Keyword line and then enter a keyword into the keywords field, as shown in Figure 2-19.

You can enter multiple keywords by pressing Return (or Enter) at the end of each one. As you type a keyword and press Return (or Enter), iPhoto encapsulates the keyword in an oval, such as the keyword band tour in Figure 2-19).

Figure 2-19: Assign keywords to a selected picture.

After you assign a keyword to a picture, iPhoto remembers the keyword so that as you move on to another picture and start entering keywords, a pop-up menu appears with previously entered keywords. You can then select the exact keyword you used before — and cut down on keyword typing mistakes and variations that would slow down searches.

To delete a keyword, click it. The keyword appears encapsulated; simply click it and press the Delete key (or choose Edit⇨Cut). You can also copy a set of keywords by clicking the first keyword and Shift-clicking the last in a sequence, choosing Edit⇨Copy, clicking in the keywords field of another picture to add keywords, and choosing Edit⇨Paste.

Rating photos with stars

The Ratings feature lets you assign a value judgment to a picture so that you can quickly find all five-star shots, all four-star shots, and so on. To assign a rating, select the thumbnail for the picture, choose Photos⇨My Rating, and pick the appropriate number of stars (or None). You can also assign a rating by dragging across the Rating field next to the title in the Info pane (refer to Figure 2-18).

Flagging pictures for processing

Back in the old days of commercial photography, if you were ordering wedding pictures, the photographer gave you a *contact sheet* — a quick print of photos in thumbnail size — and a magic marker or felt-tip pen. You, the customer, would then mark up the photos you wanted developed. That's the basic idea behind flagging pictures: You mark them for processing.

To flag a picture for processing, select its thumbnail while browsing and click the flag icon in the upper left corner of the thumbnail. You can flag a bunch of pictures by selecting them and then choosing Photos⇨Flag Photos. A red flag appears over the upper left corner of the frame of each flagged thumbnail image. (The flag doesn't change the picture in any way — it appears only on the thumbnails.) To browse only your flagged pictures, click Flagged in the Recent section of the Source pane.

After flagging pictures, you can create a new photo album with them or drag them to an existing photo album, as I describe in Chapter 3. You can automatically upload them to a MobileMe, Flickr, or Facebook album or create a project, such as a book or calendar, with them, as I describe in Chapter 6.

You can also create a new event with the flagged pictures. Choose Events⇨ Create Event from Flagged Photos. iPhoto complies immediately and creates a new event. If the pictures are already part of another event, a dialog appears, explaining that the pictures will be moved to the new event; you can click OK to go ahead, create the new event and move them, or Cancel.

You can also add flagged pictures to the selected event: Browse by event (as I describe in this chapter), select an event tile, and then choose Events⇨Add Flagged Photos to Selected Event.

To unflag one or more pictures, select their thumbnails and choose Photos⇨ Unflag Photos, or select each thumbnail and click the flag in the upper left corner of the thumbnail.

3

Organizing Your Pictures

In This Chapter

 Organizing photos into photo albums

 Backing up your photo library

 Burning a CD or DVD of your pictures

The iPhoto library can hold any number of pictures; the number is limited only by available hard drive space. At an average size of 1 megabyte (MB) per photo (and many photos occupy less space), you can store 20,000 photos in 20 gigabytes (GB) of hard drive space. And, of course, you can expand a photo library over multiple drives or create multiple libraries. For all practical purposes, you can keep shooting pictures forever.

Fortunately, you can organize even massive quantities of pictures in the iPhoto library. iPhoto provides quite a convenient organizing metaphor for assembling sets of related pictures: the *photo album.* You can organize hundreds or thousands of pictures into albums to make them easier to locate and select for projects such as calendars or books.

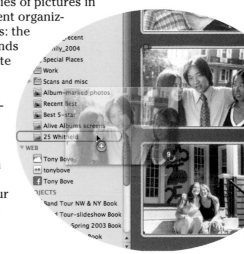

You can even create a *smart album,* which automatically includes pictures based on the criteria you set up, based on the information included with pictures. For example, you can define the criteria for a smart album to automatically include pictures from a particular camera model or that have the highest rating. This chapter shows you how to organize your iPhoto library using photo albums, and also how to manage backups and archives.

Photo Albums for All Occasions

A *photo album* is simply a way of organizing photos and placing them in a proper sequence. You select photos from your iPhoto library and arrange them in the order you want for slideshows or other projects, such as calendars or books.

You can use photo albums to assemble pictures about a particular subject, such as your favorite nature photos, or to organize pictures for a slideshow, QuickTime movie, or Web page. You can make as many albums as you like. Because the albums are *lists* of images, they don't use up hard drive space by copying the pictures — they just refer to the actual picture files in the iPhoto library. You can include the same picture in several albums without making multiple copies of the picture file and wasting space. You can delete a picture from an album without removing it from your library.

Creating albums and adding pictures

To create a new photo album, click the Create button on the right side of the toolbar and then choose Album from the pop-up menu, or choose File⇨New⇨Album (or press Command+N). The new album appears in the Albums section of the Source pane as `untitled album` — click inside the title and type a new, descriptive title, such as `25 Whitfield` in Figure 3-1).

You can organize your albums into folders in the Albums section of the Source pane (as I do in Figure 3-1, with `Band` and `Family_Recent`, for example). First, choose File⇨New⇨ Folder to create an empty folder. Then retitle the folder (just like retitling an album, as described earlier). You can then drag other albums in the Albums section of the Source pane on top of the folder title to add them to the folder.

You can then browse your iPhoto library as I describe in Chapter 2, select thumbnails, and drag them over the photo album title in the Source pane (refer to Figure 3-1). A number appears as you drag, showing the number of pictures you're adding to the album.

You can start with a full album by selecting one or more pictures first. Browse your library by any method described in Chapter 2 and select one or more picture thumbnails. Click the Create button on the right side of the toolbar and then select Album from the pop-up menu, or choose File⇨New⇨ Album. The newly created album contains the picture or pictures you selected.

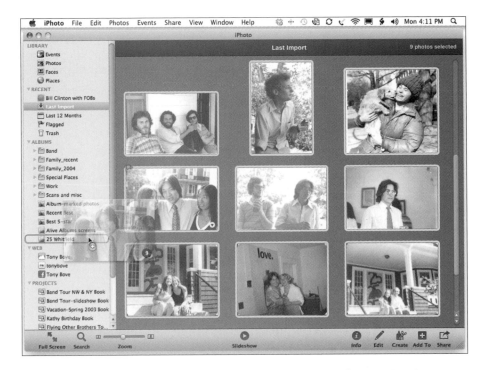

Figure 3-1: Drag multiple pictures at a time to the photo album named `25 Whitfield`.

Another way to add pictures to an album is to select one or more picture thumbnails, click the Add button on the right side of the toolbar, and then select Album from the pop-up menu. You can then scroll the pop-up menu of album tiles and select the album (or click the New Album tile to start a new album).

You know that a thumbnail is selected when an outline appears around it. Select multiple thumbnails by clicking the first one and holding down the Shift key while clicking the last one — the first and last, and all thumbnails between them, are selected automatically. You can add a nonconsecutive thumbnail to the selection by Command-clicking it (holding down the Command key). You can also Command-click a selected thumbnail to remove it from the selection.

Another way to select multiple pictures is to first reduce the thumbnail size with the Zoom slider and then drag a selection rectangle around all the thumbnails. Of course, with thumbnails that small, you may not be able to determine which pictures belong and which don't. Don't worry — in the later section "Arranging pictures in albums," I show how to remove unwanted pictures from an album.

You can also create an album by dragging a folder of pictures from the Finder into the iPhoto Albums section of the Source pane. iPhoto creates an album with the folder's name and imports all pictures contained in the folder. Using the Finder, you can add a picture to an album directly from a CD or from another location on your hard drive.

Arranging pictures in albums

To see the pictures gathered into an album, click the title of the album in the Albums section of the Source pane. The Viewer pane shows only the pictures you put in the album. You can organize the pictures within the album without having to wade through all pictures in your iPhoto library.

The sequence in which your pictures appear in the album is important — it defines the order of pictures in a slideshow or a book layout. The order in which you drag pictures to the album defines its original sequence, but you will probably want to change this sequence. To rearrange pictures in the album, follow these steps:

1. **Click the album title in the Albums section of the Source pane.**

2. **Drag the thumbnail of a picture to a new place in the sequence, or select multiple thumbnails and drag them to a new place, as shown in Figure 3-2.**

   In Figure 3-2, I'm in the process of dragging two pictures to a new place in the sequence. The pointer includes the number 2 to show that I'm rearranging two pictures.

3. **Repeat Step 2 until all pictures are arranged as you want them in the album.**

To use the same picture in more than one photo album, simply drag the thumbnail for that picture over one album, and then select and drag the thumbnail over another album. The picture appears in both albums without having to create duplicates and waste hard drive space.

You can also duplicate an entire photo album, in case you want to arrange the pictures in different ways. You don't duplicate the pictures themselves, so hard drive space is not wasted. To duplicate an album, select the album title in the Album section of the Source pane and choose Photos⇨Duplicate (or right-click the album title and choose Duplicate). A new album is created with the same title and the characters –2 added to the title. You can then retitle the album, if you want.

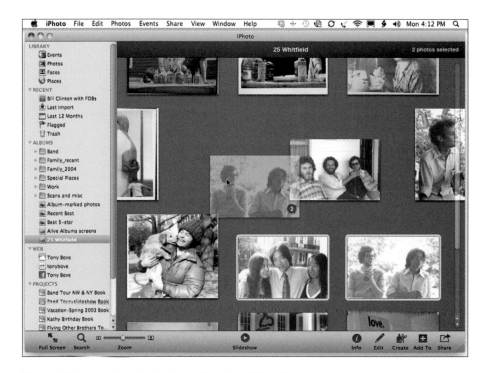

Figure 3-2: Arrange the photos in an album in a different sequence.

Removing photos from albums

You may have been a bit hasty with your selections for the new photo album. Or, perhaps you just noticed that useless shot you accidentally took of the side of a barn. Never mind — just select the thumbnail for the picture and press the Delete key on your keyboard.

If you're squeamish about using the Delete key (and who isn't?), choose Photos⇨Delete from Album.

When you remove a picture from an album, the picture isn't deleted. It remains intact in your iPhoto library. The only way to delete a picture from the library is to select the picture while browsing the Events or Photos sections of the Source pane (using any of the methods described in Chapter 2), and then pressing the Delete key or choosing Photos⇨Move to Trash (or right-clicking or Control-clicking the picture and choosing Trash from the contextual menu).

In all cases, if you delete something you didn't want to delete, you can usually undo the operation by choosing Edit⇨Undo. If you perform operations after deleting the picture, you may have to choose Edit⇨Undo several times and undo all subsequent operations before you can undo the deletion.

Using an album for your desktop and screen saver

One sure way to demonstrate your skills with a Mac is to personalize your Desktop to show your own pictures. The Desktop is the background image behind the Finder. To set your Desktop to a photo or an album, select the photo's thumbnail or select the album name in the Albums section of the Source pane and choose Share⇨Set Desktop.

You can also use any iPhoto photo album as a screen saver. The Desktop & Screen Saver preferences (choose System Preferences in Mac OS X and click Desktop & Screen Saver) let you choose not only pictures for your desktop but also animation to display when your Mac is inactive. To protect your display, you can set the Screen Saver setting to display animation if your computer hasn't been used for several minutes. Apple provides a set of animated effects, but you can use a photo album from your iPhoto library as your screen saver — the pictures appear one after the other, like a slideshow. Scroll the list of Screen Savers until you find your iPhoto photo albums. After clicking a photo album, click the Options button to display these options:

- **Present Slides in Random Order:** When you turn on this setting, the images appear in random order rather than in the sequence you arranged for the photo album in iPhoto.

- **Cross-Fade between Slides:** A cross-fade is a smooth transition from one image to another.

- **Zoom Back and Forth:** The screen effect zooms into the image to show more detail, and zooms out to show the entire picture.

- **Crop Slides to Fit on Screen:** Draw a smaller rectangle inside the image and cut away everything outside the rectangle, in order to fit the image onscreen. This option is useful for working with photos whose aspect ratios are different from the typical 16:10 ratio of the Mac screen.

- **Keep Slides Centered:** When you turn on this option, the pictures are always centered onscreen (either letterboxed or pillarboxed, or both, if the dimensions are smaller than the screen dimensions) without the need for cropping.

Creating and editing a smart album

In the Albums section of the Source pane, you can find *smart albums,* which are indicated by the gear-in-a-folder icon. iPhoto comes with a few sample smart albums, such as Best 5-Star and Recent Best, and you can create your own. Smart albums add pictures to themselves based on prearranged criteria, or *conditions.* For example, when you add ratings to your pictures, as I describe in Chapter 2, the Best 5-Star and Recent Best albums change to reflect your new ratings. You don't have to set up anything because those smart albums are already defined for you.

To create a new smart album, follow these steps:

1. **Choose File⇨New⇨ Smart Album (or press Command+Option+N).**

   The Smart Album dialog appears, as shown in Figure 3-3.

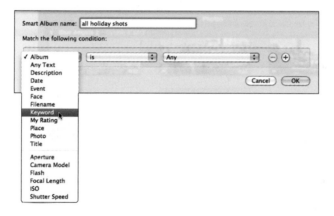

Figure 3-3: Set the first condition for a smart album.

2. **Enter a new name (a title) for the smart album in the Smart Album Name field at the top.**

3. **Choose a category of information from the Match the Following Condition pop-up menu.**

   You can choose any of the categories used for information, such as Album, Any Text, Description, Date, Event, Face, Filename, or Keyword.

4. **From the second pop-up menu (refer to Figure 3-3), choose an operator, such as Is, Contains, or Starts with.**

   The selections you make from these two pop-up menus combine to create a condition, such as `Date is after 10/6/2009`, `Any Text contains Jimi`, or `Keyword contains holiday`.

5. **To add multiple conditions, click the plus-sign (+) button (on the right), as shown in Figure 3-4.**

   You can then decide whether to match all or any of these conditions, as explained in Steps 3 and 4. The Match *xx* of the Following Conditions option is enabled by default when you set one or more conditions.

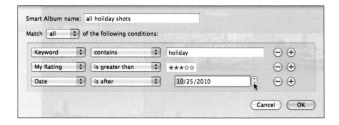

Figure 3-4: Set multiple conditions for a smart album.

6. **After setting one or more conditions for the smart album, click OK to create it (or Cancel to cancel it).**

   The smart album appears in the Albums section of the Source pane and goes to work immediately.

To edit a smart album, select it from the Albums section of the Source pane and choose File⇨Edit Smart Album. The Smart Album dialog appears with the criteria for the smart album.

Maintaining a Photo Archive

They're your pictures — why shouldn't you have multiple copies of them?

Whether or not you manage files on your hard drive, you may want to know where these pictures are stored so that you can go about your usual file management tasks — such as backing up current files and archiving files you no longer need at hand.

You may also want to move the whole iPhoto library to another Mac — after all, these Macs just keep getting better year after year. You may also want to make more copies of all your pictures and create CDs or DVDs as archives. The cost of a single blank CD or DVD is quite low compared to the cost of losing a priceless picture without a backup.

The operations I describe in this section make use of the Mac Finder and the iPhoto Library package, which is the container for the individual files that comprise your entire iPhoto library. If you move, delete, rename, or otherwise tamper with files or folders inside the iPhoto Library package, you may be unable to see your pictures in iPhoto.

Backing up your library

Routinely copying your iPhoto library to another hard drive, or including it in your Time Machine backup, is a good idea. If you have no other hard drive or removable storage device (and don't mind how long the backup may take), you can even copy your iPhoto library to the iDisk of your MobileMe service on the Internet, if you have enough space on it. You can also burn a CD or DVD with your iPhoto library, as I describe, later in this chapter, in the section "Burning a CD or DVD."

To copy the iPhoto library to another drive, locate the iPhoto Library package file using the Finder. The file is usually located within the Pictures folder in your User folder. Drag this file to another hard drive and you're all set. The copy operation may take some time if the library is huge — you can stop the operation at any time, but the newly copied library may not be complete. For best results, allow the copy operation to finish.

Burning a CD or DVD

A useful way to maintain backups of your pictures is to burn CDs or DVDs with them. If you have an Apple-supported CD-RW or DVD-R drive, you can burn CDs and DVDs with iPhoto albums. When you save (or write) information to a disc, your drive *burns* the information onto the disc's surface with a laser.

iPhoto burns a CD or DVD that can be used only with iPhoto, not with other photo programs or photo processing services. To create a CD or DVD of image files to use with other programs or services, export the pictures to files in a folder in the Finder (as I describe in Chapter 6) and use the Burn Disc command to burn the folder to a CD or DVD.

To burn a CD or DVD for use with iPhoto, follow these steps:

1. **Browse and select pictures, or choose a photo album.**

   You can browse and select an event or a location or select a photo album, or individual pictures, before choosing to burn to a disc. You can fit numerous pictures on a DVD, so you may want to select your entire iPhoto library for a DVD burn operation to use up the entire DVD space.

2. **Choose Share⇨Burn.**

   The Insert Disc dialog box appears, prompting you to insert a blank disc.

3. **Insert a blank disc and click OK.**

   The burn disc pane appears at the bottom of the Viewer pane. A disc icon appears on the panel — the green area on the disc icon represents the amount of disc space that your pictures require.

4. **Click the Burn button in the Burn Disc pane (or Cancel).**

   The burn operation starts. It may take several minutes to burn the disc; when it's done, you hear a chime and the disc automatically ejects. You can cancel the burn by clicking the Cancel button next to the progress bar, but if you're using a CD-R disc, you may not be able to use the CD after canceling.

You can show pictures you burned to a CD or a DVD while using your current iPhoto library. You can't modify the pictures on the CD or DVD, but you can view and copy any pictures and albums they contain.

To open a CD or a DVD you burned in iPhoto, insert the CD or DVD disc into your Mac. An icon for the disc appears in the Source pane. Click the disc icon in the Source pane to display the pictures and albums on the disc. Click the triangle next to the disc icon to see the photo albums on the disc. You can copy them to your current iPhoto library to work on them.

You can use photos and DVDs in many ways, including assembling documentary-style slideshows. I cover these and many other DVD topics in Chapter 12.

4

Improving Photos

*P*hotos are records of reality, but reality doesn't always comply with your wishes — the sun may be too bright, the forest too dark, or the subject too far away, or the combination of light, shadows, and distance make the scene too blurry to show details. Cameras offer automatic settings for taking pictures that compensate for some of these factors, but these settings don't always give you the best pictures.

Digital photography, on the other hand, offers unlimited ways to change images without adversely affecting the quality of the image. Unlike the technology involved with developing film, in which successive modifications to the film degrade the image quality, digital technology allows you to experiment with images at will. You can not only save the original version of the image in pristine condition but also directly change the pixels of an image without changing its resolution. The image resolution remains as high as when you started.

Go ahead and have fun with your photos. This chapter is all about using iPhoto to its fullest potential for improving and enhancing images. You find out how to adjust the brightness and contrast, remove the annoying red-eye effect in the photo subject's eyes, and retouch photos to remove blemishes and image artifacts. As the influential writer Arthur C. Clarke once said, "Any sufficiently advanced technology is indistinguishable from magic." He could have easily been talking about the editing and fine-tuning capabilities of iPhoto.

Editing Images

The obvious advantage that digital images have over prints is that you can change a digital image instantly. You can also make copies quickly and easily, and make changes to the copies without affecting the originals.

To edit a photo or an image, browse your iPhoto library and select its thumbnail, and then click the Edit tool on the toolbar. The photo or image appears in the Viewer pane, as shown in Figure 4-1, with editing buttons in the Quick Fixes pane along the right side and the Zoom slider in the lower left corner for zooming in and out. You click the Quick Fixes, Effects, and Adjust buttons in the upper left corner to switch panes from Quick Fixes to Effects or Adjust.

A row of thumbnails at the bottom of the Viewer pane shows all the pictures you're browsing — click any thumbnail to edit its image.

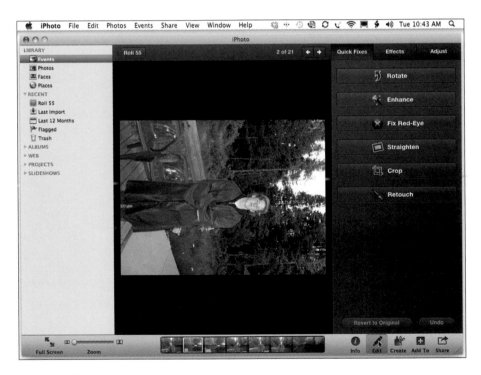

Figure 4-1: Making quick fixes on a photo.

If you select a video clip in iPhoto and click Edit, a warning appears that you can't edit the video clip in iPhoto, but you can still trim the clip — see "Trimming Video Clips" at the end of this chapter, and see Chapter 8 for details on editing video clips from iPhoto using iMovie.

Keep the following tips in mind when editing photos:

- ✔ Any changes you make to an image, such as cropping, rotating, or changing brightness or contrast, changes the image's appearance in the library and in every album where it appears.

- ✔ To change an image without changing it everywhere, make a duplicate of the image by selecting its thumbnail while browsing and choosing Photos⇨Duplicate (or Command+D). Then you can change the duplicate without changing the original.

- ✔ You can revert an image to its previous version by choosing Edit⇨Undo, thereby canceling the last edit or adjustment.

- ✔ You can always revert an image to its original version by choosing Photos⇨Revert to Original or clicking the Revert to Original button under the editing buttons in the lower right corner (refer to Figure 4-1) and then clicking OK in the warning dialog. Revert to Original removes all changes and restores the image to its original imported state.

Rotating and straightening

On some cameras, if you hold your camera sideways to take a picture of a tall object, such as a redwood tree, you end up with a photo that's horizontally oriented (the tree is on its side). You probably want to rotate the image to make it vertically oriented. You may want to rotate an image for other reasons as well — for example, to rotate photos shot by a camera held upside down or pointed down.

You can quickly and easily rotate images by using one of these methods:

- ✔ **While browsing thumbnails in the Viewer pane**: Select the thumbnail, click the pop-up menu button on the lower right side, and choose Rotate from the pop-up menu.

- ✔ **After selecting an image**: Choose Edit and then click the Rotate button in the Quick Fixes pane.

Either way, iPhoto rotates the entire image in 90-degree increments (right angles) counterclockwise. Every time you click Rotate, the photo rotates 90 degrees counterclockwise. To rotate clockwise, hold down the Option key while clicking Rotate. (You can switch to rotate clockwise when you click

Rotate, and counterclockwise by holding down Option first, by choosing iPhoto⇨Preferences, clicking the General tab, and then clicking the clockwise arrow for the Rotate option.)

Choose Edit⇨Undo if you don't like how the rotation turns out.

If the image is crooked, you can straighten it while editing. Follow these steps:

1. **Click the Straighten button in the Quick Fixes pane, as shown in Figure 4-2.**

2. **Drag the angle slider to straighten the image or set it at an angle.**

   A grid appears in order to make it easier to set the image straight. Dragging the angle slider to the right sets the image at a positive angle; to the left, at a negative angle (as much as 10 degrees either way).

3. **To finish, click Done.**

Figure 4-2: Straighten a photo by 2.5 degrees to the right (positive).

By combining rotation and straightening, iPhoto offers great flexibility for setting the image at an angle, either for special effect or to correct the perspective.

Cropping

The professionals who knew how to trim photos on a light table wielded precision knives with wild abandon and, most important, knew how to cut in straight lines. They used words such as *crop* to describe cutting away the outer edges of a photo, bringing the center of the photo to the forefront. You can crop an image to frame it better and show only what you want it to show, and combine cropping, straightening, and rotating to show only part of an image at the proper angle. And, you don't need to be able to draw or cut a straight line.

Cropping enables you to keep only a rectangular portion of the photo and remove its outer edge. Cropping is often better than stretching or resizing a photo, because the pixels within the cropped area don't change. You can use cropping to

- **Get rid of areas you don't want.** You can eliminate the outer portions of a photo to remove wasted space, crop out an ex-boyfriend who shouldn't be in the picture, or remove the fuzzy outline of a car window in a photo shot from a car.

- **Focus on the subject.** By cropping a photo, you can adjust where your subject appears in the frame of the picture, drawing more attention to your subject and improving its overall composition. Professional photographers, for example, may crop tightly around a person's face, removing most of the background.

- **Constrain the photo to fit a specific proportion.** You can use the Constrain feature to crop an image to a specific proportion. You may want to adjust the proportions of your photo to fit sizes for book layout or prints — by constraining the cropping selection, you produce better results because the picture is framed properly for the size of the print or book layout. Using the preset choices from the Constrain menu guarantees that the cropped image fits nicely in the format you need.

To crop an image, follow these steps:

1. **Browse your iPhoto library and select the thumbnail for the image, and then click the Edit tool on the toolbar.**

   After you click Edit, the selected image fills the Viewer pane and the Quick Fixes pane appears (refer to Figure 4-1).

2. **Click the Crop button in the Quick Fixes pane.**

   After clicking Crop, the cropping rectangle appears superimposed over the image in the Viewer pane.

3. **(Optional) Click the Constrain option and choose a format from the pop-up menu.**

   Constrain keeps the proportions accurate while you drag the cropping rectangle, so you don't need rulers, math expertise, and graphics skill to get it right for specific print dimensions. The Constrain option and pop-up menu underneath the Crop button offer a list of print sizes, such as

   - 4 x 6 (Postcard)
   - 2 x 3 (iPhone)
   - 8 x 10

   You can constrain these ratios in Portrait or Landscape view. You even find sizes such as 1024 x 768, a specific ratio that matches some computer screen pixels.

4. **Drag any corner or edge of the cropping rectangle to crop the image, or drag from the center to move the cropping rectangle.**

   For example, drag down the upper left corner of the cropping rectangle diagonally to define a new left corner, or reshape the rectangle by dragging an edge. As you drag, the portions of the image outside the selected area dim to show that it will be cut. You can also drag from the center of the cropping rectangle to drag the rectangle itself around the image, as shown in Figure 4-3. If you turned on Constrain in Step 3, the rectangle always stays at the correct ratio for the format you chose, but you can move the rectangle around the image and resize it. You can also drag the edges of the cropping rectangle to make it larger or smaller but still in the same proportion.

5. **Click Done to finish (or Reset to start over).**

Although many of us don't need to be extremely precise in cropping our photos, graphic artists and print-layout specialists may want precise image sizes for reproducing on printing presses. iPhoto lets you edit the image more precisely using the full display — click the Full Screen button in the lower left corner.

Figure 4-3: Drag the cropping rectangle into position.

Solving printing problems with cropped images

Problems can crop up, if you'll forgive the pun, when you try to print images that have been cropped or resized. The Constrain feature is useful because prints typically come in specific sizes such as 4 (width) x 6 (height), 5 x 7, and 8 x 10 inches. However, photos from some digital cameras can be sized at proportions of 4 x 3 or even 16 x 9, which may be fine for computer displays, DVDs, and iPhoto book layouts, but not the right proportion for typical prints. If you pay no attention to the Constrain feature, you may find that some photos have unintended white margins at the sides of the finished prints.

Use the Constrain feature if you're cropping for a print.

Although cropping has no effect on the cropping area, the other parts of the photo are removed, reducing the overall size of the photo. A photo at low resolution may, after cropping, be too low to print well at large sizes. The printer resizes the photo to fill the paper size, which makes the pixels larger and produces jagged edges. High-resolution cameras produce higher-quality prints at large sizes, even if you crop them.

Fine-Tuning Photos

Your vacation is over and you're looking over your photos. The beach shots look washed-out from way too much sunlight, and the forest shots look as dark as inside a cathedral. And, your youngest son is in the gift shop impersonating a red-eyed Martian.

You can work magic with the iPhoto Quick Fixes, Effects, and Adjust tools, improving photos that would otherwise be fuzzy, too dark, or too bright. Poor lighting is often the biggest problem with photos. But the Fix Red-Eye button in the Quick Fixes pane can remove the red spots that a flash creates in your subject's eyes. (It can also reduce the amount of red in any selected area of a photo.) You can also remove anomalies and blemishes by using the Retouch button in the Quick Fixes pane and enhance the colors in a photo with the Enhance button. The Adjust pane lets you adjust the exposure, contrast, and saturation, and the Effects pane lets you combine effects to produce professional-looking results.

Removing red-eye and red tint

Red-eye is light from the camera's flash, reflected back. Red-eye happens frequently with humans because red is the color of the eye's retinal tissue. (You get green-eye or even blue- or yellow-eye when taking pictures of some dogs and cats, whose retinal tissues aren't red.) Red-eye can be more prominent in photos shot in dim rooms, because the eye's pupils are dilated and exposing more retina.

The red-eye effect is a common problem in flash photography — so common that many digital cameras come with built-in red-eye reduction. But my shots prove that my digital camera still zaps people's eyes with red even with this reduction feature — either that or it proves that I don't know how to use the camera's reduction feature.

It doesn't matter. You have a magic wand in iPhoto that zaps red-eye. Follow these steps:

1. **Browse your iPhoto library and select the thumbnail for the image, and then click the Edit tool on the toolbar.**

   After you click Edit, the selected image fills the Viewer pane and the Quick Fixes pane appears (refer to Figure 4-1).

2. **Zoom into the photo.**

   Use the Zoom slider to zoom into the eyes. (You can click inside the navigation window that appears in the lower right corner of the iPhoto window to move the zoomed view around the image and then close the navigation window by clicking the circled *x* in the upper left corner.)

3. **Click the Fix Red-Eye button in the Quick Fixes pane.**

    A circle with four handles then appears over the image as you move your pointer, as shown in Figure 4-4. The circle defines the area that will be changed.

4. **Do one of the following:**

    - *Click the Auto-Fix Red-Eye option.* This option looks for the obvious red eyes in the image and reduces the red tint in them. However, it may not do the job the way you want — which is why you have a second choice.

    - *Adjust the red-eye area size with the Size slider, and then click on the area to change.* You can click your own areas to reduce the red tint — as close as possible to the actual red part of the eye — so that you don't change any other part of the face.

5. **To apply the change, click Done.**

    The eyes may now be a lot darker than before, but at least they don't look bright red.

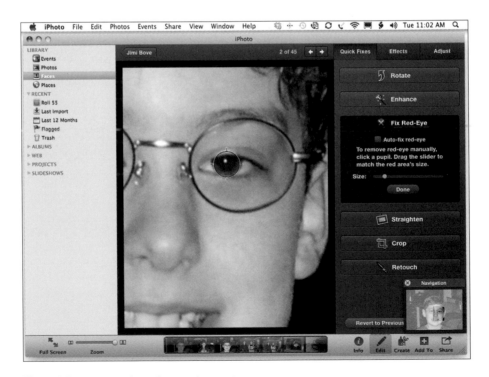

Figure 4-4: Remove red-eye from a photo.

Retouching and enhancing photos

When you begin retouching and enhancing photos, photos can begin to depart from reality. (Removing red-eye is, after all, just removing an effect that the camera put there.) You can literally alter the photo with iPhoto in such a way that even a judge and jury couldn't tell the difference. You can remove anomalies and blemishes by using the Retouch button and enhance the colors in a photo by using the Enhance button.

To retouch a photo, follow these steps:

1. **Browse your iPhoto library and select the thumbnail for the image, and then click the Edit tool on the toolbar.**

   The selected image fills the Viewer pane and the Quick Fixes pane appears (refer to Figure 4-1).

2. **Zoom in to the photo.**

   Use the Zoom slider to zoom into the area to retouch.

3. **Click the Retouch button in the Quick Fixes pane.**

   The Retouch tool displays a circle over the image as you move your pointer, as shown in Figure 4-5. The circle defines the area that will be changed. You can adjust the size of this circle by dragging the Size slider under the Retouch button.

4. **Click the circle on the image or drag over the circle.**

   Click once to retouch evenly within the circled area, or drag over the circled area as though you're using a brush. The circled area blends into the surrounding pixels, removing (or at least blurring) the blemish or spot. Life would be so much easier if getting rid of real blemishes were this easy.

5. **To apply the change, click Done.**

The Retouch feature *clones* neighboring pixels and uses them to replace the pixels in the circled area, blending them by manipulating color values. (And you thought cloning was for sheep!)

The Enhance button works on the entire photo. It performs a combination of operations, including subtle adjustments to the exposure, contrast, saturation, and other color settings to bring out more clarity and saturated color in the image.

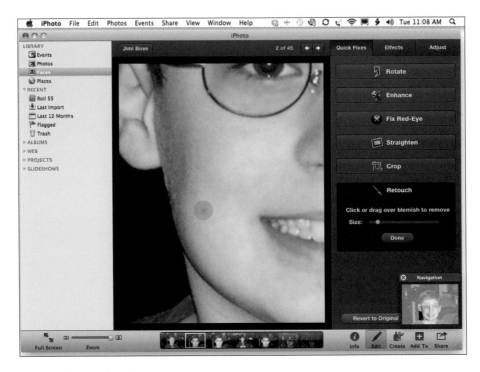

Figure 4-5: Retouch a photo.

To enhance a photo, select the picture's thumbnail and click the Edit tool, and then click the Enhance button in the Quick Fixes pane. The essential effect of Enhance is to make the colors, and the overall photo, more vivid.

Adjusting exposure, contrast, and saturation

Some of the best indoor photos are taken with light streaming through a window, using only ambient light. (Why, then, when you sit for a portrait photo, does the photographer spend more time on lights than on anything else?) With natural, ambient light, your camera reads the lighting for the entire room and reveals more depth in the background and surroundings. Ambient light from various sources, such as lamps and overhead lights, produces a softer, more balanced photo with less contrast. With a flash, only about ten feet in front of the camera is illuminated, and everything beyond fades to black.

Whatever the lighting conditions are when you take your photos, you can regain some of the detail lost in the darkness by using the Adjust pane and then adjusting the Exposure, Contrast, and Saturation sliders. These sliders show the effects of changes immediately.

To adjust these settings for a photo, follow these steps:

1. **Browse your iPhoto library and select the thumbnail for the image, and then click the Edit tool on the toolbar.**

   The selected image fills the Viewer pane and the Quick Fixes pane appears (refer to Figure 4-1).

2. **Click the Adjust tab to show the Adjust pane.**

   The Adjust pane appears to the right of the Viewer pane, as shown in Figure 4-6.

3. **Drag the sliders left or right to make changes.**

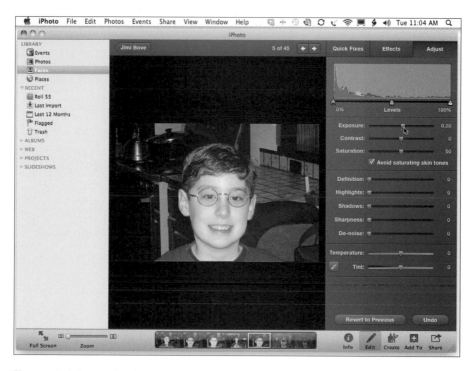

Figure 4-6: Adjust a photo's color levels, exposure, contrast, and saturation and other settings.

You can bring out details in photos taken in poor lighting conditions by adjusting the Exposure and Contrast sliders. The sliders allow you to make incremental adjustments — drag each slider gradually until you create the effect you want, or click anywhere along the slider bar to jump directly to a setting.

4. **If you don't like the last change you made, you can click the Revert to Previous button at the bottom of the Adjust pane to reset the sliders to their previous settings.**

   You can also continue to undo changes by clicking the Undo button next to the Revert to Previous button or choosing Edit⇔Undo.

Adding effects

Some scenes just look better with faded color, and others (especially historic scenes) look better in a sepia tone. Antique-looking images can evoke a moody atmosphere. The vignette effect can be effective for portraits to create an enhanced starkness around the face, and black-and-white can be useful for trying to achieve the Ansel Adams look.

You can add one or more of these effects to your image by selecting the picture's thumbnail in the Viewer pane, clicking the Edit tool, and then clicking the Effects tab in the upper right corner to show the Effects pane. The Effects pane appears to the right of the Viewer pane.

Some effects, such as B & W (black and white), can be turned on or off by clicking the effect tile once in the Effects pane. Others, such as Vignette, have levels you can set by clicking the left or right arrow inside the effect tile in the Effects pane. You can combine effects by clicking one tile and then another. Click the Revert to Original button at the bottom of the Effects pane to remove all effects, or click Undo to undo the last change.

Trimming Video Clips

To trim video clips in your iPhoto library, browse your library as I describe in Chapter 2 and double-click the thumbnail for the video clip. The player controls appear, along with a gear icon that displays a pop-up menu. Click the gear icon and choose Trim from the pop-up menu. A frame viewer appears below the video clip, as shown in Figure 4-7.

Figure 4-7: Drag the ends of the frame viewer and then click Trim.

To trim the beginning or ending of the clip, drag either the beginning or the end of the frame viewer to a new position. For example, you can drag the right end of the frame viewer (the end of the clip) to the left, and the left end of the frame viewer (the beginning of the clip) to the right, to trim both the beginning and end of the clip (refer to Figure 4-7).

Click the Play button to the left of the frame viewer to view the temporarily trimmed video clip. You can adjust the ends of the frame viewer to trim more precisely until you have it the way you want it. To save the trimmed version, click the Trim button in the lower right corner; or click Cancel to restore the full clip without trimming.

5

Enjoying Slideshows

In This Chapter

▶ Creating a slideshow

▶ Controlling slideshow playback and adding music

▶ Sharing slideshows online

▶ Exporting slideshows to QuickTime and iDVD

*Y*ou may remember the old days when slides were projected onto white walls or sheets and the click-clack sound of the slide carousel on the projector drowned out all other sound. Slideshows of this sort were the only way to exhibit photos to a group of people.

Photos look great on computer displays, and using laptops to connect directly to video projectors, you can put on shows nothing like your grandfather's slideshows. Not only do the images look fantastic, but you can also set them to music, fade between each image, mix video clips with still images, repeat the slideshow in a loop endlessly, and generally make a slideshow look as good as a professional slideshow in a boardroom or kiosk.

In this chapter, you discover how to change transitions and other settings to fine-tune your slideshow. I also describe how to choose the best pictures, share slideshows with friends, and create a movie from a slideshow.

Creating and Playing a Slideshow

Follow these steps to create a slideshow with a particular selection of images in mind:

1. **Select the pictures to use for the slideshow.**

   You can browse and select thumbnails in the Viewer pane while browsing or select one or more events in Events, one or more locations in Places, or one or more faces in Faces, as described in Chapter 2. Or, you can select the most recently browsed event, Last Import, or Flagged in the Recent section of the Source pane, or any photo album, any MobileMe, Flickr, or Facebook album, or any project. The section "Assembling pictures for an exhibition," later in this chapter, offers more details about selecting photos.

2. **Click the Slideshow tool in the toolbar.**

   The Slideshow tool looks like a CD player Play button. After you click Slideshow, the first image fills the screen and the Themes, Music, and Settings browser appears on top, as shown in Figure 5-1.

3. **(Optional) Choose a theme and some music for the slideshow, and change its settings.**

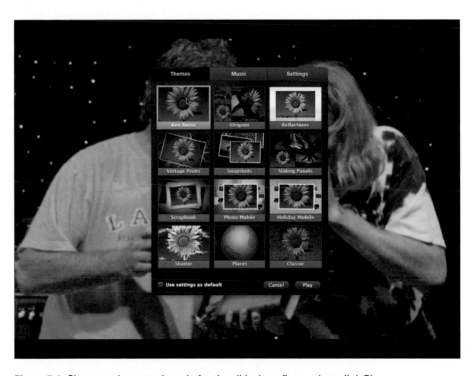

Figure 5-1: Choose a theme and music for the slideshow first, or just click Play.

The first time you play a slideshow of the selected album or pictures, the Themes, Music, and Settings browser appears (refer to Figure 5-1). See the later section "Choosing a theme and music" for details on choosing themes and music and see "Changing playback settings" for changing settings.

4. **Click the Play button in the slideshow settings (or Cancel).**

   After you click Play, the slideshow starts. iPhoto remembers the theme, music, and settings so that you don't have to choose them the next time you click Slideshow.

5. **Control playback with the slideshow controls.**

   The slideshow control panel appears whenever you move the pointer during a slideshow, as shown in Figure 5-2. Click the Pause button in the control panel to pause the show, and the button changes to a Play button; click the Play button to resume. Click the left arrow on the control panel to go to the previous slide, or the right arrow to go to the next slide — or press the left- or right-arrow keys on the keyboard. You can also pause the slideshow by pressing the spacebar. To resume playing, press the spacebar again. To stop the slideshow, click the circled *x* on the right side of the control panel (or press the Esc key).

Figure 5-2: Control slideshow playback.

6. **Save or export your slideshow.**

    Save or export it so you that you can play it again or share it with others, as explained in "Saving and Editing a Slideshow" and "Exporting Slideshows," later in this chapter.

If your slideshow doesn't look as good as you expect, check your display settings. To find out how to change them, see Chapter 1.

Setting Up Slideshow Features

Words are inadequate to express the feeling you have when you first look at a full-screen slideshow of photos you've taken. The display fades to black, and each image fills the screen for about five seconds before dissolving into the next image.

Here's the point: You can change the duration, settings, and other visual elements as you want. You can also choose from a variety of themes and hear music associated with the theme of the slideshow or music of your own choice.

Assembling pictures for an exhibition

You probably want to rearrange images in order to create slideshows that are at least interesting, if not dazzling. You can do this by choosing the best pictures and the most appropriate music.

iPhoto offers different ways to select pictures for a slideshow:

- **Show a photo album:** The advantage of using a photo album is that the pictures in an album are easy to rearrange, as I describe in Chapter 3. Select a photo album in the Albums section of the Source pane, and then click the Slideshow tool. The slideshow consists of all pictures in the album, starting with the first picture. To start with a different picture, select that picture's thumbnail first in the Viewer pane, before clicking Slideshow.

- **Show a selection of photo albums:** The same advantage of using a photo album applies (as stated in the preceding bullet), and in addition, you can play multiple albums at a time by Command-clicking each one to select it first. The slideshow combines pictures from all the albums in the sequence in which they appear in the albums.

✔ **Show all pictures for a location, an event, or a face:** Browse Events, Places, or Faces and select an event, a location, or a face (as I describe in Chapter 2). You may want to open the event, location, or face and sort the thumbnails first, to put them in a specific order (such as by date or title) for the slideshow. Then click the Slideshow tool. The slideshow starts with the first picture — to start with a different picture, select that picture's thumbnail first in the Viewer pane, before clicking Slideshow.

✔ **Show the entire library:** Browse Photos (as I describe in Chapter 2). You may want to sort the thumbnails first, to put them in a specific order (such as by date or title) for the slideshow. Then click the Slideshow tool. The slideshow starts with the first picture — to start with a different picture, select that picture's thumbnail first in the Viewer pane, before clicking Slideshow.

✔ **Show selected pictures only:** Select multiple thumbnails in the Viewer pane — either a range of pictures in consecutive order or individual pictures in nonconsecutive order. The slideshow uses only those pictures.

You may want to play a makeshift slideshow of selected pictures just to experiment with them to see whether they would work well in the final version of the slideshow. The pictures may not be ready for slideshow viewing — you may want to crop or rotate some of them, or enhance or adjust them (as I describe in Chapter 4), before playing the final version of the slideshow.

Not all photos fill the screen properly. You may want to use only photos that look good at full-display dimensions.

iPhoto uses the entire display resolution when putting on a slideshow. If your photos are smaller than the resolution of the display, iPhoto stretches them to fill the display or displays a black border. To ensure that your photos are large enough to look good in a full-screen slideshow, you can check the size in the Info pane. Select a thumbnail in the Viewer pane and click the Info tool. The Info pane displays at the top a number similar to 3072 x 2304, which is the size of the photo (3072 pixels wide by 2304 pixels high).

Choosing a theme and music

Are you ready for a performance? Possibly not — you may want to choose one of the jazzy built-in themes and set the slideshow to music.

The first time you click the Slideshow tool to play a slideshow of an album or a selection of pictures that hasn't yet been played, the Themes, Music, and Settings browser appears (refer to Figure 5-1). Click the Themes tab for the Themes pane.

In the Themes pane, click a theme for the slideshow, such as Snapshots or Sliding Panels (or Classic, if you prefer a straightforward image-by-image presentation with the dissolve effect). iPhoto even provides a Ken Burns theme — named for the famous documentary filmmaker known for using a still-photo technique for dramatic effect in his documentaries *Civil War* and *Jazz.* (Often, music as well as the voice of the narrator accompanies the still photos, and you can accomplish this effect by creating a soundtrack in GarageBand, covered in Part V of this book, and choosing that soundtrack in the Music pane.)

While playing a slideshow, you can click the Slides icon in the playback control panel (refer to Figure 5-2) to open the Themes pane and choose a different theme, or the Music icon to open the Music pane and choose music.

Apple also thoughtfully provides nice music to go along with your slideshows. Music makes a slideshow come alive, by turning ordinary (and extraordinary) photos into something that resembles parts of a Ken Burns documentary. (Okay, so maybe your family vacation doesn't rank up there, no matter what you may think.)

Click the Music tab in the Themes, Music, and Settings browser for the Music pane, as shown in Figure 5-3. At the top is the Play Music During Slideshow option, which you can turn off by clicking to remove the check mark, or leave on. Under that is the Source pop-up menu, which lets you choose the source of your music.

Figure 5-3: Choose music for the slideshow.

The list under the Source pop-up menu changes, depending on the choice you make in the Source pop-up menu:

- **Sample Music** displays music provided by Apple.
- **Theme Music** displays popular music licensed by Apple to go with the themes.
- **GarageBand** displays your own creations in GarageBand.
- **iTunes** displays your entire iTunes library.
- **iTunes Playlists** displays playlists by name, including Genius and Purchased playlists and smart playlists.
- **A playlist in your iTunes library** (such as White Shoe playlist in Figure 5-3) displays the songs in the playlist.

You can also search for songs in your iTunes library by first selecting iTunes from the Source pop-up menu, clicking inside the Search field underneath the list, and then typing a word or part of a word. iPhoto begins searching immediately for artists, song titles, and albums in your iTunes library that match.

To listen to a song first, click the song in the list and then click the CD-style Play button to the left of the Search field; click the button again to stop.

To use the song for the slideshow, select it in the list and click Play in the lower right corner of the Music pane. The song repeats for the duration of the slideshow.

To use a playlist, select the playlist in the list and click Play in the lower right corner of the Music pane (refer to Figure 5-3). The playlist starts with the first song and continues to the end of the playlist before starting over. (You can adjust the timing of your slideshow to play as long as the music plays, or to make the music repeat. See the later section "Changing playback settings.")

The Custom Playlist for Slideshow option lets you create a playlist on the fly, just for this slideshow. Click the option and a box appears below it (refer to Figure 5-3). You can then drag songs from the list above into the box to create the custom playlist. You can even drag the tracks up and down in the custom playlist box to rearrange them.

To play the slideshow after choosing a theme and music, click Play in the lower right corner of the Themes or Music pane. iPhoto saves the slideshow settings for the photo album or selected pictures.

Changing playback settings

The first time you click the Slideshow tool to play a slideshow of an album or a selection of pictures that hasn't been played, the Themes, Music, and Settings browser appears (refer to Figure 5-1). Click the Settings tab to see the Settings pane of the browser, as shown in Figure 5-4.

Figure 5-4: Change the slideshow duration and other settings.

While playing a slideshow, you can click the Gear icon in the playback control panel (refer to Figure 5-2) to open the Settings pane.

The Settings pane lets you change the duration of the slideshow, set transitions, scale images to fit the screen, shuffle the slide order, repeat the slideshow endlessly, and show titles and captions, as described in this list:

✔ **To set the duration for a specific amount of time,** click the Play Each Slide For a Minimum of . . . Seconds setting, so that slides appear onscreen for the duration you want (while the music repeats). The up and down arrows for the Seconds button lets you adjust the number in tenths of a second. The number of seconds you choose applies to every slide in the slideshow.

If you use a photo album for your slideshow, the timing is saved with it. You can try different timings by setting up multiple photo albums and changing the settings for each one.

- ✔ **To fit the slideshow to the length of a song or playlist,** click the Fit Slideshow to Music option. The duration of each slide is adjusted so that the slideshow and song (or playlist) finish at the same time.

- ✔ **To repeat the slideshow in a loop,** keep the Repeat Slideshow option turned on. If you turn off this option, iPhoto plays the slideshow and, at the end, returns to the Viewer pane. This option may be useful for previewing, but you may want your slideshows to repeat, especially if you're using a slideshow in an exhibit or on a demonstration table.

Some themes are already equipped to use special transitions between slides, but others, such as Classic and Ken Burns, let you choose your own transition between slides. To set a different transition and the transition speed, follow these steps in the Settings pane:

1. **Click the Transition option (refer to Figure 5-4), and then select a transition from the pop-up menu.**

2. **To set the speed of the transition, drag the Speed slider under the pop-up menu.**

3. **Set the direction of the transition by clicking the up, down, left, or right arrows in the circular button next to the Speed slider.**

   A preview of the transition appears in the tiny frame next to the circular button.

If you've diligently added titles and descriptions to your pictures as I describe in Chapter 2, you can use one or both for captions or use places or dates as captions. Click the Show Captions option, and pick what to use from the pop-up menu: Titles, Descriptions, Titles and Descriptions, Places, or Dates.

You can also set the slideshow to show a title slide at the beginning with the name of the photo album or selection: Choose the Show Title Slide option. If you want to experiment with the slide order, choose Shuffle Slide Order.

To save your settings without playing the slideshow, click the Use Settings As Default option. Doing so doesn't mean that other slideshows will use these settings — just that the particular slideshow based on this selection of pictures or photo album will always start with these settings.

Saving and Editing a Slideshow

If you base your slideshow on a photo album, the slideshow settings are saved with that album. However, you may want to save the slideshow itself — especially if you selected pictures by browsing or if you want to fine-tune the settings and save them permanently. Follow these steps:

1. **After playing a slideshow, leave the thumbnails selected in the Viewer pane. If you selected a photo album, leave the photo album selected.**

2. **Click the Create tool on the toolbar and choose Slideshow from the pop-up menu that appears.**

3. **Enter a name for the slideshow in the Name field (or use the name supplied) and click Create.**

   iPhoto creates a new section of the Source pane (if it hasn't been created already) named Slideshows and saves the selected pictures as a permanent slideshow.

Select the slideshow's name in the Slideshows section of the Source pane. You can then click the Play or Preview buttons to view the saved slideshow, click Themes to change its theme, click Music to change its music, or click Text Slide to add a text slide, such as a title slide or credits. Click Settings to open the Slideshow Settings pane, shown in Figure 5-5.

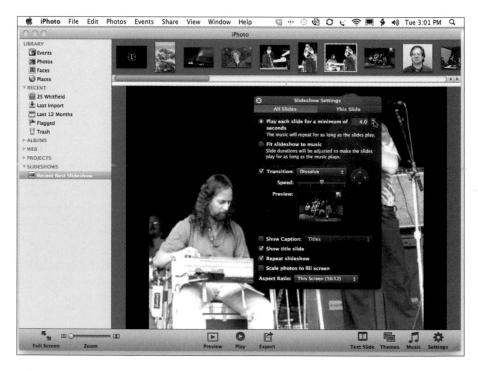

Figure 5-5: Change settings for a saved slideshow.

In the Slideshow Settings pane, click All Slides at the top to make changes to all slides at one time, or click This Slide to make changes to settings for only this slide. Using this powerful feature, you can edit your slideshow to your heart's content, by changing the duration, transition, and other settings for each slide.

Exporting Slideshows

A slideshow on your computer is wonderful for those who can pull up a seat and watch. If you have a laptop, iPad, iPod, or iPhone, you no doubt already appreciate the slideshows you can show others on the spot. But to reach a larger audience, or different audiences at different times, you have some options:

✔ **Share your slideshow online.**

   The entire slideshow can be made available online (in the Gallery section of your MobileMe account) for others to view. See Chapter 6 for details.

✔ **Export your slideshow in a format suitable for an iPad, iPod, or iPhone or for Apple TV.**

   You can export the slideshow in format sizes that work well with these devices.

✔ **Export your slideshow to a QuickTime movie.**

   You can post a QuickTime movie on a Web page and include it with other scenes in an iMovie presentation.

✔ **Import your slideshow into iDVD to make a DVD.**

   You can use your slideshow, including music, with iDVD, which gives you tools to improve the slideshow and burn a DVD disc. I describe how to import slideshows into iDVD in Chapter 12.

In addition, you can share individual pictures with others via e-mail, Flickr, or Facebook and publish individual pictures on a Web page. I describe how to do all these tasks in Chapter 6.

Exporting to an iPad, iPod, or iPhone, or to Apple TV

Slideshows can appear horizontally (in *Landscape mode*) on an iPad, iPod touch, iPod nano, or iPhone screen, and if you rotate the screen 180 degrees to the opposite horizontal position, it adjusts accordingly. All the controls you expect in a DVD player are on the screen at the touch of a finger. You can also view slideshows on an iPod classic.

Or, you can just sit back on your couch and let Apple TV offer up your slide-shows. *Apple TV* is sort of a large iPod that wirelessly streams content from one or more iTunes libraries to play on your high-definition (HD) television and audio system.

To export your slideshows for these devices, follow these steps:

1. **Save the slideshow as I describe in "Saving and Editing a Slideshow," earlier in this chapter.**

2. **Select the slideshow in the Slideshows section of the Source pane and click the Export button in the middle of the toolbar, along the bottom of the iPhoto window (refer to Figure 5-5).**

   The Export dialog appears, as shown in Figure 5-6.

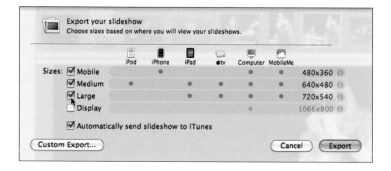

Figure 5-6: Export a slideshow in several formats at a time.

3. **Choose one or more format sizes for your exported slideshow.**

   If you choose more than one, multiple slideshow files are created and transferred to iTunes for synchronizing with these devices.

4. **Select the Automatically Send Slideshow to iTunes option to send the slideshow to iTunes in one step.**

5. **Click Export to start the export operation, which may take quite a bit of time.**

The QuickTime resolution for slideshows

You have some choices to make about how you plan to use a slideshow before exporting a QuickTime movie. You can make a movie as large as your display (which is how iPhoto typically plays slideshows). However, pixel resolution affects file size dramatically, and you need to make a movie that everyone can play. If you specify 1024 x 768 pixels (the typical lowest display setting for slideshows on an iMac), the resulting movie may still be too large to send as an e-mail attachment — if that's what you want to do with it. Your movie's screen size may also be too large for other people's displays.

Although you can type any number you want as a pixel dimension, you should maintain the 4:3 aspect ratio that digital cameras and displays use. You can, however, reverse the ratio and specify 480 x 640 pixels, if all photos in the slideshow are vertically oriented.

A resolution of 800 x 600 is okay for just about all computer displays, but 640 x 480, the suggested resolution, is by far the most commonly used. With 640 x 480 pixels, the resulting file size is small and easy to handle by e-mail or another means (such as publishing on a Web page). For example, a slideshow of ten photos, at a 640 x 480 pixel image size, creates a QuickTime file that is 1MB; the same slideshow at 800 x 600 pixels creates a 1.5MB file, and at 1024 x 768 pixels, a 2.3MB file.

Remember: Music takes up a considerable amount of space. A slideshow saved as a QuickTime file with music is a lot larger than the same file saved without music. With music, the file size jumps to 1.6MB for a slideshow with ten photos at a 640 x 480 resolution. Without music, you'd have . . . a silent movie.

Exporting a QuickTime movie file

QuickTime is sort of a container for multimedia built into every Mac and available to any PC user intelligent enough to use iTunes — it's installed with every Windows version of iTunes.

When you create a QuickTime movie file, even those dudes with Dells and geeks with Gateways can play it. You send it to them on a CD or DVD, or you can also publish a QuickTime file on a Web site for anyone to play.

To put your slideshow into a QuickTime file, follow these steps:

1. **Save the slideshow.**

   See the section "Saving and Editing a Slideshow," earlier in this chapter, for specific instructions.

2. **Click Export.**

   The Export dialog appears (refer to Figure 5-6).

3. **Click Custom Export and choose a QuickTime format.**

   The Save As dialog box opens, with the Export pop-up menu of format choices. From the pop-up menu, choose Movie to QuickTime Movie or Movie to MPEG-4, depending on which format you want.

4. **Click Options to set QuickTime video and sound options, such as compression settings and filters, and then click OK.**

   An explanation of all possible settings for QuickTime movies is beyond the scope of this book. (See the nearby sidebar "The QuickTime resolution for slideshows.")

5. **Type a name for the QuickTime movie and choose where to save it on your hard disk, and then click the Save button.**

To view the finished movie, open the movie file using QuickTime Player or any other application that plays QuickTime movies. Your slideshow looks like a professional presentation and now you can share it with the world.

For more information about exporting QuickTime movies, see Chapter 11.

Sharing Pictures Online

In This Chapter

▶ Sharing photos and images by e-mail

▶ Publishing pictures on Facebook and Flickr

▶ Sharing pictures with MobileMe

▶ Publishing pictures to your iWeb site

▶ Exporting pictures to files

*P*eople generally save pictures for posterity, nostalgia, history, and hundreds of other reasons, but for the most part, they save pictures so that others can see them.

Going online creates a whole new set of possibilities for sharing your pictures. You can share pictures you never considered sharing — a school play, the family vacation — even business opportunities. If you need to share photos, images, or video clips, you can probably do it more cheaply and easily online.

E-mail is perhaps the most ubiquitous medium for sharing images and photos. It's practically effortless and costs nothing with an Internet connection, so why not? In a quick instant, you can e-mail photos to friends and family (perhaps too quickly, because you didn't want your mother to see those shots from the local pub.)

If you use the MobileMe service, you can share photo albums, slideshows, and movies by inviting family and friends in an e-mail message containing just a single link, and your family and friends can add comments and upload their own pictures if you permit it. You can also publish and manage your Facebook or Flickr albums, send pictures and video clips to iWeb to use in your own Web site, and export these items to files that you can then use with other programs.

Attaching Pictures to E-Mail

Sending a photo attached to an e-mail message is perhaps the most common use of the Internet, other than browsing the Web, of course. E-mail is a helpful way to send an image to one person or a thousand people at the same time (although I discourage spamming — please don't send me photos unless I know you). You can even combine several photos and images in one e-mail, if they're small: E-mail servers typically limit message size to about 5MB or 10MB. Adding one photo or image to an e-mail is easy and almost always works.

Every photo that you're considering sending in a single e-mail must be encoded for e-mail transmission, which makes the photo's file about 40 percent larger.

If you have an e-mail account and you're ready to send a message, attaching a single photo or image is simple. Follow these steps:

1. **Browse and select one or more thumbnails for photo or images (but not video clips).**

   Browse your iPhoto library as I describe in Chapter 2, and select each thumbnail.

2. **Click the Share tool on the toolbar and choose Email from the pop-up menu, as shown in Figure 6-1 (or choose Share➪Email).**

   The e-mail message appears in the Viewer pane with e-mail themes on the right. (The Snapshots theme is selected.)

3. **Choose a theme for the e-mail message.**

   You can choose any of the themes on the right for your message; I chose the Celebration theme in Figure 6-2.

4. **(Optional) Choose Optimized or Actual Size from the Photo Size pop-up menu.**

   The Optimized choice offers faster downloading; Actual Size offers higher quality.

5. **Add the To address, type text on the Subject line, and change your From address, if you want.**

   If you have multiple e-mail accounts, they appear on the From pop-up menu so that you can choose one.

Choosing Email from the pop-up menu

Figure 6-1: Share the selected photo by e-mail.

6. **Type text in the e-mail message.**

   The theme offers placeholders for inserting text, such as a name and date for the Celebration theme (refer to Figure 6-2).

7. **Click Send at the bottom of the e-mail message to send the message.**

iPhoto creates an e-mail message encoded in HTML (the same type of code used for Web pages) and compresses the photo. However, some people don't like to receive HTML-encoded e-mail, and sometimes you want to send the original uncompressed image. If you want to send the photo without HTML, or in its original file format with no loss in quality (and no compression), create a new e-mail message using your e-mail program (such as Mail) and leave its window open. Then switch to iPhoto and drag the thumbnail for the photo directly into the message window to attach the file.

Figure 6-2: An e-mail message that's almost ready to send.

If you want to use PDF as the file format (which is universal for viewing anything from a single photo to a slideshow or photo book — don't share using the Email selection. See Chapter 7 to find out how to save a PDF file and use the Mail application to attach the PDF file to the message.

Sharing with Facebook

Facebook is the fastest-growing, free-access social networking site as of this book's publication, with hundreds of millions of active users worldwide. If you're one of them (as I am), you already know that you can upload photos, images, and video clips to your personal profile by using the Safari browser on your Mac. But far more convenient is managing your Facebook albums directly in iPhoto — adding and deleting photos and editing their information, for example.

To create a new album or add photos or images to an existing album in your Facebook account, follow these steps:

1. **Browse and select one or more thumbnails for pictures.**

   Browse your iPhoto library as I describe in Chapter 2.

2. **Click the Share tool on the toolbar and choose Facebook from the pop-up menu (refer to Figure 6-1), or choose Share⇨Facebook.**

   If this is the first time you're using your Facebook account with iPhoto, follow the instructions to allow iPhoto to publish to your Facebook account. You have to log in to your Facebook account by using your e-mail address and password. After setting up iPhoto to work with Facebook, repeat this step.

   Your Facebook albums appear on a pop-up menu, as shown in Figure 6-3.

Figure 6-3: Select a Facebook album, your profile's Wall, or a new Facebook album.

3. **Select one of these options from the pop-up menu shown in Figure 6-3:**

   • *New Album:* Creates a new Facebook album

   • *An existing Facebook album:* Adds the photos or images to an already existing album

   • *Wall:* Posts the photos or images to your Facebook profile's Wall

   After you select New Album, a Facebook album, or Wall, a dialog appears with the album name and privacy settings, as shown in Figure 6-4.

4. **If you chose New Album, type a new album name for the new Facebook album (refer to Figure 6-4).**

5. **To control privacy, change the Photos Viewable By option from Everyone to Friends of Friends or Only Friends.**

Figure 6-4: Publish the selected picture on Facebook.

6. **Click Publish to publish the photos or images to the Facebook album (or click Cancel to cancel).**

   iPhoto may take a few seconds or minutes to upload the pictures to Facebook.

You can view the albums you've uploaded to your Facebook account by clicking your Facebook account name in the Web section of the Source pane. You can then select the album and manage its pictures and information, as shown in Figure 6-5.

You can also use your browser to view the album in Facebook by clicking the right arrow next to the album title at the top of the Viewer pane after selecting the Facebook album (refer to Figure 6-5).

Select your Facebook account name

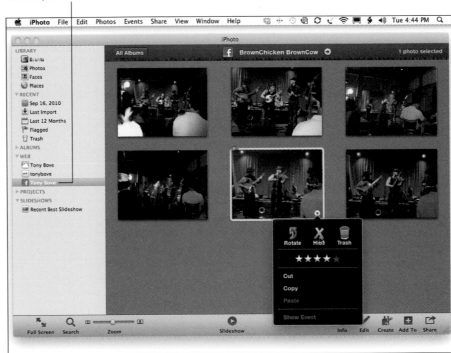

Figure 6-5: Manage photos in the Facebook album.

After you've created a Facebook album, you can then edit the album in iPhoto in two ways:

- **Add other pictures to a Facebook album.** Choose the album in Step 3 in the preceding step list.

- **Edit the picture information published in the Facebook album.** After clicking your Facebook account name in the Web section of the Source pane and selecting the album, click the Info button to edit the title, description, and keywords, as I do in Figure 6-6. You can also delete pictures from the Facebook album by selecting their thumbnails and choosing Photos➪Delete from Album.

Figure 6-6: Add keywords and edit the album information.

Sharing with Flickr

The *Flickr* photo-and-video site doubles as an online community: You can give your friends, family, and other contacts permission to add comments, notes, and tags to your pictures. Besides being popular for sharing photos, Flickr is widely used by bloggers as a photo repository. You can upload photos, images, and video clips to Flickr using the Safari browser on your Mac, but uploading pictures directly from iPhoto is far more convenient.

To create a new album or to add photos or images to an existing album (a *set* in your Flickr account's *photostream*), follow these steps:

1. **Browse and select one or more thumbnails for pictures.**

   Browse your iPhoto library as I describe in Chapter 2.

2. **Click the Share tool on the toolbar and choose Flickr from the pop-up menu (refer to Figure 6-1), or choose Share⇨Flickr.**

If this is the first time you're using your Flickr account with iPhoto, follow the instructions to allow iPhoto to publish to your Flickr account. You have to log in to your Flickr account with your username and password. After setting up iPhoto to work with Flickr, repeat this step.

Your Flickr sets appear on a pop-up menu, as shown in Figure 6-7.

3. **Select an option from the pop-up menu shown in Figure 6-7:**

   - *New Set:* Creates a new Flickr set (album)

   - *An existing Flickr set:* Adds the photos or images to a set you've already created

   - *Photostream:* Posts the photos or images to your Flickr account's photostream

   After you select New Set, a Flickr set, or Photostream, a dialog appears with the set name and privacy level and size settings, as shown in Figure 6-8.

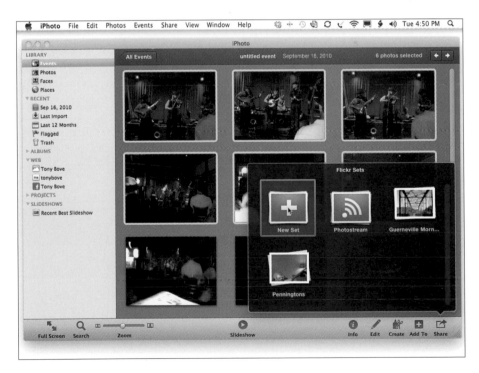

Figure 6-7: Select a Flickr set (album), your account's photostream, or a new Flickr set.

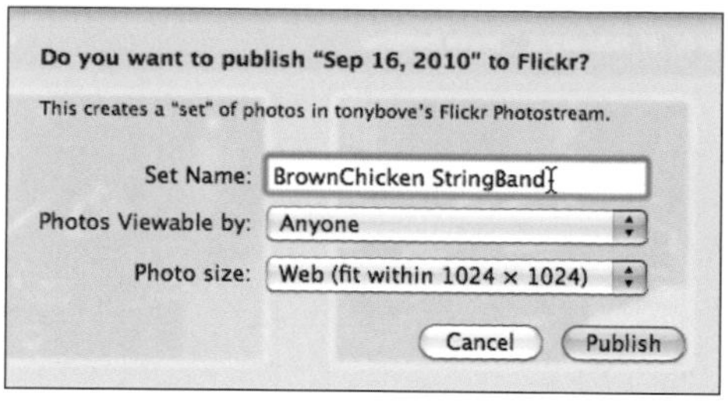

Do you want to publish "Sep 16, 2010" to Flickr?

This creates a "set" of photos in tonybove's Flickr Photostream.

Set Name: | BrownChicken StringBand |

Photos Viewable by: | Anyone |

Photo size: | Web (fit within 1024 × 1024) |

Cancel | Publish

Figure 6-8: Publish the selected picture on Flickr.

4. **If you chose New Set, type a new set name for the new Flickr album (refer to Figure 6-8).**

5. **To control privacy for the uploaded pictures, change the Photos Viewable By option from Anyone to Only You, Your Friends, Your Family, or Your Friends and Family.**

6. **(Optional) Choose a different size from the Photo Size pop-up menu (refer to Figure 6-8).**

   Web is the standard size for fast uploading, Optimized is better for printing, and Actual Size is the original picture size.

7. **To publish the pictures, click Publish (or Cancel to cancel).**

   iPhoto may take a few seconds or minutes to upload the pictures to Flickr.

You can view the sets (albums) you've uploaded to Flickr by clicking your Flickr account name in the Web section of the Source pane. You can then select the set and manage its pictures — including clicking the Info button to add a description, as I do in Figure 6-9.

You can also view the Your Photostream section of your Flickr account in your browser by clicking the right arrow next to the set title at the top of the Viewer pane after selecting the Flickr set (refer to Figure 6-9).

After you've created a Flickr set, you can then edit the set in iPhoto in two ways:

✓ **Add other pictures to a Flickr set.** Choose the set in Step 3 in the preceding step list.

✓ **Edit the picture information published with the Flickr set.** After clicking your Flickr account name in the Web section of the Source pane and selecting the set, click the Info button to edit the title and description, as I do in Figure 6-9. You can also delete pictures from the Flickr set by selecting their thumbnails and choosing Photos➪Delete From Album.

Selecting your Flickr account

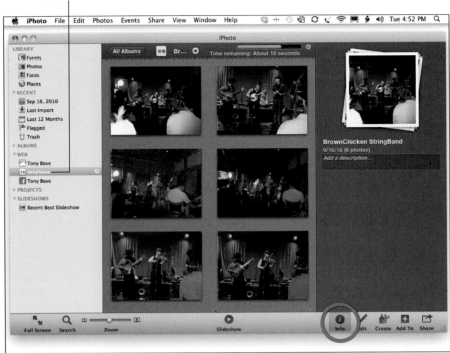

Figure 6-9: Manage the published set on Flickr and edit its information.

Sharing with MobileMe

You may already use MobileMe with your Mac — the service not only offers the iDisk hard drive on the Web for storing files but also pushes new e-mail, contacts, and calendar events to an iPad, iPhone, or iPod touch. What you may not know is that MobileMe also offers the Gallery section for sharing pictures with other people — they can view your pictures using any current Web browser and, if you give permission, download pictures and even contribute (upload) some of their own.

To create a new album or to add photos or images to an existing album in your MobileMe Gallery, follow these steps:

1. **Browse and select one or more thumbnails for pictures.**

   Browse your iPhoto library as I describe in Chapter 2.

2. **Click the Share tool on the toolbar and choose MobileMe Gallery from the pop-up menu (refer to Figure 6-1), or choose Share⇨MobileMe Gallery.**

If this is the first time you're using MobileMe, follow the instructions to acquire a MobileMe account. If this is the first time you're using your MobileMe account with iPhoto, you have to log in to your MobileMe account with your username and password. After setting up MobileMe to work with iPhoto, repeat this step.

Your albums in the MobileMe Gallery appear on a pop-up menu, as shown in Figure 6-10.

3. **From the pop-up menu shown in Figure 6-10, choose New Album to create a new album or select an existing album to add the photos or images to.**

   After you select New Album or an existing album in your MobileMe Gallery, a dialog appears and lists the album name and privacy settings, as shown in Figure 6-11.

4. **If you chose New Album, type an album name for the new album (refer to Figure 6-11).**

5. **To control the privacy level of uploaded pictures, change the Album Viewable By option from Everyone to Only Me, or choose Edit Names and Passwords to add the names and passwords of people you want to allow access to your album.**

Figure 6-10: Select an album or create a new one on MobileMe.

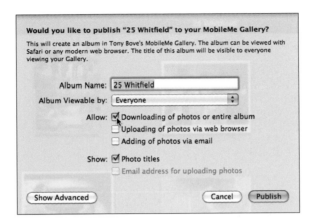

Would you like to publish "25 Whitfield" to your MobileMe Gallery?

This will create an album in Tony Bove's MobileMe Gallery. The album can be viewed with Safari or any modern web browser. The title of this album will be visible to everyone viewing your Gallery.

Album Name: [25 Whitfield]

Album Viewable by: [Everyone ▲▼]

Allow: ☑ Downloading of photos or entire album
☐ Uploading of photos via web browser
☐ Adding of photos via email

Show: ☑ Photo titles
☐ Email address for uploading photos

(Show Advanced)   (Cancel) (Publish)

Figure 6-11: Publish selected pictures in your MobileMe Gallery.

6. **(Optional) Set the Allow options to allow the downloading of photos, uploading of new photos, and e-mailing of new photos by other people.**

You can allow album visitors to download pictures to their own computers, upload new pictures to the Gallery album, or e-mail pictures to automatically add them to the Gallery album.

7. **(Optional) Set the Show options to show photo titles and an e-mail address that other people can use to upload photos.**

Turn on the Photo Titles option to show picture titles. If you allow album visitors to e-mail pictures to automatically add them to the Gallery album, turn on the Email Address for Uploading Photos option to show the e-mail address that others can use.

8. **Click Publish to publish the pictures (or Cancel to cancel).**

It may take from a few seconds to several minutes to upload the pictures to your MobileMe gallery.

You can view the albums you've uploaded to a MobileMe Gallery by clicking your MobileMe account name in the Web section of the Source pane. You can then select the album and manage its pictures and album information, as shown in Figure 6-12.

You can also view the album in MobileMe from your browser by clicking the album's Web address at the top of the Viewer pane after selecting the MobileMe Gallery album (refer to Figure 6-12).

You can invite people to view your MobileMe Gallery albums by clicking the Tell a Friend button, which creates an e-mail message with a link to your MobileMe Gallery. You can also find the link in the upper left corner of the MobileMe Web page displaying the album or at the top of the Viewer pane by selecting the MobileMe Gallery album (refer to Figure 6-12).

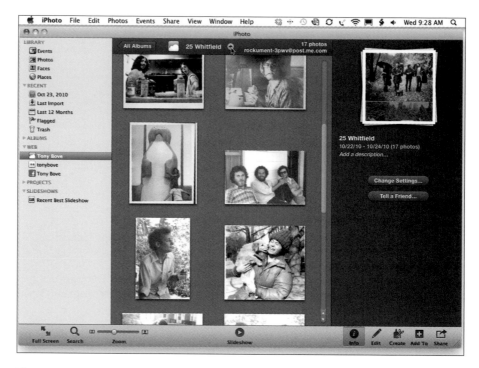

Figure 6-12: Manage the album in your MobileMe Gallery and edit its information.

After you create a MobileMe album, you can edit the album in iPhoto in two ways:

- ✔ **Add other pictures to a MobileMe album** by choosing the album in Step 3 of the preceding step list.

- ✔ **Edit the picture information published in the MobileMe album.** After clicking your MobileMe account name in the Web section of the Source pane and selecting the album, click the Info button to edit the title and description. You can also delete pictures from the MobileMe album by selecting their thumbnails and choosing Photos➪Delete From Album.

Publishing to Your iWeb Site

Publishing on the Web is by far the most universal method of distributing photos online. Everyone in the world can see your photos on a Web page — as long as they can find the Web page. (You can create a Web page whose address you never tell anyone, but Google may still find it!)

You can publish photos on the Web from iPhoto in three ways:

- ✓ Use your MobileMe Gallery, as I describe in the previous section.
- ✓ Send your pictures to iWeb as I describe in this section.
- ✓ Export your photos to files in a folder on your hard drive and use Web publishing software to post the files, as I describe in the next section.

To send your pictures to iWeb, follow these steps:

1. **Browse your library and select one or more thumbnails of pictures to export.**

   Browse your iPhoto library as I describe in Chapter 2, and select one or more thumbnails of pictures to send.

2. **Choose Share➪iWeb➪Photo Page to send the pictures to your iWeb Web page or Share➪iWeb➪Blog to send it to your iWeb blog.**

   iPhoto automatically starts iWeb and sends the pictures as a new photo album for the Photos page (if you chose Photo Page) or the Blog page (if you chose Blog), using as the album title either the event title (if you browsed Events, Photos, Faces, Places, or Recent collections) or the album title (if you browsed photo albums).

To find out more about iWeb, see Chapter 15.

Exporting Pictures to Files

If you want to save a picture in its original file format with no loss in quality (and no compression), or in another file format such as JPEG or TIFF, or with adjustments you made to the picture (as I describe in Chapter 4), you can export the picture from iPhoto to a file on your hard drive. iPhoto can save images and photos in their original formats or in JPEG, TIFF, or PNG formats, in full, large, medium, or small sizes or even a custom size.

Exporting to your hard drive

To export pictures to files on your hard drive, follow these steps:

1. **Browse your library and select one or more thumbnails of pictures to export.**

   Browse your iPhoto library as I describe in Chapter 2, and select one or more picture thumbnails to export.

2. **Choose File➪Export.**

The Export Photos dialog appears, as shown in Figure 6-13.

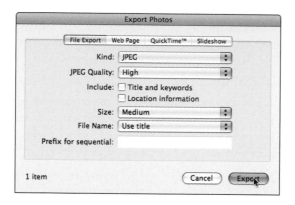

Figure 6-13: Export a photo by using the Export Photos dialog.

3. **Click the File Export tab (the leftmost tab).**

The File Export pane appears, with options for exporting photos into different file formats.

4. **Choose the appropriate file format from the Kind pop-up menu.**

The Kind pop-up menu lets you pick from these formats:

- *Original:* The original format for the photo (used by the digital camera — typically JPEG but can be another format), *before* any improvements were made.

- *Current:* The original format for the photo *after* any improvements were made (such as cropping or color adjustments).

- *JPEG:* Joint Photographic Experts Group (JPEG), the standard image format for Web pages. Use this choice to ensure that the photo is in a standard version of JPEG (if your digital camera's Original format is specialized).

- *TIFF:* Tagged Image File Format, the standard format for desktop publishing software.

- *PNG:* Portable Network Graphics (PNG-24) format, a lossless alternative to JPEG.

5. **If you select JPEG, choose its quality from the JPEG Quality pop-up menu.**

You can specify Low (for the lowest level of quality and the highest level of compression), Medium, High, or Maximum quality (for minimal compression). Low is good enough for tiny images and keeps the file size extremely small.

6. **Include titles, keywords, and location information.**

   You can choose to include titles, keywords, and location information as tags within the file that other applications can use.

7. **Specify the image size.**

   You can specify the image size to be small, medium, large, full size, or a custom size. If you specify the Custom option, the Max pop-up menu appears for choosing to set the maximum width, height, or dimension, and a field below the pop-up appears for entering the maximum number of pixels for either width, height, or dimension.

8. **Specify how to create the filename.**

   The File Name pop-up menu lets you choose from these options:

   - *Use Title:* Use the picture's title.

   - *Use Filename:* Enter a filename when saving.

   - *Sequential (and then enter the prefix to use before the number):* Specify a sequentially numbered filename with a text prefix.

   - *Album Name with Number:* Use the photo album name with a sequentially numbered suffix.

9. **Click the Export button and choose a folder for saving the file.**

Exporting pictures as a Web page

You can export one or more pictures as a Web page — a HyperText Markup Language (HTML) page with thumbnail versions of the images that link to larger versions — directly from iPhoto. If you already have a Web site, you can use your usual method of uploading the page to your site. The iPhoto Export function doesn't use layouts such as iWeb — its no-frills design is simple and easy to modify using any HTML editing program.

To publish a Web page of pictures by using the Export function, follow these steps:

1. **Browse your library and select one or more thumbnails of pictures to export.**

   Browse your iPhoto library as I describe in Chapter 2, and select one or more picture thumbnails to export.

2. **Choose File⇨Export.**

   iPhoto displays the Export Photos window.

3. **Click the Web Page tab.**

   The Web Page pane appears, as shown in Figure 6-14.

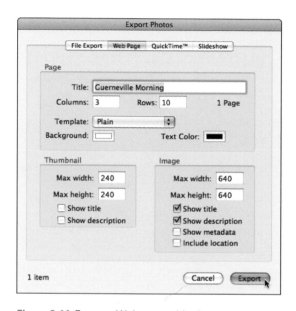

Figure 6-14: Export a Web page with pictures.

4. **Customize the page layout.**

   You can specify the number of columns and rows for the page, a page template (Plain or Framed), and the background color and text color. The Web page uses thumbnails as links to larger photos. You can specify the size (Max Width and Max Height) of thumbnails in the Thumbnails section and the size (Max Width and Max Height) of the larger image in the Image section. You can also choose to show each picture's title, description, tags (metadata), and location.

5. **Click the Export button and save the page on your hard drive.**

   The main page with thumbnails, and its associated photos, are saved in files ready to be uploaded to your Web site. You can open the pages in a Web browser, even though they exist only on your hard drive until you upload them to your site.

Making Prints and Photo Books

George Eastman's Kodak camera went on the market in 1888 with the slogan "You press the button, we do the rest," implying that you could leave all the complex parts of the process to his company, such as making prints, framed portraits, photo books, and calendars. Now, with Apple's iPhoto online service, this slogan is real — you simply click a button and the printed material arrives at your door.

Paper is still the most useful medium for showing photos to anyone. You still want prints to put in frames that you can hang on your walls. Your grandmother still hasn't figured out how to use a computer, anyway. Using iPhoto, you can create prints on your own color printer and print as many as you want.

If you want excellent photographic prints, you can use the Apple printing service and just press the button for at-your-door delivery. You can even publish copies of a photo book or a photographer's portfolio using this service: After organizing photos into a book layout that can include titles and captions, you can order professionally printed books worthy of a spot in the Library of Congress.

This chapter walks you through all the details of printing as well as creating a project such as a photo book.

Printing Photos and Images Yourself

The trees may not like it, but paper remains the most universal medium for showing photos and images. True, with digital photography, the noxious chemicals of film processing are gone and the darkroom has been turned into a walk-in closet, but you may still need to make prints of some kind.

In fact, digital photography makes it easier than ever to produce exactly the prints you want without wasting money on prints you don't want. For example, you can print individual photos on your own color printer to see how they look in print form before ordering a high-quality print on photographic paper. You can even print your own greeting cards.

Read this section to discover how to easily set up your printer to take advantage of printing your own pictures.

Picking a desktop printer and paper

Printing pictures from iPhoto is just about the easiest thing you can do. However, your results may be of low quality, especially if you use a standard office printer. Office printers used for invoices and documents don't do justice to color photos — you need a *color* printer. You can use a decent inexpensive color printer (most cost less than $200), and higher-quality color printers are surprisingly affordable (about $300 and more).

Be sure to factor in the number of prints you can make with a single set of ink cartridges, and the cost to replace the cartridges. Desktop printers designed to print photos typically use six different ink colors rather than just the four colors used by most color inkjet printers. The extra colors make photo prints look outstanding.

A second factor to consider is the type of paper used for printing. The plain typing paper that you use in a laser printer or copier is too thin and can't absorb enough ink to show colors well. You can still use regular copy paper for test prints that show the size of the image and its content. Paper labeled *high resolution* for use with inkjets is heavier and might be better for test prints — it's not glossy, but it has a smooth finish on one side. The best paper for finished prints or greeting cards is either matte paper, glossy photo paper, or (if you can afford it) glossy film, made with polyethylene rather than with paper.

Setting up pages for your printer

When using a printer with iPhoto (as with most Mac applications), you can access page layouts and printer-quality features in the Print dialog. Browse Events, Photos, Faces, Places, Recent collections, or photo albums in the Source pane, as I describe in Chapter 2, and select one or more pictures to print. Then choose File⇨Print. The Print Settings dialog appears, as shown in Figure 7-1.

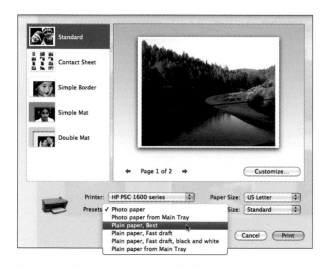

Figure 7-1: Choose the printer and select a theme.

The Print Settings dialog offers these themes for printed photos:

- ✔ **Standard:** Create prints just like the ones from a photo service. iPhoto makes conforming to standard print sizes with your color printer easy because iPhoto automatically resizes images to fit properly for the paper size and print size you choose. Standard is useful if you intend to use store-bought picture frames, which are measured for specific sizes such as 4 x 6 and 8 x 10.

- ✔ **Contact Sheet:** Make a quick print of thumbnails of the pictures. Contact sheets can be useful for comparing the quality of several photos at one time, making test prints of an entire album, or even repeating the same photo in a grid for cutting up wallet-size prints.

- ✔ **Simple Border:** Do the same thing as the Standard theme but improve it with a simple white border surrounding the image.

✔ **Simple Mat:** Do the same thing as the Standard theme but improve it with a mat border surrounding the image.

✔ **Double Mat:** Do the same thing as the Standard theme but improve it with a double mat border surrounding the image.

Choose one of these themes in this list and the preview image in the dialog box changes to show how the printed image will look. Your next step is to choose from the Printer pop-up menu which printer to use. (An HP PSC 1600 is chosen in Figure 7-1.)

After choosing the printer, you can choose options for paper size, presets, and print size:

✔ **Paper Size:** Choose a paper size, such as US Letter, Index Card (3 x 5 inches), or A2 Envelope. (You have too many choices to list here.) You can also specify a custom size, depending on your printer, by choosing Custom.

✔ **Presets:** Many color printers offer presets such as Photo Paper; Plain Paper, Best; and Plain Paper, Fast Draft (refer to Figure 7-1).

✔ **Print Size:** Choose the size of the print area on the paper, such as Standard (the standard printing area, defined by the printer), 8 x 10 (inches), 5 x 7, or 4 x 6.

Don't choose a large print size, such as 8 x 10, for a low-resolution image, because the picture stretches over a large area and doesn't look as good as it does at smaller print sizes. A photo shot with a 4-megapixel or even 3-megapixel camera should be okay.

Before clicking the Print button, consider customizing your photos for the print job so that they look better in print.

Customizing the printed photos

You can crop and adjust photos before printing them by clicking the Customize button in the Print dialog (refer to Figure 7-1). The Viewer pane changes to show the selected photos for printing, as shown in Figure 7-2. You can click thumbnails in the top row to switch from one photo to another, or from one page to another.

On the toolbar along the bottom are these tools:

- ✔ **Print Settings:** Opens the Print Settings dialog (refer to Figure 7-1) to change print settings.

- ✔ **Themes:** Shows a pop-up menu for choosing a different theme for your photos — the themes are listed in "Setting up pages for your printer," earlier in this chapter.

- ✔ **Background:** Shows a pop-up menu for changing the background color behind the photos to one that looks good for the chosen theme.

- ✔ **Borders:** Shows a pop-up menu for changing the border around the photos to one that works for the chosen theme.

- ✔ **Layout:** Shows a pop-up menu for changing the page layout for the photos to one that works for the chosen theme.

- ✔ **Adjust:** Shows the Adjust pane for adjusting the exposure, contrast, saturation, and other aspects, of the photo image (refer to Figure 7-2).

- ✔ **Settings:** Opens the Settings dialog to change the font of the title or the number of photos per page, show crop marks, and specify other layout settings.

Figure 7-2: Adjust photos before printing them.

You can also roughly crop the photo image by clicking the image in the Viewer pane. A slider appears for zooming in to the center of the image. (You can see the slider panel just behind the Adjust pane in Figure 7-2.) You can also use the hand tool in the slider panel to drag the image around in the window. By combining zooming and hand-dragging, you can roughly crop the image.

You may need to crop a photo to adjust its proportions to fit certain sizes. Photos from most digital cameras are sized at proportions of 4 (width) x 3 (height) pixels, which is fine for computer displays, DVDs, and iPhoto book layouts, but isn't the right proportion for standard prints. If you don't crop to adjust the proportions, you may find that some photos have unintended white margins at the sides of the finished prints. iPhoto makes this adjustment easy with the Constrain feature for cropping, which offers choices for standard print and display formats. When cropping is constrained, the cropped photo fits the format properly. To find out more about cropping with the Constrain feature, see Chapter 4.

Printing to a printer or a PDF file

After you specify your printer settings and customize your photos, as I explain in the preceding sections, click the Print button to start the printing operation. The standard Print dialog appears; click the down arrow next to the Printer pop-up menu to see more options:

- **Printer and Presets pop-up menus:** You can change the printer and the printer's presets.

- **Copies:** Specify the number of copies — if you print a set of photos, this number specifies the number of copies in the entire set. Click the Collated option to automatically collate pages for multiple-page prints.

- **Pages:** Click the All option for iPhoto to print all pages in a multiple-page print, or specify a page range with the From option to print only the range of pages.

To save the pages as a Portable Document Format (PDF) file that other people can open using Preview (on a Mac), Adobe Reader (on a Mac or PC), or the Safari browser (or another browser that supports PDF), choose Save As PDF from the PDF pop-up menu in the lower left corner of the Print dialog. You can then click the Save button to save the PDF file.

In the center of the Print dialog, the pop-up menu that's usually set to iPhoto also enables you to adjust many other settings — a mess of settings, in fact (too many to explain them all in this book). Here are some tips for choosing settings:

✔ To change the layout before printing or saving as a PDF file, choose Layout from the center pop-up menu. You can then set the pages per sheet, choose a border, and select the Reverse Page Orientation (horizontal to vertical or vice versa) option to change which end of the page comes out of the printer first.

✔ With some printers you can specify a perfect match with the type of paper you're using by choosing Paper Type/Quality from the center pop-up menu and choose a printer-specific paper type (such as HP Premium Plus Photo Paper, for my HP PSC 1600) from the Paper Type pop-up menu (not all printers offer this pop-up menu).

✔ You can set the quality of the print job (Fast Draft, Normal, or Best, for example) from the Quality pop-up menu.

✔ You can also choose Color Matching or Paper Handling or other types of options.

✔ For adaptive lighting, photo brightening, smoothing, sharpness, and automatic red-eye removal, choose Real Life Digital Photography from the center pop-up menu.

✔ To see a summary of all options and settings, choose Summary from the center pop-up menu. (Many of these settings are described in detail in books about Mac OS X, such as *Mac OS X Snow Leopard All-in-One For Dummies,* by Mark L. Chambers.)

If you run out of ink for your printer, iPhoto provides the convenient Supplies button in the lower left corner of the Print window. The button launches your browser and goes directly to the Apple Store printing-supplies page for your chosen printer.

Ordering Prints

You can order, directly from iPhoto, prints that are of much higher quality than prints you can make with a color printer. All you need is an Apple Store or iTunes account. Select the size and quantity of the photos to be printed and, in one click, transmit the photos directly to Apple. Your finished photos, printed on high-quality, glossy photographic paper, are mailed or delivered by express to you.

To order prints, you need to connect to the Internet. Then browse Events, Photos, Faces, Places, Recent collections, or photo albums in the Source pane, as I describe in Chapter 2, and select one or more pictures for ordering prints. With your photos selected, follow these steps:

1. **Click the Share tool on the toolbar and choose Order Prints from the pop-up menu, or choose File⇨Order Prints.**

2. **If this is your first time ordering prints, the Set Up Account window appears. If you already have an Apple Store or iTunes account, sign in with your ID and password.**

   To create a new account, click the Create Account button, which opens another page in the Set Up Account window in which you can fill in your personal information, including your e-mail address and a password. Click the Continue button, and then click the Accept button to accept the Apple Terms of Use agreement. Enter your billing information and your shipping address and phone number, and click Continue to establish your account.

   After you sign in to your account, the pictures you selected appear in the Order Prints window, as shown in Figure 7-3.

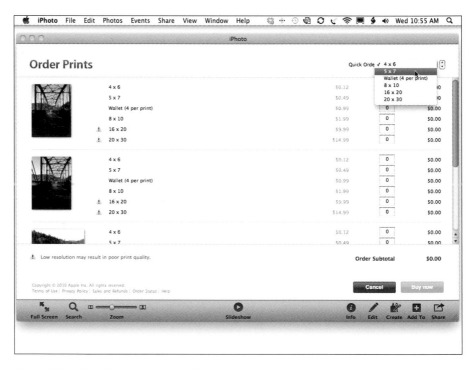

Figure 7-3: Order prints from Apple online.

3. **Enter the quantity of prints in the rightmost column of the Order Prints window for each print size, or choose one print size for all photos from the Quick Order pop-up menu (refer to Figure 7-3).**

   If you selected multiple pictures for prints, you can enter a different quantity and select different print sizes for each picture — scroll the Order Prints window to see the rest of your selected pictures. The total cost updates as you make your selections.

4. **Click the Buy Now button to finish placing your order.**

A low-resolution warning (an exclamation point in a yellow triangle) appears if a picture isn't high enough in resolution for a particular print size. You can still order that print size for the picture, but the quality will probably be poor.

Making Photo Books

iPhoto provides an automatic photo book layout capability that helps you assemble a book from a photo album, an event, or a selected set of pictures. You can then print the photo book on a color printer, use it as the basis for a slideshow, or order a professionally printed and bound version that looks as good as most books on library shelves (better, in fact, because yours hasn't been mishandled yet).

Your first step is to choose pictures for the photo book. Browse Events, Photos, Faces, Places, Recent collections, or photo albums in the Source pane, as I describe in Chapter 2, and select one or more pictures for the book. You can also select an entire event or a photo album to create a book of those pictures.

Pictures are sequenced in a photo book based on the sequence in which you select the pictures, or the sequence of pictures in a photo album if you select an album. If you know in advance how you want the pictures to be arranged, it may be quicker to create a photo album of the pictures in the sequence you want (as I describe in Chapter 3) and then select the photo album to create the photo book. If you want to change the sequence, you can rearrange the pictures while fine-tuning the photo book layout.

After selecting pictures or a photo album, click the Create tool on the toolbar, which turns into a pop-up menu — choose Book from the menu. The Photo Book Assistant appears in the Viewer pane, as shown in Figure 7-4. The sections that follow walk you through the various tasks involved in creating your Photo Book.

Figure 7-4: Choose a photo book layout theme and color.

Your first choice is the book type and size. Here's how it works:

1. **Click Hardcover, Softcover, or Wire-Bound for the book type along the top of the Photo Book Assistant (refer to Figure 7-4).**

   Your choice in this step determines which layout themes are available. (For example, in Figure 7-4, I chose Hardcover, which offers a variety of themes.)

2. **Click the size icon (XL for extra large or L for large) in the lower left corner of the Photo Book Assistant (refer to Figure 7-4).**

   The size icons are directly above the theme title (Picture Book in Figure 7-4). Your choice in this step also determines which layout themes are available. (For example, in Figure 7-4, I chose L.)

3. **Choose a layout theme from the carousel-like menu in the center.**

   As you select each theme, iPhoto displays a sample layout of pages of the book in the bottom section of the Photo Book Assistant (refer to Figure 7-4). All the themes offer special title pages and ways to vary the layout in order for you to customize your book. Some present the pictures with accompanying captions and text; others offer creative positioning but without captions.

4. **(Optional) Click a color tile in the lower right corner of the Photo Book Assistant (refer to Figure 7-4) to change the background color of the book theme.**

   The color tiles are directly above the Cancel and Create buttons. Each theme is already designed with a background color, but you can change it to one that still fits the theme.

5. **To see more information about book ordering options and prices, click the Learn More button in the lower left corner of the Photo Book Assistant.**

6. **After selecting a theme, click the Create button (or Cancel to cancel).**

   iPhoto creates a photo book and saves it in the Projects section of the Source pane, using the photo album name or event title if you selected a photo album or an event (with the suffix *Book*) or *untitled book* — either of which you can change by clicking inside the photo book name in the Source pane and editing it. iPhoto then displays All Pages view.

7. **Customize your book layout in the All Pages view.**

   In All Pages view, you can double-click any page to edit it and then drag photos to rearrange them on the page. To display tools that let you customize your layout, just click directly on the page, a photo, or some text. iPhoto flows the pictures through the pages automatically.

   To see more about customizing your photo book layout, such as fine-tuning page layouts and editing titles and captions, visit the Tips section of the author's Web site at www.tonybove.com.

8. **Place your order for the photo book.**

   When you're ready, click the Buy Book button in All Pages view to place your order and a professionally printed and bound book will be delivered to your door.

iPhoto converts your book layout into a form that can be transferred to the book printing service. Depending on how big your book is, transferring may take a few minutes.

If you didn't edit all available text areas of the themed layout, a warning tells you that the default text hasn't been edited and won't be included — those text areas will remain blank. You can continue with your order by clicking OK, or click Cancel to cancel it.

Seeing the Low Quality warning message means that you ignored the yellow warning indicators about printing pictures at certain sizes. You can continue with your order by clicking OK, or click Cancel to cancel it.

When you first use the service, you either log in to your existing Apple Store or iTunes account or set up an account with your credit card, as I describe in the "Ordering Prints" section, earlier in this chapter. After you log in, the Order Book window appears. Choose the number of copies from the Quantity pop-up menu. Use the Ship To and Ship Via pop-up menus to specify the shipping address and method. If you need to see or change your account information, click the Account Info button. After making changes, click the Buy Now button to make the purchase (or click Cancel to cancel). Follow the instructions (the helpful folks at Apple are always improving them) to finish the purchase process.

Part II

Winning an Oscar with iMovie

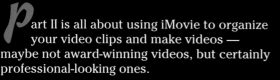art II is all about using iMovie to organize your video clips and make videos — maybe not award-winning videos, but certainly professional-looking ones.

🖝 Chapter 8 gets you started with iMovie. You find out what it can do, how to bring in video clips from a random-access video recorder, video camcorder, digital camera, iPhone, or iPod as well as from other sources.

🖝 Chapter 9 describes how to organize and browse video clips by events, skim through them quickly, and play them full-screen. You also find out all about cropping and rotating the video picture, adding the Ken Burns zoom and pan effects, marking your favorites, marking and deleting your rejects, and sorting your clips.

🖝 Chapter 10 shows you all the iMovie editing features, including arranging clips in a project, adding photos, spicing up clips with video effects and transitions, and adding titles and credits. You also can read all about editing the soundtrack, including recording through the microphone and adding music.

🖝 Chapter 11 describes the best methods of sharing your videos online, including sharing them with others using MobileMe, uploading them to YouTube, transferring them to your own Web site with iWeb, exporting them as QuickTime files, and sending them to iDVD for publishing on disc.

8

Gathering All Your Videos

In This Chapter

▶ An overview of moviemaking and what you can do with iMovie

▶ A tour of iMovie and what you need in order to run it

▶ Importing videos from various types of video cameras

▶ Importing videos from other sources

*P*eople seem to pay more attention to video than to any other medium. As the wise sage (and wisecracking baseball player) Yogi Berra once said, "You can observe a lot just by watching." Now that people have the tools to make their own videos and show them to the world, they're making new videos for others to watch at a phenomenal pace. At the time this book was written, more than 24 hours of new videos were uploaded to the YouTube site every minute of every day!

You can get into this act with any type of video recording device, but even the best ones aren't easy to use for editing hastily recorded video clips into ones that looks as appealing as professionally recorded videos. Using iMovie, you can not only edit your video clips properly but also enhance them with Hollywood-style transitions and special effects, balance the audio with the video, add music from your iTunes library, add photos and clips from iPhoto, and create videos you can be proud of. You can even use the automatic iMovie features and themes to create videos that look like movie trailers and TV news segments. You can then watch them on your iPhone, iPad, or iPod or on Apple TV; share them with other people using MobileMe; upload them to Facebook; Vimeo, and YouTube; and even burn a DVD. You can even send newsworthy content directly to a service such as CNN iReport or create a video podcast for the iTunes store.

If you have an iPhone 4, you can not only record video clips with its camera but also edit the video clips directly on your iPhone using the iMovie app (available in the App Store for $4.99). You can trim the lengths of clips, splice them into two clips, rearrange them in sequence, stylize them using one of several themes (such as Travel or Playful), add a soundtrack from your music library on your iPhone, and export the edited video clip to the Camera Roll album on your iPhone. You can then sync your iPhone to your Mac and use the edited video clip in an iMovie project. (For details on using the iMovie app, see the tips section of my Web site at www.tonybove.com).

What You Can Do with iMovie

You shoot the video, but that's about all you need to do with a video recording device. iMovie can

- ✔ **Import video:** iMovie enables you to import from a wide variety of devices — from HDD, DVD, and flash memory cameras and recorders that connect to your Mac by USB (Universal Serial Bus) to DV and mini-DV tape camcorders that connect by FireWire (also known as IEEE 1394 DV terminal). You can instantly use video clips imported into iPhoto from a digital camera or an iPhone or iPod nano.

  You can even record directly into iMovie by using the iSight camera that's built into current iMac and MacBook models.

- ✔ **Organize video clips:** iMovie helps you organize all your video clips from these different sources into a video library organized by event. For example, you can group all video shot for a single event, even if the video clips come from different sources and were recorded in different formats. You can also find people in your shots by using iMovie's people finder.

- ✔ **Create a movie using editing tools and effects:** You can assemble these clips, along with sounds or music from iTunes and photos and clips from iPhoto, into a *project* for editing into a single video. iMovie provides the basic, no-frills editing tools you need in order to put together a video from a set of clips and adjust the audio so that it sounds better. You can pick out the good parts of clips, snip out the slow or boring parts, trim the beginnings and endings of clips, and shuffle scenes around to your heart's content. Bring to life photos from your iPhoto library with pan and zoom effects to make scenes worthy of a Ken Burns documentary.

Sprinkle a glittering trail of fairy dust over a festive scene, or add haunting visual effects such as fog and ghost trails. When you're finished with your finishing touches, add the end credits, rolling commentary, and opening title.

✓ **Share videos you've made:** Pending a Hollywood distribution deal, you may want to share your video with friends using MobileMe, let all your Facebook friends view it, or even publish it on YouTube or Vimeo. You can even send a clip to CNN iReport or create a video podcast for the iTunes store. iMovie makes sharing and publishing videos a snap. And don't forget that this is Apple: You can, obviously, play your new video in iTunes on your Mac and on your iPad, iPod, or iPhone or on Apple TV.

What You Need for iMovie

Assuming that you already have a properly configured Mac running the newest version of OS X, you still need these items:

✓ **Lots of free hard drive space:** For tape-recorded (uncompressed) video, you need about 13GB to store an hour of standard-definition (SD) video and 40GB to store an hour of high definition (HD) video, so make sure you have enough space. An hour of video compressed in MPEG-4 (recorded by some camcorders and the iPhone and iPod touch) occupies about 2 GB, depending on the bit rate.

✓ **A video camera or another type of recording device:** You might have the iSight camera built into your iMac, an iPhone 3GS or iPhone 4, a fifth-generation iPod nano, a flash-based Advanced Video Coding High Definition (AVCHD) camcorder, a high-definition video (HDV) camcorder that uses digital video (DV) cassette tapes, or any type of digital video camera or camcorder that can connect to your Mac using a USB or FireWire cable. (All Macs support USB, and desktop Macs and the MacBook Pro also support FireWire.)

Most video recorders also keep track of the time and date and store this information with the video. When you first use a new recording device, be sure to set its date and time in order for the date and time to be correct when the video is imported to iMovie.

 Avoid the temptation to throw out your old camcorder and tapes. Considering the level of control iMovie has over a digital camcorder, you can use one as a go-between to connect your older camcorder or VCR to your digital camcorder and to connect the digital camcorder to your Mac.

Exploring the iMovie Window

On most Macs, you find the iMovie icon in the Dock and in the Applications folder. Double-click the icon to open iMovie, and the dialog shown in Figure 8-1 appears.

iPhoto Video Thumbnails

iMovie needs to generate thumbnails for the videos in your iPhoto library. This process may take several minutes.

You can postpone this operation by clicking Later, but your iPhoto videos will be unavailable until the next time you restart iMovie.

Later   Now

Figure 8-1: iMovie gathers any video clips in iPhoto.

Click Now to gather the video clips you have in iPhoto, or Later to do it later. iMovie doesn't copy the clips; it simply links to them and creates thumbnails for them so that you can use them in your projects.

iMovie then displays its window, as shown in Figure 8-2. iMovie shows a video clip as a *filmstrip* — a series of thumbnail images joined together. You can move the pointer along any filmstrip to skim it and see the video — the thin, red vertical line that appears in the filmstrip is the *playhead*. (It represents lingo from the days of recording and playing tapes.) A single thumbnail image represents a video frame within the clip.

The following list describes the window elements and how to use them:

- **Project pane:** This pane holds these items:
  - The *Project Library* lets you browse the list of projects.
  - The *Project Browser* (not shown), which fills the Project pane, holds the filmstrips for the project you select.
- **Viewer pane:** When playing or skimming, the video appears in this pane.
- **Toolbar:** The tool buttons and controls appear here.
- **Event Library:** Browse the list of source video clips, which are sorted by event.

✔ **Event Browser:** After you select an event, the source video clips appear as filmstrips in the Event Browser, which fills the Source Video pane.

✔ **Source Video pane:** The Event Browser and other media browsers (not shown) appear in this pane.

The Event Library and Project Library are empty at first. You import video clips from all your sources: video recorders and camcorders and the iPhoto library.

Project pane   Project Library (and Project Browser, not shown)

Toolbar   Viewer pane

Event Library   Event Browser   Source Video pane   Media Browser

Figure 8-2: The iMovie window.

Importing Source Video Clips

iMovie caters to whatever video recording devices you want to use:

✔ You can record directly into iMovie using an iSight camera or FireWire-based DV tape recorder or camcorder.

✔ With random-access video cameras such as the Flip Ultra HD, Canon Vixia HF10, or iPod nano (fifth generation), you can select and import individual video clips randomly without having to play them.

✔ iMovie also supports digital video (DV) tape recorders such as mini-DV camcorders that use FireWire (also known as IEEE 1394 DV terminal) to connect to your Mac. These devices are usually supplied with the appropriate FireWire cable. The Import window offers a viewer and Rewind, Fast Forward, and Play controls — you can import the entire tape or use the controls to import portions of the tape.

✔ Browse the Event Library for video clips imported into iPhoto from a digital camera or an iPhone, iPod touch, or iPod nano.

iMovie supports the most popular video formats used by camcorders and video recorders, such as AVCHD and MPEG-4 — specifically, H.264/MPEG-4 Part 10, also known as AVC (Advanced Video Coding) — as well as Apple's iFrame Video format. You can also import MPEG-4 and QuickTime files and projects you already created by using iMovie HD. To find out about exporting and importing movie file formats, see Chapter 11.

If your video recorder or camcorder supports the iFrame Video format, you should use this format for your shots. The iFrame Video format is designed by Apple to speed up importing and editing by keeping the content in its native recorded format while editing. Select the Video or Format settings from your video recorder or camcorder's Recording menu and choose iFrame if the menu offers it, or 960 x 540 at 30 fps (frames per second). iFrame is the default video setting on certain new camcorder models, such as the Sanyo VPC-FH1A.

Choosing import options for HD video, stabilization, and people

When you first choose File⇨Import and select a movie, camera archive, or previous project, or when you first click the Camera tool to import from a camera, camcorder, or recorder, a couple of options appear that are common to these import methods — namely, HD video import options, analyzing for stabilization, and analyzing for people in the video picture. As you're working the steps for importing video in the following sections, it's helpful to know what the HD, stabilization, and people options are all about.

Some video cameras record in the high-definition (HD) video format 1080i, which offers a resolution (the dimensions of the image) of 1920 x 1080 pixels at the highest setting. Some camcorders are labeled as recording 1080i-format video but record at lower resolutions, such as 1440 x 1080 pixels. If you import HD video, the 1080i HD Import Setting dialog appears, as shown in Figure 8-3.

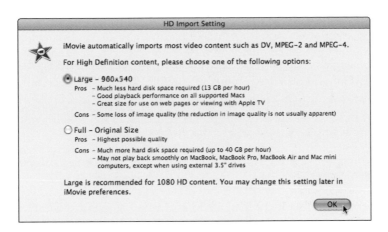

Figure 8-3: Import HD video in either Large or Full size.

If you are *not* using the 1080i format, just click OK. If you *are* using the 1080i format, choose a size for the video resolution:

✔ **Large** is recommended for most uses (including viewing on Apple TV) because it saves hard drive space and plays back more smoothly on some computers. The Large option has a high enough quality to view on a high-definition television (HDTV) without noticeable differences in quality. This option reduces to 13GB the 40GB that an hour of full-size 1080i video occupies.

✔ **Full** is available if you need to use the video for broadcasting or exporting to Final Cut Express or Final Cut Pro, but is useful only if the camcorder records in true 1920 x 1080 resolution. This option better preserves the original quality of the video, but can use up to 40GB of hard drive space per hour, depending on the bit rate set for the camera when recording.

To set iMovie to always use Large or Full size, choose iMovie➪Preferences, click the Video tab, and choose the size from the Import HD Video As pop-up menu.

During the import operation, iMovie gives you the option to analyze your video for stabilization or people, or both:

✔ **Stabilization analysis:** Use the Smooth Clip Motion option for video clips in your project to smooth the motion and reduce the shakiness in videos recorded by hand. iMovie stabilizes video by analyzing the camera motion in the video and then moving the picture the opposite way to steady it when played. To make enough room to move the image without moving past the edge, iMovie zooms in a little, which may crop out elements of the picture. More motion in the clip means more zooming (and cropping). You can decide later whether to use the Smooth Clip Motion option because iMovie keeps intact the original version of the clip.

✔ **People analysis:** Find video clips with people in them faster, as you can see in Chapter 9. This ability comes in handy when you're creating movie trailers, as I show in Chapter 10.

Analyzing for stabilization or people can take a *lot* of time. Therefore, you should analyze the video during the import operation.

If you're importing more than an hour of video, you might want to do the analysis later (perhaps overnight). You can leave the Analyze option turned off and, later, after adding the video clip to a project, select the clip and choose File➪Analyze Video➪Stabilization or choose File➪Analyze Video➪Stabilization and People to do both at one time.

Importing video files and previous projects

To import a video file, choose File➪Import➪Movies. To import a previously created iMovie HD project (from an earlier version of iMovie known as iMovie HD), choose File➪Import➪iMovie HD Project.

A dialog appears so that you can select the movie or project file from your hard drive, as shown in Figure 8-4.

Follow these steps:

1. **Choose a hard drive from the Save To pop-up menu.**

2. **Choose Add to Existing Event and an event from the pop-up menu, or choose Create New Event.**

   If you choose Create New Event, you can change the title of the event.

3. **(Optional) Choose Optimize Video and select Large Size or Full Size from the Optimize Video pop-up menu.**

4. **Choose Copy Files to copy the files into the iMovie clips library and leave the originals intact, or choose Move Files to move the files into the library and delete the originals (to save space).**

5. **Click Import (or Cancel to cancel).**

iMovie creates a new event for the video file or imported video clips in the project.

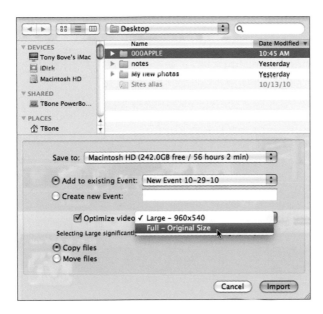

Figure 8-4: Choose a movie or project file that's on your hard drive.

Using video already imported into iPhoto

You may have imported video clips from a digital still camera or camera phone (such as an iPhone or iPod touch) into your iPhoto library. If you clicked Later to gather the video clips you have in iPhoto (refer to Figure 8-1), you can gather them now. Select iPhoto Videos in the Event Library (refer to Figure 8-2), and the video clips appear in the Source Video pane.

iMovie doesn't copy the clips; it simply links to them and creates thumbnails for them so that you can use them in your projects. You can browse iPhoto video clips the same way as iMovie clips, and you can move the clips to events in the Event Library to organize them, as I describe in Chapter 9.

Recording directly into iMovie

If you have an iSight camera or a similar webcam attached or built into your Mac, you can use the device to record video directly into iMovie. You can also use a tape-based digital video camcorder (such as a mini-DV camcorder) with iMovie — without recording to the tape — to record video directly from the camcorder's lens and microphone to your hard drive over a FireWire cable.

To record directly into iMovie, follow these steps:

1. **Click the Camera tool on the far left side of the toolbar to open the Import window (or choose File⇨Import from Camera).**

   The Import From window appears with a Camera pop-up menu in its lower left corner, as shown in Figure 8-5.

Figure 8-5: Record directly to iMovie (using iSight).

2. **Turn on your camera and choose it from the Camera pop-up menu.**

   If you're using a FireWire-based camcorder or webcam, connect it to your Mac and turn on Camera mode. (If you're using iSight, it's already on.) Then choose the video camera (such as iSight or the webcam or a FireWire-based camcorder) from the Camera pop-up menu in the lower left corner of the Import From window.

   On most DV camcorders, you put the camcorder in Camera mode but *don't* click the Record button on the camcorder to record on tape. In fact, you don't need a tape cassette in the camcorder. Because you're recording directly to your hard drive, you don't use the camcorder's record-to-tape mechanism — the video goes directly from the camcorder's circuitry to your computer. However, some camcorders don't pass the video through in this manner, and the opposite is true: You must insert a DV tape cassette and press the Record button. If this is the case, you can still record directly to a hard drive with the tape paused (or record to tape at the same time and then rewind the tape for later use).

You should now be able to see in the Import window the view from the video camera (refer to Figure 8-5).

3. **(Optional) Change the video picture size from the Video Size pop-up menu.**

   The sizes offered with the iSight camera are 1024 x 576 pixels and 640 x 480 pixels (which is what I set it to in Figure 8-5). The sizes for attached camcorders depend on the type of camcorder you've connected.

4. **Click the Capture button to start recording video.**

   A dialog appears, as shown in Figure 8-6.

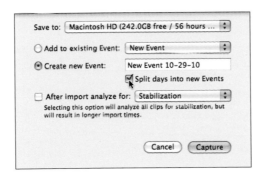

Figure 8-6: Save the recorded video.

5. **Choose from the Save To pop-up menu a hard drive on which to save the video, and then choose Add to Existing Event and an event from the pop-up menu, or choose Create New Event.**

   If you choose Create New Event, you can change the title of the event and have the Split Days Into New Events option (refer to Figure 8-6), to create separate events for each day of video recording.

6. **(Optional) Choose the After Import Analyze For option and select Stabilization, People, or Stabilization and People.**

   After importing, iMovie can immediately start analyzing your video for stabilization or people, or both, as I describe in "Choosing import options for HD video, stabilization, and people," earlier in this chapter.

7. **Click Capture to start capturing video.**

8. **To stop, click the Stop button in the lower right corner. Start and stop recording as often as you like.**

   Every time you stop recording, iMovie takes a few moments to generate thumbnails for the video. You can then click Capture to start recording again. Every time you start again, the dialog appears so that you can create a new event or continue adding to the same event; choose which one you want and click Capture.

9. **When you're finished recording, click Done.**

   The recorded clips appear in the Source Video pane, assigned to events that appear in the Event Library.

Importing from a random-access video camera

iMovie supports random-access devices that use USB to connect to your Mac, such as HDD or DVD or a flash memory video camera (such as a Flip Ultra HD or the Canon Vixia HF10) or a fifth-generation iPod nano, which includes a video camera. These devices are usually supplied with the appropriate USB cables. The Import window displays all clips on the device — you can import them all or select the ones you want to import. Just follow these steps:

1. **Connect the camera to your Mac using the supplied USB cable.**

   The Import window opens automatically, as shown in Figure 8-7, showing all clips stored on the device.

   (An iPod nano with a video camera is shown in the figure.)

2. **You can select any clip and click the Play button to view it; click the Next or Previous button to select the next or previous clip, respectively.**

3. **Choose to import all clips or only selected clips.**

   Click Import All if you want to import all clips (or Done to cancel). To import only some clips, click the Automatic/Manual switch in the lower left corner to Manual. You can then deselect the check box under any clip so that iMovie skips it, and click Import Checked to import the selected clips (or Done to Cancel).

   After you click Import All or Import Checked, the Save dialog appears so that you can save the clips. (Refer to Figure 8-6 for the options; an Import button appears in place of the Capture button.)

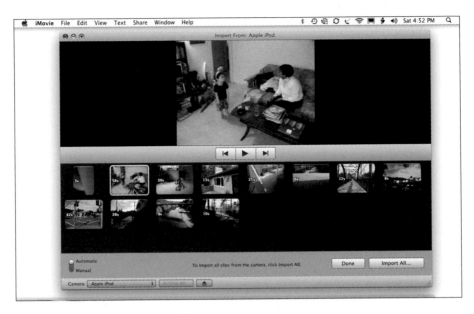

Figure 8-7: Import all clips from a USB recording device.

4. **Choose from the Save To pop-up menu a hard drive on which to save the clips, and then choose Add to Existing Event and select an event from the pop-up menu, or choose Create New Event.**

   If you choose Create New Event, you can change the title of the event and have the Split Days Into New Events option to create separate events for each day of video recording.

5. **(Optional) Choose the After Import Analyze For option and select Stabilization, People, or Stabilization and People.**

   After importing, iMovie can immediately start analyzing your video for stabilization or people (or both), as I describe in "Choosing import options for HD video, stabilization, and people," earlier in this chapter.

6. **Click Import to start the import operation.**

   iMovie displays a progress bar under each clip as it imports the clip. You can click the Stop button to stop importing before it finishes. After the import is finished, the Import window closes and the clips appear in the Source Video pane, assigned to events that appear in the Event Library.

Importing from DV tape or cassette

DV and mini-DV camcorders not only record digital video onto tape — they also can play back the tape. When the camcorder is in *Camera mode,* its microphone and lens are ready to record when you press the Record button. When the camcorder is in *VTR (video tape recorder)* or *VCR (video cassette recorder)* mode (also known as Play mode), the camcorder plays the tape when you press the Play button and you can also rewind and fast-forward the tape.

If your camcorder has Sleep mode, make sure it's disabled or set to a time increment long enough to allow your video to play in full at normal speed. If possible, connect AC power to the camcorder during this process to save battery life.

To start importing from a FireWire camcorder tape, follow these steps:

1. **Turn the camcorder to VTR/VCR mode, and then connect it to your Mac with the supplied FireWire cable.**

   The Import window opens automatically (see Figure 8-8), showing a blue screen for the viewing area.

2. **Choose your camcorder from the Camera pop-up menu in the lower left corner of the Import window.**

Figure 8-8: Import an entire tape from a DV camcorder.

3. **To import the whole tape, skip to Step 4; otherwise, click the Automatic/Manual switch in the lower left corner to Manual and move to the portion you want to import.**

   You can then use the Rewind, Fast Forward, and Play controls in the Import window, as shown in Figure 8-9, to review your tape first and decide which portions to import.

4. **To import the entire tape, click the Import button; to import only a portion of the tape, start playing the tape before the moment you want to start importing, and then click Import.**

   After you click Import, the tape is paused and iMovie displays the Save dialog to choose a hard drive and an event for the video. (Refer to Figure 8-6 for the options; an Import button appears in place of the Capture button.)

5. **Choose a hard drive from the Save To pop-up menu, and then choose Add to Existing Event and an event from the pop-up menu, or choose Create New Event.**

   If you choose Create New Event, you can change the title of the event and have the Split Days into New Events option to create separate events for each day of video recording.

Figure 8-9: Import only the part of the tape that's playing.

6. **(Optional) Choose the After Import Analyze For option and select Stabilization, People, or Stabilization and People.**

   After importing, iMovie can immediately start analyzing your video for stabilization or people (or both), as I describe in "Choosing import options for HD video, stabilization, and people," earlier in this chapter.

7. **Click the Import button to start importing.**

   If you chose automatic importing, iMovie rewinds the tape in the device and imports its contents from beginning to end, separating the scenes into clips. iMovie does this by automatically detecting a break in time — which happens when you stop recording with the camcorder, even for just a few seconds. After the import is finished, the Import window closes.

   If you chose manual importing, iMovie starts playing the tape and imports the video as the tape plays. Click Stop to stop importing. Start and stop recording as often as you like — every time you stop recording, iMovie takes a few moments to generate thumbnails for the video. You can then use the Fast Forward and Rewind buttons to find another portion of the tape, and click Import again to import another portion. Every time you start recording again, the dialog appears so that you can create a new event or continue adding to the same event: Choose which one you want and click Import. When you're finished importing, click Done.

   After the import is finished, the clips appear in the Source Video pane, assigned to events that appear in the Event Library.

9

Organizing and Improving Video Clips

*I*n moviemaking, the clapstick helps the sound editor synchronize sound with picture because in film, the picture and sound are recorded separately. But the most important function of the slate is to help the director and editor identify a particular *take* in the raw footage from the cameras. As the director, you can then edit these takes (or *clips,* in video lingo) and rearrange them as you see fit. Though the most important part of moviemaking is getting the shots, the second is working with clips.

A video project with a lot of clips can quickly become hard to manage if you don't organize the clips in some way. This chapter explains how to group video clips by event, select the ones you want to use, and adjust those clips so that they play exactly the way you want them to play.

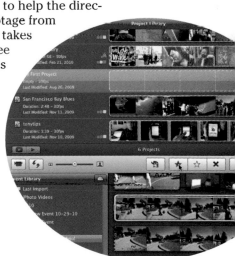

It Happened One Night: Grouping Clips by Event

Events are a handy way to organize your video clips — if you were shooting a movie, each day's work could be organized as an event; if you took videos of a weeklong vacation, for example, the entire vacation could be a single event.

iMovie checks the date and time stamp as it imports clips, so the information is readily available. Each event appears in the Event Library, listed within its year — clicking the triangle for a year in the Event Library displays all the events in a single year. You can also merge multiple events, such as several days of shooting, into one event or split a single event into two events. If you would rather see the Event Library at the top of the iMovie window, you can swap that library with the Project Library by clicking the Two Arrows button next to the Camera button on the left side of the toolbar.

Here are some things you can do in the Event Library:

- **To browse an event's video clips,** select the event in the Event Library, as I did in Figure 9-1 with *Pennington family visit*. The clips appear as filmstrips in the Event Browser (which fills the Source Video pane to the right of the Event Library).

- **To browse multiple events,** hold down the Command key as you click the events in the Event Library. Select a year in the Event Library to browse all events within it.

- **To retitle an event,** double-click the event's title in the Event Library to highlight the title, and then type a new title.

    You don't have to keep the date as part of the title. To show the date underneath the title of each event, choose iMovie⇨Preferences, click the Browser tab, and then click the Show Date Ranges in Event Library option.

- **To merge events,** browse multiple events in the Event Library as I describe in the first bullet in this list, and then choose File⇨Merge Events. A dialog appears so that you can type the name of the merged event. Type the name and click OK. After combining the dates for the clips, iMovie places the merged event in the Events Library, perhaps in a new position (depending on the dates).

- **To split an event into two events,** select the event title in the Event Library, and click the video clip you want to make the first clip of the new event. When you click the filmstrip representing a video clip, iMovie selects four seconds of video beginning at the point, which is good enough for this purpose. (For more details about clicking and selecting video in filmstrips, see "Selecting and Playing Clips," later in this chapter). Then choose File➪Split Event before Selected Clip.

✏ **To move a selected clip (an entire filmstrip) or a selected portion of a clip from one event to another,** drag it from the Source Video pane over the title of the other event in the Event Library.

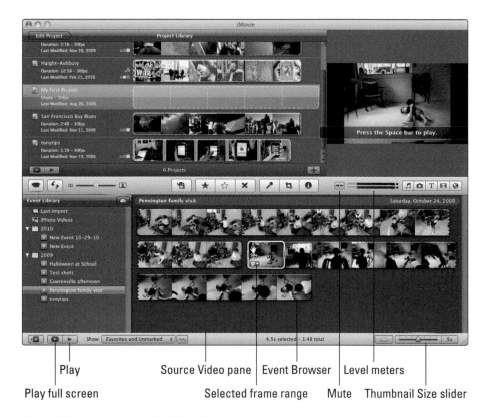

Play

Play full screen

Source Video pane   Event Browser   Level meters

Selected frame range   Mute   Thumbnail Size slider

Figure 9-1: Browse an event's video clips.

If you used different hard drives to store imported clips, you can sort the Event Library by hard drive by clicking the Hard Disk icon at the top of the Event Library. You can then browse the events on a hard drive by selecting the drive.

Selecting and Playing Clips

iMovie shows a video clip as a *filmstrip* — a series of thumbnail images joined together. A single thumbnail image represents an important video frame (also known as a *key frame*) within the clip. A ragged edge appears on the right side the filmstrip if the clip is too long to fit in the pane, indicating that the clip continues to the next line — and the filmstrip on the next line has a ragged edge on its left side to show that it's a continuation of the same clip.

iMovie displays one thumbnail for every five seconds of video in a clip. You can change the number of seconds by dragging the Thumbnail Size slider in the lower right corner of the iMovie window (refer to Figure 9-1). Drag to the right to shorten the filmstrip by using fewer thumbnails for each clip (more seconds per thumbnail), or drag to the left to make the filmstrip longer by using more thumbnails for each clip (fewer seconds per thumbnail). Changing the size of the filmstrip is only for viewing purposes; it doesn't change the video itself.

Skimming and watching clips at full-screen size

As you may already have noticed, moving the pointer across a filmstrip — without even clicking — shows a hyperactive version of the video. The images in the filmstrip move, and so does the larger image in the Viewer pane. This process is named *skimming* because you can quickly skim backward and forward to see frames in the video. The Viewer pane shows the video frame at the point of the *playhead* (the thin, red vertical line that appears in the filmstrip).

You can hear the audio portion of the video as you skim. The two narrow grooves on the right side of the toolbar (refer to Figure 9-1) are audio *level meters* — one for each channel of stereo sound. The meters show green, and then orange, and then red as the volume level increases. The red part, at the far right, appears only when the volume is at its highest. If the red dots to the right of the meters appear (they're *clipping indicators*), the volume is way too high. The clipping indicators stay on to remind you that clipping occurred in the audio. You can reset these indicators by clicking them.

Hearing the audio while skimming can be distracting but might also be useful for locating a particular moment in the video. To silence the audio temporarily, click the Mute button (the Sound Wave icon — refer to Figure 9-1), or choose View➪Audio Skimming to deselect it on the menu. To turn the audio back on, click the Mute button again (or choose View➪Audio Skimming again). Muting the sound doesn't affect the audio in the video — it just turns down the sound for skimming.

The following list explains handy commands for watching your video:

- **To watch the video in the Viewer pane** (and hear its audio), press the spacebar to start playing from the playhead. Press the spacebar again to stop playing the video. To play the video clip from the beginning, click the Play button below the Event Library; click the button again to stop playing.

- **To play the video at full-screen size,** click the Play Full Screen button (the Play icon enclosed by a TV tube) below the Event Library to play the video from the beginning, or press Command+G (or choose View↔ Play Full-Screen) to start playing from the playhead.

  While the video plays full-screen, you can control playback and even jump from one to clip to another, from one event to another, or even from one project to another. (You can see how to create a project in Chapter 10.) Move the pointer to reveal the buttons and *thumb strip,* as Apple calls it (the strip of thumbnails under the image), as shown in Figure 9-2. The buttons and thumb strip disappear after a few seconds of not moving the pointer or clicking.

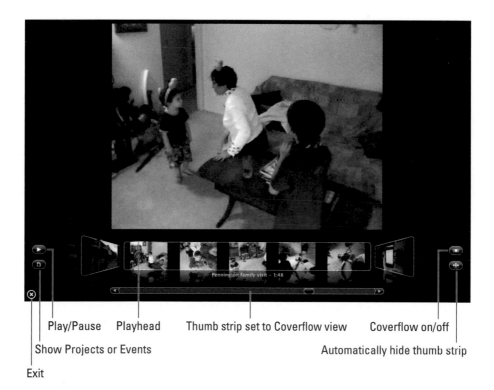

Play/Pause   Playhead   Thumb strip set to Coverflow view   Coverflow on/off

Show Projects or Events   Automatically hide thumb strip

Exit

Figure 9-2: Play a clip at full-screen size, with the Coverflow view of the source video.

- **To keep the thumb strip displayed in full-screen view,** click the Automatically Hide Thumb Strip on-off button so that it's turned off (dark gray rather than blue).

- **To rewind or fast-forward,** skim the thumb strip forward or backward (refer to Figure 9-2); the playhead appears in the filmstrip inside the thumb strip. You can also press the arrow keys to move frame by frame.

  In Figure 9-2, the thumb strip is set to the Coverflow view (as in iTunes) of all your events and video sources. Click the Coverflow on-off button to switch the thumb strip from Coverflow view to the single filmstrip view, or back to Coverflow view. Click the Show Projects or Events button to show either project in the thumb strip, or events and sources of video.

- **To exit the full-screen view and return to the iMovie window,** press the Esc (Escape) key or click the circled X in the lower right corner.

- **To play only the selected video,** press the slash (/) key (or choose View⇨Play Selection).

Selecting a video frame range

When you click the name of a filmstrip in the Event Browser (inside the Source Video pane), a yellow selection border appears around the range of frames selected (refer to Figure 9-1). The yellow-bordered selection is, appropriately enough, the *frame range*. iMovie automatically selects four seconds of video as the frame range, beginning at the point where you clicked. You can drag the edges of the yellow border to extend or shorten the frame range.

To select an entire clip, hold down the Option key while clicking the filmstrip, as shown in Figure 9-3. After selecting an entire clip, you can Command-click a second clip to add it to the selection or Shift-click a second clip to select a range of clips between them.

The automatic four-second frame range (which you can see in Figure 9-1) helps you build an evenly paced video — you can skim to find perfect scenes and just click to select them, and each section is exactly four seconds long. But the frame range doesn't have to always be four seconds. To change the duration of the frame range selected by a single click, choose iMovie⇨Preferences, click the Browser tab, and drag the slider under the Clicking in Events Browser Selects option to longer or shorter than 4.0 seconds. If you'd rather fix the one-click frame range to be an entire clip, choose the Clicking in Events Browser Selects Entire Clip option.

Selected frame range (an entire clip)

Figure 9-3: Option-click to select an entire clip.

Sorting and Deleting Clips

While skimming a video, you can mark the best frame ranges as your favorites and mark the worst as rejects. You can then sort your video clips to show only the favorites to use in projects, or rejects to delete to save hard drive space. You can also show only favorites and unmarked frame ranges, rejecting those portions of a clip you don't want so that they aren't included in a project.

iMovie starts out by showing all the unmarked clips and clips marked as favorites.

If you changed the type of clips you're showing in the Event Browser, you can go back to showing all clips, even ones previously marked for deletion, by choosing All Clips from the Show pop-up menu below the Event Library.

Marking frame ranges as favorites or rejects

While skimming, select a frame range and then click the Mark As Favorite button (the icon with the filled-in, five-point star) on the toolbar. A green bar appears over the top of the frame range, as shown in Figure 9-4. That frame range is now marked as a favorite.

To mark the selected frame range for deletion, click the Reject button (the x icon) to the right of the Mark As Favorite and Unmark buttons on the toolbar. A red bar appears over the top of the frame range when you choose All Clips.

Show pop-up menu   People   Reject   Frame range marked as a favorite

Mark as favorite   Unmark

Figure 9-4: Mark a selection in a clip as a favorite.

To remove the favorite or rejection mark for the selected frame range, click the Unmark button (the icon with the empty five-point star) to the right of the Mark as Favorite button.

Showing only favorites or rejects

After you've marked some video, you can show only the marked video in the Event Browser (or any other source library you're browsing in the Source Video pane — this trick works with iPhoto Video selections as well). Choose an option from the Show pop-up menu below the Event Library:

- **Favorites Only:** Shows only the video frame ranges marked as favorite.
- **Favorites and Unmarked:** Shows all frame ranges marked as favorite or left unmarked.

> ✔ **All Clips:** Shows all clips in the selected events or iPhoto Video library, marked or not.
>
> ✔ **Rejected Only:** Shows only the frame ranges marked for deletion. Use this option to keep rejected frames from appearing in clips and in your projects, and to preview the frame ranges you've rejected before you delete them.

To hide frames of video that shake too much, click the squiggly-line button next to the Show pop-up menu. The excessively shaky video segments disappear from the Source Video pane. You can then drag clips from the Source Video pane to a project and be sure to not include any shaky video segments. Click the button again to show all segments.

The bored ultimatum: Deleting rejected videos

To delete rejected frame ranges, choose Rejected Only from the Show pop-up menu (or choose View⇨Rejected Only) and then click the Move to Trash button in the upper right corner above the rejected filmstrips.

To reclaim the hard drive space occupied by the video you've deleted, empty the Trash on your Mac. You can do that quickly without leaving iMovie by right-clicking (or Command-clicking) the Trash icon in the Dock and choosing Empty Trash; or, you can temporarily leave iMovie by clicking the Desktop to show the Finder and then choosing Finder⇨Empty Trash, and then click the iMovie window to return.

Showing only clips with people

If you're in a hurry to grab the shots you took with people in them, iMovie gives you a button for it: the People button, to the right of the Shaky button next to the Show pop-up menu (refer to Figure 9-4). This button appears only if you had the video clip analyzed for people while importing. (See Chapter 8 for details.) If you haven't yet analyzed the clip for people, select the clip and choose File⇨Analyze Video⇨People (or choose File⇨Analyze Video⇨Stabilization and People to do both at one time).

Click the People button to show only segments that have people in them. All other segments disappear from the Source Video pane (but not from your library).

You can then drag clips from the Source Video pane to a place in a project that requires people shots — such as the movie trailer themes provided with iMovie (shown in Chapter 10). Click the People button again to show all segments again.

Nip/Tuck: Improving Clips

Most of the work of producing a video consists of improving individual clips to make them more visually appealing or more effective at communicating. Though many special effects, transitions, and overall improvements are usually performed after creating a sequence of clips in the Project Browser (as I describe in Chapter 10), you can quickly improve the clips you're browsing by event, before using them in a project.

By far the most common editing technique is to do away with unwanted sound in a clip by lowering the volume. You can lower the volume of the sound on a clip-by-clip basis and control the volume within each video clip.

Don't worry about messing up your video — the changes you make can always be reversed. Choose Edit⇨Undo to undo your last action. To remove changes and settings and restore the clip to its original state, open the same tools you used to make the changes (as described in this section) and restore only the settings you want. For example, if you make video and audio adjustments to a clip, you can reopen the video adjustment and audio adjustment windows and click Revert to Original in either window (or both windows) to remove changes.

Cropping and rotating a clip

As you can see in Chapter 4, you can *crop* a photo in iPhoto — cut away the outer edges of the image to bring the center of it to the forefront. You can do the same with video: Use iMovie to crop the image in a clip to get rid of something you don't want at the edges or to focus on the subject in the center of the picture. Note, however, that if you're working with standard or lower-resolution video, cropping may make the image in the video appear grainy.

You may want to rotate a clip's image, especially if you shot the video by holding your camera sideways or if you shot the clip with an iPhone in portrait rather than landscape orientation. You can rotate and crop the clip's image at the same time. Follow these steps:

1. **Select the clip in the Event Browser, and click the Cropping tool on the toolbar, as shown in Figure 9-5, to show the cropping view inside the Viewer pane.**

2. **To rotate the image in the video clip, click the curling right-arrow or left-arrow button at the top of the cropping view in the Viewer pane.**

Cropping tool   Rotate left/right

Figure 9-5: Open the cropping view to crop or rotate the image in a clip, or both.

The image rotates 90 degrees. Every time you click the left or right Rotate button, the image in the clip rotates 90 degrees.

3. **To crop the image, click the Crop button at the top of the Viewer pane (refer to Figure 9-5).**

After you click Crop, the cropping rectangle appears superimposed over the image in the Viewer pane, as shown in Figure 9-6.

4. **Drag any corner or edge of the cropping rectangle to crop the image, or drag from the center to move the cropping rectangle.**

As you drag, the portions of the image outside the selected area dim to show that it will be cut. You can also drag from the center of the cropping rectangle to drag the rectangle itself around the image.

5. **When you're finished adjusting the cropping rectangle, click Done.**

To remove the cropping and restore the clip's image to fit in the frame, click the Fit button at the top of the cropping view.

Cropping rectangle

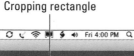

Figure 9-6: Adjust the cropping rectangle to crop the image in the clip.

Imitating the famous Ken Burns effects

You can zoom into a video clip image and pan across the image, and you can combine zooming and panning in ways that suggest movement or the passing of time. Whether or not filmmaker Ken Burns is a household name, his documentaries (such as *Ken Burns' Jazz*) have been watched by millions, and Apple pays him respect by naming this zooming and panning effect after him — the Ken Burns button at the top of the cropping view in the Viewer pane (refer to Figure 9-6).

Ken Burns uses variations of this effect with photos in his documentaries with great success. You can use these effects on any source video clips, including clips you create with photos from your iPhoto library. (See Chapter 10 for details on adding photos to a project.)

To add the Ken Burns effect, follow these steps:

1. **Select a clip in the Event Browser, and click the Cropping tool on the toolbar.**

The cropping view appears inside the Viewer pane.

2. **Click the Ken Burns button at the top of the cropping view.**

   Two cropping rectangles appear superimposed over the image in the Viewer pane, as shown in Figure 9-7, marked with these two words:

   - *Start* (in green) shows the cropped image at the start of the zoom or pan.

   - *End* (in red) shows the cropped image at the end of the zoom or pan.

Figure 9-7: Adjust the Start and End cropping rectangles of the Ken Burns zooming and panning effect.

3. **Click inside the Start cropping rectangle and then adjust its position and edges.**

   Drag any corner or edge of the cropping rectangle to crop the image, or drag from the center to move the cropping rectangle, to show how the zoom or pan should start. As you drag the rectangle, the yellow arrow shows the path of the zoom or pan to the End cropping rectangle.

4. **Click and adjust the End cropping rectangle the same way as in Step 3.**

   Click inside the End cropping rectangle and adjust it in the same way as in Step 3 to show how the zoom or pan should end. As you drag the rectangle, the yellow arrow shows the path of the zoom or pan from the Start cropping rectangle.

5. **Click Done to apply the Ken Burns effect.**

To make the cropping rectangles easier to select, or to reverse the zoom and pan effect, you can exchange the positions of the End (red) and green (Start) cropping rectangles by clicking the small button with two arrows inside the selected cropping rectangle.

To remove the Ken Burns effect and restore your video to its original size, click the Fit button.

Making audio and video adjustments

You can adjust the audio in video clips, especially ones that are louder or softer than others, so that they sound better when included in a project. You can also adjust the video image itself, to increase or decrease exposure, brightness, contrast, and saturation, and adjust the colors of the entire image according to a white point in the image.

To make adjustments, follow these steps:

1. **Select a clip in the Event Browser.**

2. **Click the Gear icon that appears when you move the pointer over the lower left corner of the selected filmstrip, as shown in Figure 9-8.**

   The Clip Adjustments pop-up menu appears.

Figure 9-8: Choose Audio Adjustments from the Clip Adjustments menu.

3. **To adjust audio settings, choose Audio Adjustments from the Clip Adjustments pop-up menu, and make your adjustments.**

   The Audio pane appears as shown in Figure 9-9. It offers a slew of controls to help make clips sound more in harmony with each other. (Forgive the pun.)

   If you prefer, you can double-click the selected clip in the Event Browser to show the Inspector window, and then click the Audio pane.

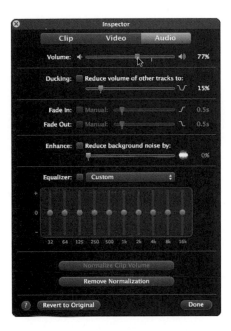

Figure 9-9: Make adjustments to the clip's audio, including overall volume.

Make audio adjustments:

- *Volume slider:* To adjust the audio volume, drag the Volume slider to the volume level you want for the clip.

- *Ducking:* Control the selected clip's audio priority over the competing audio of other clips or sounds you may add in a project. By default, the priority is set to 15 percent, which gives other sounds higher priority. You can increase or decrease it now, or after you've added the clip to a project.

- *Fade In and Fade Out:* These controls in the Inspector window's Audio pane work only with clips already added to a project. See Chapter 10 for more details on working with a project and adjusting its soundtrack.

- *Enhance:* Reduce the background noise in a clip. Drag to the right to reduce noise in the clip by a greater percentage, or to the left to restore the audio to its original state of zero percent reduction.

- *Equalizer:* iMovie provides an equalizer to fine-tune the sound spectrum frequencies in a precise way. The equalizer increases or decreases specific frequencies of the sound to raise or lower highs, lows, and midrange tones. You can adjust frequencies by clicking and dragging sliders that look like mixing-board faders — just like the iTunes Equalizer.

- *Normalize Clip Volume:* You can also normalize the audio for a set of clips, bringing them into the same volume range. For example, if one clip is too loud and a second one is too soft, yet a third one is too loud, you can normalize all three to the same range. Click Normalize Volume to set the selected clip's volume to its maximum level without distortion. Then select another clip, and click Normalize Volume again — iMovie adjusts the volumes of the two clips to the same range. You can continue selecting and normalizing clips to bring them all into the same range.

You can undo audio normalization at any time by clicking Remove Normalization in the Inspector window's Audio pane. You can restore the audio to its original state by clicking Revert to Original.

4. **To adjust video settings, click the Video tab in the Inspector window.**

Or, choose Video Adjustments from the Clip Adjustments pop-up menu (refer to Figure 9-8). The Video pane appears, as shown in Figure 9-10.

The Video pane has these controls:

- *Exposure, Brightness, Contrast, and Saturation:* Drag these sliders to the right to increase the setting or to the left to decrease the setting.

- *White Point:* If your clip's white areas look off-white or if its colors seem too warm or too cold, click a point in the image in the Viewer pane that should be white (or at least gray) when the Video pane is open, and iMovie adjusts the video's colors accordingly. You can also choose a new color for the white point in the color in the Video pane of the Inspector window (refer to Figure 9-10). You can choose a bright color for a radical adjustment or just make the clip look a little warmer or cooler by selecting a light orange or blue.

- *Levels:* Drag the left slider to the right to change the black level in the clip, which darkens the picture. Drag the right slider to the left to change the white level in the clip, which lightens the picture.

- *Auto:* Click the Auto button at the bottom of the Video pane to automatically set the white and black levels.

You can undo the video adjustments all at one time and restore the video to its original state by clicking Revert to Original.

5. **When you're satisfied with your changes, click Done in the lower right corner of the Inspector window.**

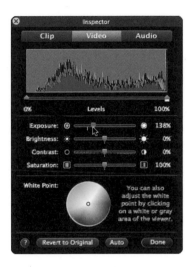

Figure 9-10: Adjust the exposure, saturation, and white point to adjust colors in the video.

You can also edit the audio portion of the video clip directly in the Event Browser. Click the audio waveform button in the lower right corner of the Event Browser window, as shown in Figure 9-11, to show the audio waveform underneath each video clip. You can then drag the volume line in the wave-form up (to raise the volume) or down (to lower the volume), and the wave-form representing the audio moves up or down with it.

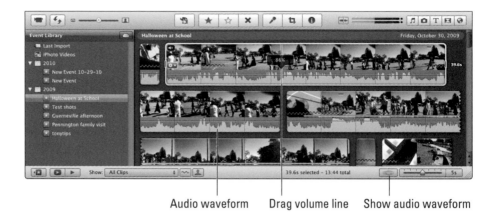

Audio waveform   Drag volume line   Show audio waveform

Figure 9-11: Click the audio waveform button and drag the volume line to adjust the audio part of a clip.

You can even edit only a portion of the audio — click the audio waveform once for a clip and a yellow rectangle appears, defining the area to make your adjustment. Drag the edges of the rectangle to cover the area of the waveform to adjust, and then drag the volume line to adjust the volume, as shown in Figure 9-12. Two yellow fade points appear at either end of the volume line, showing where the volume adjustment begins and ends — the volume is set to automatically fade down or ramp up to accommodate the adjustment. You can adjust the fade points to shorten or lengthen each fade. (To find out how to fade audio between video clips in a project, see Chapter 10.)

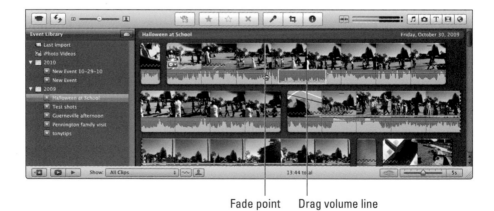

Fade point   Drag volume line

Figure 9-12: Change the volume of an area of the waveform and adjust its fade points.

Editing a Blockbuster Sequence

In This Chapter

▶ Arranging video clips in a project

▶ Adding photos from your iPhoto libraryw

▶ Adding effects, transitions, titles, and credits

▶ Recording through the microphone

▶ Adding music and editing the soundtrack

Movie directors are often lauded for their creative editing. Alfred Hitchcock raised editing to a new level — he used tricks such as cutaways to show what an actor is reacting to, or tight editing to show only the parts of a scene he wanted to show, leaving the audience to imagine the rest. A director often creates a rhythm for a movie established by the lengths of its edited clips, and uses a chronological ordering to help advance the story line and introduce suspense.

The level of suspense you want to create in a vacation or wedding video is up to you. The editing choices you make to arrange your video clips in a sequence can be either wholly original or shamelessly imitative of the great directors of Hollywood — the goal is to engage the audience. People expect a music video to cut quickly from scene to scene in time to the music. The audience wants to be thrilled, so make your videos the best they can be. Experiment with all the tricks and effects you know to see what you can do.

This chapter shows you how to start a project and experiment freely with your video clips. You can try anything that iMovie can do, without damaging any of your source video clips. Arrange clips in any order, trim unwanted frames from clips, slow down or speed up some clips (or even run them in reverse), and then add background music, sound effects, voice-overs, animated maps, and photos spiced up with the Ken Burns effect. iMovie offers several styles for adding text (such as titles and credits) and transitions to move smoothly from one clip to the next. It even offers ready-made *themes* that automatically style your videos with effects, transitions, title and credit graphics, and text styles.

Starting a Project

To edit video scenes into a movie to share with others, you first create a project in the Project Library and edit the project in the Project Browser. The project defines a sequence of video clips (and photos, transitions, and sounds, for example). The project is simply a set of links to the imported clips (which contain the video footage). The changes you make to a project don't affect the original clips or media.

When you create a project, you can define its aspect ratio so that it looks good on a widescreen or standard video display or TV. You can also choose an optional theme for the movie that adds effects such as video-in-a-frame, special transitions, and highly graphical titles and credits.

You can start a project in either of two ways, depending on how you want to work:

- **Create the project, name it, and define its aspect ratio and theme now.** Click the plus-sign (+) button in the lower right corner of the Projects pane or choose File⇨New Project. You can then name the project (use the title you want for the movie), set the aspect ratio, and pick a theme, as shown in Figure 10-1. You can always change these settings at any time.

- **Create the project and provide its name, aspect ratio, and theme later.** Drag clips to the Project pane. iMovie creates the project automatically, and you can start editing it. You can rename the new project at any time in the Project Library. You can also set the aspect ratio and theme at any time by selecting the project in the Project Library and choosing File⇨Project Properties.

Figure 10-1: Start a project and set its aspect ratio (Standard selected), frame rate, and theme. (Comic Book is selected.)

Setting the aspect ratio and frame rate

The *aspect ratio* defines the horizontal and vertical pixel dimensions of the video picture. iMovie offers these aspect ratios:

- **Widescreen (16:9):** The ratio for high-definition (HD) TVs, widescreen makes the video picture appear much wider than it is tall. On a standard TV, the video picture appears with black areas above and below (also known as *letterbox* format).

- **Standard (4:3):** Use the standard ratio for just about all other uses. The video picture is square and fills the screen of a standard-definition (SD) TV, enhanced-definition (ED) TV, or computer display. On a high-definition (HD) TV, the video picture appears with black areas on the left and right of the video (also known as the *pillarbox* format).

When you start a new project by clicking the plus-sign (+) button in the lower right corner of the Projects pane or choosing File➪New Project, you can choose the aspect ratio from the Aspect Ratio pop-up menu (refer to Figure 10-1). You can also set or change the aspect ratio after creating a project by selecting the project in the Project Library and choosing File➪Project Properties.

The *frame rate* defines the number of frames per second. In the United States, the frame rate is set to 30 frames per second (fps), which is compatible with televisions that use the NTSC format (also referred to humorously as "never the same color"). You can use the Frame Rate pop-up menu (refer to Figure 10-1) to change to 25 fps, which is the rate used by the PAL format in other countries, or to the Cinema setting of 24 fps. Originally, 24 fps was used in the nonlinear editing of film-originated material — 24 fps is now increasingly used for aesthetic reasons to deliver film-like motion characteristics.

Choosing a theme for titles and transitions

iMovie can automatically jazz up your movie with titles, transitions, and video-in-a-frame effects based on themes such as Comic Book, News, Sports, Photo Album, and Filmstrip (and more).

When you start a new project by clicking the plus-sign (+) button in the lower right corner of the Projects pane or choosing File➪New Project, you can choose a theme (refer to Figure 10-1). You can also set or change the theme for a project at any time by selecting the project in the Project Library and choosing File➪Project Properties.

As you move the pointer over a theme, it shows a preview of what the movie will look like. Click a theme to select one, or click the None theme if you want to start without one.

After choosing a theme, you can leave the Automatically Add Transitions and Titles option turned on so that iMovie automatically inserts a theme-style introductory title over the first clip, a credits title over the last clip, and cross-dissolves and themed transitions between clips. As you add clips to your project, iMovie automatically inserts a themed transition or cross-dissolve between clips (according to which element works best for the theme). Turn off this option if you'd rather add transitions, titles, and credits manually.

Even if you choose a theme for the project, you can still include standard, nonthemed transitions and titles in it. See "Transition-spotting" and "Dial T for Titles and Credits," later in this chapter, for details on adding these elements manually.

If you choose the None "theme," you can still automatically add transitions — select the Automatically Add option and choose a transition from the pop-up menu. As you add clips to your project, iMovie automatically inserts the selected transition between clips. Keep this option turned off if you'd rather add transitions manually.

Making a movie trailer

Sometimes, the trailer is better than the movie. But for home movies, you have never had a way to create trailers as exciting as these. The iMovie movie-trailer templates make it supereasy to arrange your video clips into well-edited trailers.

When starting a project (as I describe in the earlier section "Choosing a theme for titles and transitions"), you can scroll to the movie trailer templates just below the themes (refer to Figure 10-1). You can choose from 15 movie trailer templates, such as Action, Adventure, Blockbuster, Documentary, Epic Drama, and Romantic Comedy. And, these templates include music: Apple went to Abbey Road to record the legendary London Symphony Orchestra for the original soundtrack of each template (and you have every right to use this music for your personal use).

After you pick a movie trailer, the Project Browser displays the Outline pane along with the Storyboard and the Shot List tabs, as shown in Figure 10-2, to allow you to edit the project. You can click the text fields (such as Movie Name and Release Date) and type your own text into the Outline pane. You can also scroll the Outline pane to change items such as the studio name and logo style and the credits.

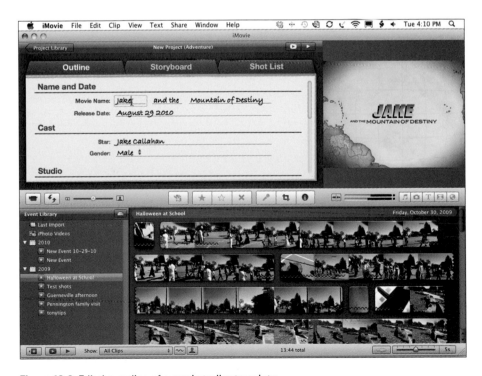

Figure 10-2: Edit the outline of a movie trailer template.

To add your video clips to the movie trailer template, click the Storyboard tab to show the Storyboard pane, as shown in Figure 10-3. You can then click each scene in the Storyboard pane and click a video clip in the Event Browser to drop it into the storyboard scene. You can also edit the text of transitions in the movie trailer and add character names and personalize the titles in scenes.

The Shot List pane shows all clips used in the movie trailer, sorted by type of scene (such as Action, Landscape, Medium, or Wide). To substitute a new clip for an existing clip in the trailer, you can click the clip in the Shot List pane or the Storyboard pane and then click the new clip in the Event Browser to replace it.

After you fill all scenes in the movie trailer template, iMovie tells you that it's finished. You can then click Watch to watch the trailer or click Done to finish editing the trailer and return to the Project Library.

Figure 10-3: Add video clips to the movie trailer template's storyboard.

You can convert your movie trailer template project into a real iMovie project so that you can change the arrangement of clips, perform all kinds of editing tricks, and add special effects (which I describe in this chapter). After finishing your movie trailer project, click Done to return to the Project Library. Select the movie trailer project and choose File⇨Convert to Project.

Adding and Arranging Project Clips

The Project Browser lets you rearrange video clips into a proper sequence. To add video to your project, select a frame range, an entire clip, or several clips at once, as I describe in Chapter 9, and drag the selection to the Project Browser, as shown in Figure 10-4. You can select frame ranges and entire clips from any event and add them to your project.

After you drag a frame range to the Project Browser, the range appears as a whole clip in the Project Browser even if it's only part of a source video clip — to differentiate them, I call them *source clips* and *project clips.* When you drag multiple source clips to the Project Browser, they remain separated as project clips.

Figure 10-4: Drag a selected frame range to the project.

As you drag more frame ranges from source clips to the Project Browser, you can place them in sequence with the other project clips. Simply drag a clip to a specific location in the sequence between other project clips. If you drag a source clip *over* a project clip in the Project Browser, rather than between two project clips, a pop-up menu appears with Replace, Insert, Audio Only, and Cancel options. Choose Replace to replace the project clip with the source clip you're dragging, or Insert to insert the source clip at the point of the playhead in the filmstrip. (Yes, you can insert a source clip in the middle of a project clip.) Choose Audio Only to bring just the audio of the source clip into the project. (See "Editing the Soundtrack," later in this chapter, for more details about adding audio from clips).

Rearranging project clips

To rearrange project clips in the Project Browser sequence, you can use the techniques described in this list:

- **Click each clip and drag it to a new location**. iMovie automatically moves the other clips to make room for it.

- **Move multiple clips at a time** by clicking the first clip and either Shift-clicking the last clip for a consecutive range of clips or Command-clicking each subsequent clip to add it to the selection. With the clips highlighted, click and hold down the mouse button to drag the selection to the new location.

The Project Browser shows not only the project clips in sequence but also the title and credits. I show you how to adjust the titles and credits in the later section "Dial T for Titles and Credits."

Trimming project clips

Most of the work of producing a video consists of editing the project clips to make them more interesting or more effective at communicating. You may want to "tighten up" the project clips so that they start and stop at exactly the right moments or remove unwanted beginnings or endings. The following commands and techniques are handy to know as you trim clips:

- **To quickly trim a project clip,** select the frame range of the video in the clip you want to keep and then choose Clip⇨Trim to Selection.

- **If you trimmed too much at the end and want just a few frames of it back,** choose Clip⇨Trim Clip End⇨Move Right or press Option-right arrow to add more frames at the end from the source clip.

✔ **If you trimmed too much from the beginning,** choose Clip⇨Trim Clip End⇨Move Left, or press Option-Left arrow, to add more frames at the beginning from the source clip. As you add frames, they appear outside the selected frame range (at either the beginning or end).

✔ **To see the entire clip while trimming,** select the project clip and choose Window⇨Clip Trimmer (or click the Gear icon pop-up menu at the beginning of the clip and choose Clip Trimmer from the menu). The Clip Trimmer, shown in Figure 10-5, appears below the Project and Viewer panes, temporarily replacing the Event Library and Event Browser. The Clip Trimmer shows the entire source clip, with the selected portion for the project clip highlighted. Drag the start-point or end-point selection handles to trim the selection for the project clip. To be more precise, click near the start point or end point and then press Option-left arrow or Option-right arrow to move the start point or end point frame by frame.

✔ **To preview the newly trimmed project clip before leaving the Clip Trimmer,** click the Play button in the upper right corner of the Clip Trimmer (to the left of the Done button — refer to Figure 10-5). When you're finished trimming, click Done.

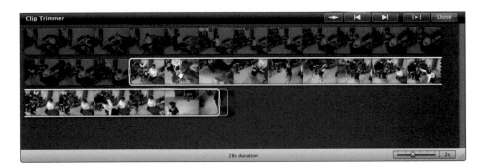

Figure 10-5: Trim a project clip in the Clip Trimmer.

Adding Photos from iPhoto

Documentary filmmaker Ken Burns is known for the technique of using still photos for dramatic effect rather than reenacting a scene from history with actors. When you add photos from your iPhoto library to your project, iMovie automatically applies the Ken Burns pan and zoom effects, introduced in Chapter 9, to make it appear that the camera is sweeping across the image and moving closer or farther away from it.

To browse photos in your iPhoto library, click the Photos button — the Camera icon on the right side of the toolbar under the Viewer pane (or choose Window➪Photos). The iPhoto Browser appears next to the Event Browser, as shown in Figure 10-6.

These techniques can help you find the photos you want to add to your movie project:

- ✔ Your iPhoto library's events appear if you select Events in the list at the top of the iPhoto Browser. You can skim events to find a photo, just as you can with iPhoto (as I describe in Chapter 2).

- ✔ Select a photo album or keepsake (such as a photo book) to see only the photos in that album or keepsake.

- ✔ You can also enter a photo's title or part of a description in the Search field at the bottom of the iPhoto Browser to display photos that match your search term.

iPhoto Browser   Photo button

Search field   Show Photos pop-up menu

Figure 10-6: Browse photos in iPhoto by event, select an album, or search the iPhoto library.

✔ To see only the photos that match the selected event in the iMovie Event Library, click the Show Photos option at the bottom of the iPhoto Browser, which has a pop-up menu set to Within Event Date Range (refer to Figure 10-6). You can change the range by choosing Within 1 Day of Event, 1 Week of Event, or 1 Month of Event from the pop-up menu. The iPhoto Browser shows only images that were taken (or imported) in that date range.

To add a photo to the video project, follow these steps:

1. **Select the photo in the iPhoto Browser and drag it to the position you want it to appear in the project sequence, just like a source clip.**

   iMovie sets the photo clip's duration to 4.5 seconds and applies the Ken Burns effect, but of course you can change both settings.

2. **(Optional) To change the duration, select the photo clip in the Project Browser and then double-click it — or click the Gear icon at the beginning of the photo clip and choose Clip Adjustments, as shown in Figure 10-7.**

   The Inspector appears with the Clip pane open, as shown in Figure 10-8.

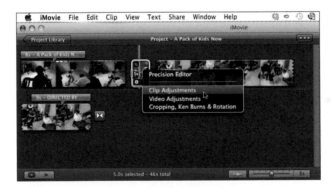

Figure 10-7: Choose Clip Adjustments to change the photo clip's duration.

Figure 10-8: Change the photo clip's duration and add a video effect.

3. **(Optional) Enter a new duration in the Duration field.**

   You can specify that all photo clips (also known as *stills*) have the same duration by clicking the Applies to All Stills option.

4. **(Optional) Choose a video effect for the photo clip by clicking the Video Effect button, which displays the Video Effects pane (for a sneak preview, see Figure 10-9), and then click an effect.**

   See the later section "FlashForward: Adding Video Effects" for details on these effects.

5. **Click Done when you finish making adjustments.**

6. **(Optional) To change or remove the Ken Burns effect, click the photo clip in the Project Browser and then click the Crop button in the clip (or the Cropping tool on the toolbar).**

   You can then change the Ken Burns effect as I describe in Chapter 9, or click Fit to remove the effect.

FlashForward: Adding Video Effects

Ever since movies such as *Star Wars,* people have grown accustomed to seeing marvelous special effects — so much so that it sometimes takes a special effect to get their attention. Not everyone can be as inventive as George Lucas, but you can experiment with some iMovie special effects to transform clips into visual eye candy. You can not only speed up or slow down project clips and run clips in reverse but also apply video effects automatically, such as Aged Film, Glow, Dream, Heat Wave, Sci-Fi, and X-Ray.

The Jedi warrior shown earlier, in Figure 10-7, might appear more convincing with a video effect — such as a glow or a sci-fi look. To set a video effect, follow these steps:

1. **Select a project clip in the Project Browser and then double-click it.**

   Alternatively, click the Gear icon at the beginning of the project clip and choose Clip Adjustments (or choose Window⇨Clip Adjustments). The Inspector appears with the Clip pane open (refer to Figure 10-7).

2. **Click the Video Effect button, which displays the Video Effects pane, as shown in Figure 10-9.**

3. **Move the pointer across an effect to see a preview of the effect in the Viewer pane.**

4. **Click an effect to select it for the clip, and then click Done in the Inspector's Clip pane.**

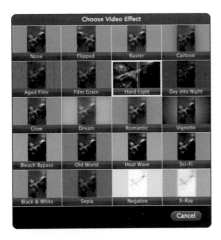

Figure 10-9: Set a video effect for the selected project clip.

Here are a few reasons why you might want to use video effects:

- **Aged Film:** Make your video look like newsreel footage with this effect, which creates a visual effect of scratched film, with a supergrainy texture and lines and specks.

- **Black & White:** Turn your clip into black-and-white to simulate early television pictures, or to emulate the *Wizard of Oz.* (Everything's in black-and-white until Dorothy lands in Oz and opens the door.) Sometimes, a video shot on a gray day looks better in black-and-white.

- **Hard Light:** Although this effect isn't a substitute for good lighting when recording video, it can help alleviate the problems associated with poor lighting and making the picture brighter or darker or with less or more contrast.

- **Sepia Tone:** Create the brown-and-white look of a very old photo, which can help convey antiquity and nostalgia.

- **Romantic:** Add a blurry, fuzzy-edged look to everything for those hazy, dreamy, or romantic scenes; you also see this effect used in TV commercials featuring aging stars because it hides facial wrinkles.

Speeding, slowing, and reversing clips

Suppose that you want to show your child's first swing of a baseball bat in slow-motion instant replay for dramatic effect. Or, perhaps you have a funny clip of an infant jumping and running around that would crack up viewers if it were run much faster and then shown in reverse.

iMovie offers Slow Motion, Fast Forward, and Instant Replay options on its Clip menu. To use these options, select the video clip in the Project Browser, choose File⇨Optimize Video, and then choose Full – Original Size or Large (960 x 540). (If either option is grayed out, the clip has already been optimized for that size or that size isn't available.) What optimization does is convert the video using the Apple Intermediate Codec, which makes a bigger video file, but one that can be modified for speed or reversed smoothly. The Full choice preserves HD resolution (or whatever the original size was).

Optimizing the video converts it to Apple's native editing format. The iMovie conversion is quick, but the video quality is a bit degraded. To ensure that your original clip isn't converted, iMovie copies it first to a folder within the iMovie Original Movies folder in the `Movies` folder inside your user folder. You can then import the original clips again from that folder if you want to use them again without speed adjustments.

After optimizing the video clip, choose one of these commands:

- **Clip⇨Slow Motion:** Then choose 50%, 25%, or 10% (the percentage to slow it down).

- **Clip⇨Fast Forward:** Then choose 2x, 4x, 8x, or 20x (the multiple to speed it up).

- **Clip⇨Instant Replay:** Then choose 50%, 25%, or 10% (the percentage to slow down the instant-replay copy of the clip).

The Instant Reply option extends the clip by copying the video and then slowing down the copied video, just like an instant replay in a sports broadcast.

To apply a special effect on a copy of a project clip and still play the original version — for example, to follow a normal clip with the same clip in reverse — select the project clip and then Option-click and drag the clip to a new insertion point in the sequence. iMovie copies the project clip.

To set a more precise speed for a project clip or set it to run in reverse, follow these steps:

1. **Select the clip in the Project Browser, and then double-click it.**

   The Inspector appears with the Clip pane open.

2. **If you see the Convert Entire Clip button, click it.**

   If your video was recorded in a format other than iFrame Video (the native iMovie format, as I explain in Chapter 8), or if it needs to be optimized as I describe earlier in this section, the Speed section of the Clip pane shows the Convert Entire Clip button.

   After you convert the clip (if it was necessary), the Clip pane shows the Speed settings, as shown in Figure 10-10.

Figure 10-10: Change the speed of a clip or run it in reverse.

3. **Drag the Speed slider to the right (toward the Hare icon) to speed up the clip, or to the left (toward the Tortoise icon) to slow down the clip.**

   The duration of the clip appears in the field below the percentage of speed increase (or decrease).

4. **Click the Reverse option for Direction to run the clip in reverse.**

5. **Click Done to finish.**

Making clips run in reverse may seem like a cheap gimmick — humorous when applied to skiers, high-divers, departing planes, or buildings being demolished, for example. But it can also be a useful way to fix a problem or add a touch of professionalism to a video. For example, if you zoomed into a stationary subject with your camcorder without also zooming out, and later you discover that you wish you had zoomed out, you can copy the project clip and then reverse the direction of the copy. You end up with two clips: the zoom-in and the reverse of the zoom-in, which looks just like a zoom-out. Put them together and the scene is complete.

When you change the speed of a video clip, the sound's speed also changes, which can be irritating for recorded voices. And, when you reverse a clip, recorded voices may sound like The Beatles at the end of the song "Rain." Nature sounds, however, may sound fine backward or forward, or even a bit slowed down or sped up. If you don't like how a clip sounds, you can adjust the audio portion and even add a different soundtrack, as I describe in the later section "Editing the Soundtrack."

Adding an animated map

One of my favorite scenes in *Raiders of the Lost Ark* is the animated map that shows the route Indiana Jones took across the globe. iMovie has already mapped the world for you, so you can put a similar animated map in your video. Here's how:

1. **Click the Maps button (the Globe icon on the right side of the toolbar under the Viewer pane). Or, choose Window⇨Maps and Backgrounds.**

   The Maps and Backgrounds Browser appears next to the Event Browser with thumbnails for the animated map types (refer to Figure 10-11).

2. **Move the pointer across a map to see a generic preview in the thumbnail.**

Inspector   Maps, Backgrounds, and Animations Browser

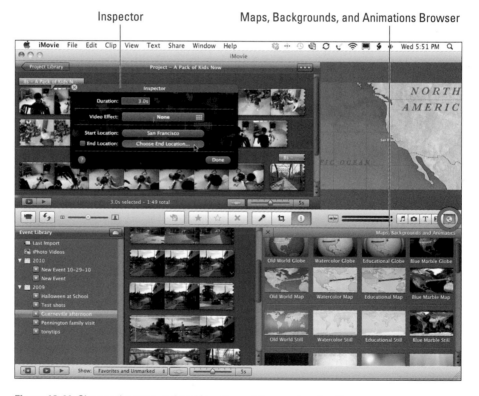

Figure 10-11: Choose the start and end locations of the map's animation.

3. **Choose a map type and drag it to the Project Browser, just like a source clip.**

   The Inspector appears (refer to Figure 10-11).

4. **Set the start or end location of the animation for the map by clicking the Choose Start Location or Choose End Location button and entering the city name.**

   As you enter the first characters of the city name, suggestions appear. Click a suggestion to select it, and then click OK.

5. **(Optional) Change the duration in the Duration field.**

6. **(Optional) Add a video effect, as I describe earlier in this chapter).**

7. **Click Done.**

Transition-Spotting

Though Alfred Hitchcock could create a movie like *Rope,* with each shot running continuously without a cut for as long as seven minutes, the rest of us likely have many individual clips that need to be cut together in a way that isn't too jarring. A *transition* provides a seamless way for one clip to end and another to begin.

Movies and professionally produced television shows typically use nothing but a simple cut from one clip to the next, even though professionals have an arsenal of transitions they can use, such as dissolve, wipe, and overlap. Transitions are usually kept simple because they can detract from the video and call attention to the video editing process. But sometimes a transition makes sense artistically, or it can be useful for suggesting the passage of time or to hide a flaw in the video itself. For example, the hit TV show *Six Feet Under* uses a cross-dissolve-to-white (or washout-to-white) transition between each major scene for artistic effect. The transition is used consistently throughout the show and the series, providing a sense of unity in the work. Other popular transitions include fading in from black in the beginning of a movie, and fading out to black at the end (or fading into credits).

If you chose a theme when you started your project, and chose the option to automatically add transitions, iMovie has already populated your video with transitions between clips that make sense for the chosen theme. (If you haven't chosen a theme, see "Starting a Project," earlier in this chapter.) However, you can change or edit the transitions, as well as add more transitions — especially after splitting a clip into two clips.

To split a project clip into two clips, drag across the project clip to select a frame range for the first clip and then choose Clip➪Split Clip.

Adding transitions between project clips

To see the available transitions and add one to your project, follow these steps:

1. **Click the Transitions button (the Hourglass icon on the right side of the toolbar under the Viewer pane).**

   The Transitions Browser appears next to the Event Browser (shown in Figure 10-12), with thumbnails for the transitions, including ones associated with the theme you chose.

2. **Move the pointer across a transition to see a generic preview in the thumbnail.**

3. **To add a transition, drag it from the Transitions Browser to a location between two project clips in the Project Browser (refer to Figure 10-12).**

   If a transition already exists at that location, the new one replaces it. If you chose a theme and the option to automatically add transitions when you started the project (or later), iMovie displays a dialog informing you that automatic transitions and titles are turned on. Click the Turn Off Automatic Transitions button to add the transition (or Cancel to cancel).

   After you turn off automatic transitions, the automatic transitions and titles that iMovie already put into your project are still there, so you don't lose them. However, you need to add transitions manually if you want them as you add more clips to the project.

4. **To see the transition in action, move the pointer in front of it to move the playhead in the project clip, and then press the spacebar to start playing. Press it again to stop.**

Editing transitions

iMovie offers a few different ways to edit transitions, and the edits available to you may depend on the transition itself. To change the length of a transition or to select a different one, follow these steps:

1. **Select and then double-click the transition, or choose Window➪ Transition Adjustments.**

   The Inspector appears.

Standard transition

Thermal transition

Dragging a transition between two clips

Transitions Browser

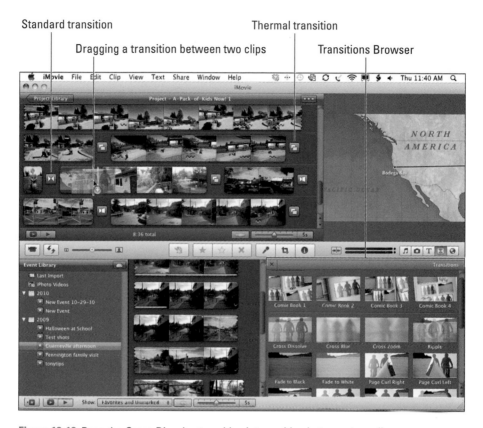

Figure 10-12: Drag the Cross Dissolve transition into position between two clips.

2. **To change the duration, enter the number of seconds (in tenths of a second) in the Duration field.**

3. **To change the transition, click the Transition pop-up menu and then select another transition.**

   Before selecting one, you can skim over the transition thumbnails to see a preview in the Viewer pane.

 Some themed transitions show still images from your project clips in separate frames. After clicking a themed transition in the Project Browser, numbers appear above the project clips before and after the transition that correspond to the numbered frames in the transition, as shown in Figure 10-13. To change the still image shown in any numbered frames of the transition, click its number and drag to a new location in the filmstrip to show a different part of the project clip in that frame.

Themed transition   Frames in the transition

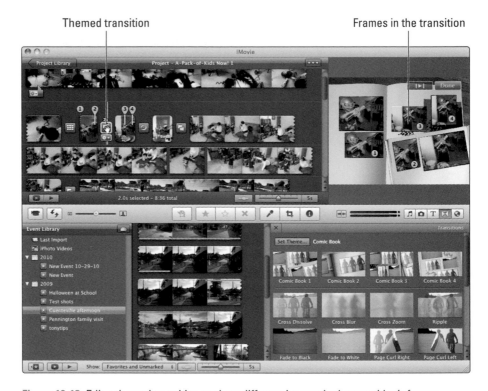

Figure 10-13: Edit a themed transition to show different images in the transition's frames.

The Precision Editor gives you more control over the project clips and the transition between them, which are lined up along a horizontal timeline. To improve a transition using the Precision Editor, follow these steps.

1. **Select the transition and choose Window⇨Precision Editor (or choose Precision Editor from the gear icon's Actions pop-up menu underneath the Transition icon).**

   The Precision Editor replaces the Event Library and Event Browser to show you a timeline view of the transition and the preceding and following project clips, as shown in Figure 10-14.

   A magnified filmstrip view shows exactly where one project clip ends and the next begins. The grayed-out parts reveal the portions of the clips that were trimmed, and the cut point where one clip ends and the other begins, or the transition between the clips. You can skim each clip to identify precisely where the cut or transition occurs.

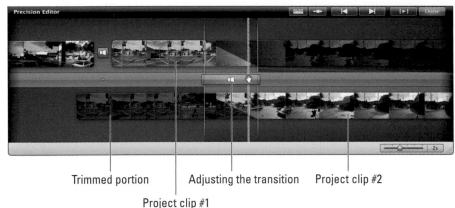

Trimmed portion   Adjusting the transition   Project clip #2

Project clip #1

Figure 10-14: Adjust the transition between two project clips more precisely by using the Precision Editor.

2. **To change the cut between two clips, move the pointer back and click the first clip at the point where you want the cut to occur, and then do the same for the second clip.**

    The Precision Editor automatically adjusts the cut to be exactly where you clicked in both clips.

3. **To change the transition between two clips, drag the transition horizontally along the timeline (refer to Figure 10-14) so that it occurs where you want it to occur between the two clips.**

4. **To adjust the transition duration, drag the right and left edges of the transition.**

5. **To play back the edited transition, click the Play button to the left of the Done button in the upper right corner of the Precision Editor pane (refer to Figure 10-14).**

    Alternatively, you can move the pointer to a position before the transition and press the spacebar.

Dial T for Titles and Credits

All movies should have titles. Even *Untitled* is a good title. Titling gives you the chance to be witty, even in a vacation video. As for credits, you make up names for all those strange job titles, such as gaffer, key grip, and associate executive producer.

iMovie simplifies the making of titles and credits. After choosing a theme for your project (see the earlier section "Starting a Project"), iMovie puts titles and credits in your project and spins interesting effects for them based on the theme. The title and credits can appear superimposed over the video, or against a background. You can still edit the text of the titles and credits and change them to suit your needs, as described in this list:

- ✔ **If you chose a theme and the option to automatically add transitions and titles,** the Project Browser shows yellow-green markers for the title on the first clip and the credits on the last clip. To change the text, move the pointer to the clip with the title or credits, select the text in the Viewer pane, and then type over the text, as shown in Figure 10-15. Click the Done button in the upper right corner of the Viewer pane to finish.

- ✔ **If you didn't choose a theme,** you can add custom titles and credits to your project and then make adjustments to them. Even if you chose a theme and the option to automatically add titles and credits, you can adjust or change them and add more custom titles and credits.

Title marker   Editing the title

Figure 10-15: Edit the title automatically added by the theme.

To add titles and credits to your project and edit those in it, follow these steps:

1. **Click the Titles button — the T icon on the right side of the toolbar under the Viewer pane (or choose Window⊅Titles).**

   The Title Browser appears next to the Event Browser (refer to Figure 10-15), with thumbnails for the title and credit styles, including ones associated with the theme you chose.

2. **Move the pointer across a title or credit style to see a generic preview in the thumbnail.**

3. **To add a custom title or credits, drag a title or credit style from the Title Browser to a project clip in the Project Browser.**

   As you hover over the video clip with the title or credit style, a blue shadow appears over the clip — you can drag the shadow over the first third of the clip or the last third of the clip or the entire clip. After you drag the title or credit style, a blue marker appears over the clip showing its duration, as shown in Figure 10-16.

Custom credits   Themed credits

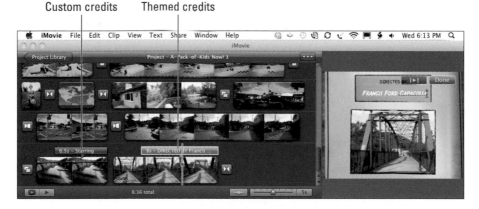

Figure 10-16: Custom and themed credits for the last set of clips.

4. **(Optional) To change the duration for a title, select and then double-click the marker for the title or credits (or select the marker and choose Window⊅Clip Adjustments).**

   The Inspector appears.

5. **(Optional) Change the duration in the Inspector dialog by entering the number of seconds (in tenths of a second) in the Duration field, and click Done.**

   You can also change the duration of the title or credits by dragging the marker's right or left edge.

6. **(Optional) To move the title to a new position in the clip, drag the marker from the middle and position it where you want it.**

7. **To change the color, font, or style of the text, select the text in the Viewer pane and click the Show Fonts button in the upper left corner of the Viewer pane.**

   You can skim over each font and see a preview in the Viewer pane. You can also choose a different color for the font by clicking the color bars, and choose a different size for the font by clicking the numbers.

8. **Click Done when finished choosing a font, size, and color.**

Editing the Soundtrack

Editing the sound is as important, if not more important, than editing the picture. Viewers usually barely notice flaws in a moving picture compared to flaws in the sound, which linger in the mind and can be irritating. (For example, a scratchy newsreel is fine to watch as long as the sound isn't scratchy.) Fortunately, iMovie makes editing the soundtrack as easy as editing video clips.

Another indispensable feature of iMovie is its ability to record a voice-over or some narration. I explain how to record with iMovie in this section, but you should also check out the coverage of recording vocals and other sounds in GarageBand in Chapter 20.

Recording through the microphone

Every Mac has the built-in capability to record sound. You can use the built-in microphone on the Mac models that have one or attach an external USB microphone. To add a voice-over or any recording through the microphone (such as a harmonica or ambient sound), follow these steps:

1. **Click the Voiceover button (the Microphone icon) in the center of the toolbar.**

   The Voiceover window appears.

2. **Choose a microphone from the Record From pop-up menu.**

3. **To check the sound level, speak into the microphone and check the volume-level meters.**

   The levels should be a bit more than halfway across for the best sound quality. Try to keep the meters in the green area. (Yellow is too loud, and red means that your voice is distorted, or *clipped,* in the recording.)

4. **Drag the Input Volume slider to the right to make it louder (for a soft voice) or to the left to make it softer (for a loud voice).**

5. **(Optional) Drag the Noise Reduction slider far to the right to reduce ambient noise in the recording.**

   If you want to retain some background sound as part of your recording, drag the slider to the left.

6. **(Optional) Turn on voice enhancement to make your recorded voice sound as smooth as a crooner or torch singer.**

7. **To hear the sound while you record your voice-over, get out your headphones or earbuds and turn on the Play Project Audio While Recording option.**

   You need the headphones or earbuds so that the microphone doesn't pick up the sound of the video's playback and start a feedback loop.

8. **When you're ready to begin recording, move the pointer into the Project Browser and click the point in the project clip where you want the voice-over to begin.**

   iMovie displays the message *Get Ready* in the Viewer pane and counts down from three to one.

9. **Begin speaking at the end of the count, when the word *Recording* appears.**

10. **To stop recording the voice-over, press the spacebar or click anywhere in the iMovie window.**

    A purple marker appears under the project clip to mark your recording.

To continue recording more voice-overs in the project, click another point in the project clip where you want the next voice-over to begin and iMovie then sets you up for the next recording.

You can drag the marker to move the voice-over to a different spot in the clip or to another project clip. You can also make the voice-over itself shorter by dragging the right end of the voice-over marker to the left. Making the voice-over shorter cuts off the end of the recording.

Adding music and sound effects

Music can make your videos a lot more exciting and establish a mood. Imagine the opening scenes of *Apocalypse Now* without the eerie music of the Doors and Jim Morrison singing "This is the end. . . ." — it just wouldn't be the same.

Sound effects are useful for triggering excitement, surprise, or humor. iMovie offers a long list of sound effects organized by folder. Here are a few techniques you'll find handy as you work with music and sound effects:

> ✐ **To browse sound effects and music,** click the Music button — the Music Note icon on the right side of the toolbar under the Viewer pane (or choose Window⇨Music and Sound Effects). The Music and Sound Effects Browser appears next to the Event Browser (refer to Figure 10-17), with a list of music sources including iMovie Sound Effects and iLife Sound Effects.

Dragging a sound effect

Figure 10-17: Drag a sound effect to the project.

To browse sound effects, open either iMovie Sound Effects or iLife Sound Effects by clicking its triangle. Select a folder in the Music and Sound Effects list, and then select a sound effect in the list below the Music and Sound Effects list. You can also use the Search field to search for the sound effect by name. Click the sound effect to hear it (or click the Play button at the bottom of the Music and Sound Effects browser).

✐ **To add a sound effect,** select and drag it from the Music and Sound Effects Browser to a project clip in the Project Browser (refer to Figure 10-17).

After dragging the sound effect, a green marker appears below the project clip, as shown in Figure 10-18. You can add as many sound effects as you like, and even overlap them by dragging them over the same area of the same project clip.

✐ **To move a sound effect to another position,** simply drag the marker.

Sound effect marker

Figure 10-18: Select the sound effect marker to adjust its position and length.

✔ **To make a sound effect shorter or longer,** drag the right end of the marker to the left. Many sound effects repeat over and over, so you can make them longer or shorter.

✔ **To browse music in your iTunes library,** scroll the Music and Sound Effects list to iTunes; open the list under iTunes by clicking its triangle; and select Music, Movies, Podcasts, Books, Purchased, or Genius or a playlist. You can also use the Search field to search for a song or an artist by name. Click the song in the list below the Music and Sound Effects list to hear it (or click the Play button at the bottom of the Music and Sound Effects Browser).

✔ **To add a song from iTunes to your movie,** select and drag it from the Music and Sound Effects Browser to a project clip in the Project Browser.

After you drag the song, a green marker appears below the project clips, as shown in Figure 10-19. To start the song later in the video, drag the left edge of the music marker to the position in the project clip where you want the clip to start. If you move the project clip while editing the movie, the music moves with it so that it's always in sync with that point in the video.

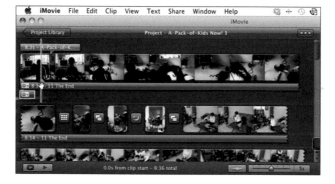

Figure 10-19: Select the song marker to adjust its position.

If your video is longer than the song, you can add another song by dragging it to project clip after the first song ends, or to any other point. You can also drag to a point that includes the other song to overlap songs.

✔ **To trim the audio clip in the Clip Trimmer,** select the audio marker and choose Window⇨Clip Trimmer. The audio track appears in the Clip Trimmer window, as shown in Figure 10-20, so that you can trim the beginning or end of the soundtrack.

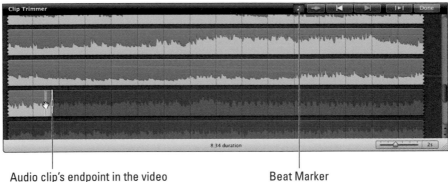

Audio clip's endpoint in the video   Beat Marker

Figure 10-20: Trim the soundtrack in the Clip Trimmer.

Syncing your audio and video

To sync video clips to the beat of the music, you can add beat markers to the audio clip in the Clip Trimmer. Drag the Music Note icon in the upper right section of the Clip Trimmer (refer to Figure 10-20) to a section of the audio clip and release it to mark the clip at that point. You may find it easier to right-click (or Control-click) the spot in the Clip Trimmer that you want to mark and then choose Add Beat Marker from the menu that appears. The markers appear as thin, vertical, white lines with dots.

You can also start the audio track playing from the beginning, and as the song plays, tap the M key for every beat corresponding to a new video clip. Remember, though: If you tap the M key just as you hear the beat, the video clip will probably appear late, so try marking immediately *before* hearing the beat. After adding beat markers, choose View⇨Snap to Beats and then select a source clip or frame range and drag it to the project. iMovie automatically snaps the clip to the beat and cuts off the end of the clip if it's too long to fit before the next beat. You can continue dragging clips that snap directly to the beat. This technique is particularly effective for aligning photos in a slide-show or Ken Burns-style documentary to the soundtrack.

Controlling volume and fading

You can control the volume and fading for a voice-over, sound effect, or music clip directly in the Project Browser. Click the Audio Waveform button in the lower right corner of the Project Browser window, as shown in Figure 10-21, to show the audio waveform underneath each audio clip. You can then drag the volume line in the waveform up (to raise the volume) or down (to lower the volume), and the waveform representing the audio moves up or down with it — just as I show when making adjustments to video clips in Chapter 9.

Fade button   Show audio waveform

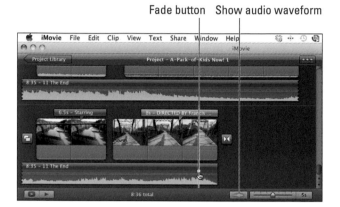

Figure 10-21: Click the Audio Waveform button and drag the Fade button to fade the audio at the end.

To fade the audio at the beginning or end, click the tiny, white Fade button on the volume line at the beginning or end, and drag it toward the middle; for example, in Figure 10-21, I drag the Fade button at the end to the left to fade out the song. You can adjust the fade points to shorten or lengthen each fade.

You can also edit only a portion of the audio — click the audio waveform once for a clip, and a yellow rectangle appears defining the area to make your adjustment. Drag the edges of the rectangle to cover the area of the waveform to adjust, and then drag the volume line to adjust the volume.

To more precisely control the volume level of a voice-over, sound effect, or music clip, select its marker in the Project Browser and choose Window⇨Audio Adjustments. The Inspector's Audio pane appears.

To adjust the audio volume, drag the Volume slider in the Inspector's Audio pane to the volume level you want for the clip. Drag the sliders for the Fade In and Fade Out controls to increase or decrease the fade into the sound clip and out of the sound clip. These and the other audio adjustment options are all described in Chapter 9, so check them out there.

Premiering Your Video to the World

In This Chapter

▶ Adding a video to your iTunes library

▶ Sharing a video by way of MobileMe

▶ Publishing a video on YouTube

▶ Using a video with other iLife applications

▶ Exporting a video to a file with custom settings

*F*inally, a distribution deal! Call your agent! Suddenly, everyone wants to see your video.

And you're in a great position to distribute that video. You can share videos with people you know using MobileMe and publish videos for the world to see on Facebook, Vimeo, or YouTube. Carry videos in your iPhone, iPad, or iPod or show them at home on your Apple TV, and use iDVD to burn DVDs for just about any DVD player. You can even create a video podcast and send it directly to Apple's Podcast Producer 2. iMovie can export high-definition (HD) video at full 1920-x-1080 pixel resolution.

You can even use a video in other Apple applications, including iDVD, iWeb, and GarageBand, by saving it in the Media Browser. And, you can export a video as a digital movie that can play on just about any current-model computer. You can even send your movie to Final Cut Express or Final Cut Pro to edit it further.

This chapter shows how to make your videos available to just about anyone with a hankering to watch them.

Adding Videos to Your iTunes Library

If the iPad, iPod, and iPhone and Apple TV are like spaceships, iTunes is the space station they use as a dock to retrieve their supplies. iTunes is the central repository of all content for these devices. If you have an iPad, iPod, or iPhone, you should already know how to synchronize them with content from your iTunes library. (If you don't, see *iPod and iTunes For Dummies,* by yours truly.) So, it makes sense that if you want to play your newly created video on an iPad, iPhone, or iPod, or stream video to Apple TV, all you need to do is move the video into your iTunes library. You can then sync the iPad, iPhone, or iPod and stream the video directly from iTunes to your Apple TV.

iMovie helps you quite easily put video into your iTunes library. You can even specify videos of different sizes for different devices at the same time, and iMovie converts the videos and dumps them into the Movies section of your iTunes library. All you need to do to see them is to open iTunes and click Movies in the Library section of the iTunes Source pane.

To send a video to your iTunes library, follow these steps:

1. **Select the video project in the Project Library and choose Share⇨iTunes.**

   A dialog appears, as shown in Figure 11-1, with a grid showing the video picture sizes that work with different devices.

2. **Select as many sizes as you want to create multiple versions of your video, or choose just the size you want for one version.**

   iMovie can help you decide: Click a target device to play the video, such as the iPhone, and iMovie automatically selects all sizes that work with that device. After clicking the target device, you can keep the multiple sizes selected to create multiple versions of your video (such as Mobile, which work for an iPhone) or deselect sizes you don't want.

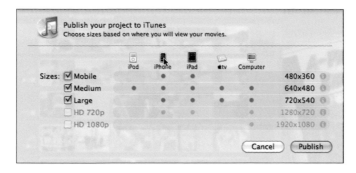

Figure 11-1: Click a device to automatically select the right video picture sizes for the device.

3. **(Optional) Move the pointer over the *i* next to the pixel dimensions for the size to display information about the video rendered at that size.**

The first bit of information — H.264 or 3GP — is the compression method; the second is the frame rate in frames per second (fps); the third is the maximum rate at which the video can be streamed over the Internet, expressed in kilobytes per second (Kbps) or megabits per second (Mbps); and the fourth is the video file size in megabytes (MB).

Some size options aren't available if the project's video clips are set to a lower size — for example, if your original source clips weren't recorded in HD, iMovie doesn't offer the Large size.

4. **Click Publish to send the video to your iTunes library (or Cancel to cancel).**

After iMovie renders the video in the size or sizes you selected, an icon appears next to the project's name in the Project Library to indicate that the project has been rendered. After the video has been transferred to iTunes, the Shared To pop-up menu appears on the title bar of the project set to iTunes. The pop-up menu includes the Visit button to go to iTunes.

The newly rendered video shows up in the Movies section of the iTunes library, as shown in Figure 11-2 — click Movies in the Library section of the Source pane. You can now include the video in syncing operations with your iPad, iPhone, or iPod and stream the video to Apple TV.

To remove versions of your video project from iTunes, select the project and choose Share⇨Remove From⇨iTunes.

Select Movies

Figure 11-2: Open iTunes to find the video in the Movies section.

Sharing Videos with MobileMe

You may already use MobileMe with your Mac and, as I describe in Chapter 6, you can upload pictures to the Gallery section of MobileMe to share with other people. You can also share videos in your MobileMe Gallery so that others can watch them using a current Web browser and, if you give permission, download them.

To share a video on MobileMe, follow these steps:

1. **Select its project and choose Share⇨MobileMe Gallery.**

   If you aren't already signed in to the MobileMe service, a window appears so that you can sign in to your account.

2. **Click the Sign In button to show the next window, and then enter your member name and password and click the Sign In button to sign in.**

If you don't have a MobileMe account, click the Learn More button to find out more about it.

After you sign in, a dialog appears, as shown in Figure 11-3.

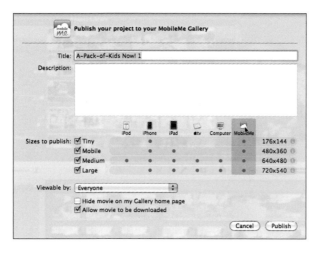

Figure 11-3: Share your video with others using MobileMe.

3. **Fill in the Title and Description fields.**

   You also see a grid showing the video picture sizes that work with different devices.

4. **Select one size or as many sizes as you want to create multiple versions of your video.**

   Click a target device to automatically select all sizes that work with the device. Some size options aren't available if the project's video clips are set to a lower size.

5. **To control privacy for the uploaded video, change the Viewable By option from Everyone to Only Me, or choose Edit Names and Passwords to add names and passwords of people you want to allow access to your video.**

6. **Click Publish to publish the video (or Cancel to cancel).**

   After the video has been uploaded to your MobileMe Gallery, the Shared To pop-up menu appears on the title bar of the project set to MobileMe, the pop-up menu includes the Visit button to go to the video's Web page, and the Tell a Friend button lets you send a notification (by e-mail) to others to watch the video.

You can invite people to view your MobileMe Gallery by sending an e-mail with a link to it. You can find the link in the upper left corner of the MobileMe Web page displaying the Gallery.

To remove versions of your video project from the MobileMe gallery, select the project and choose Share➪Remove from➪MobileMe.

Uploading Videos to YouTube, Facebook, Vimeo, or CNN iReport

YouTube (www.youtube.com) and *Vimeo* (http://vimeo.com) are popular video sharing sites you can use to serve your videos to anyone on the Internet, and the services are free. Companies use YouTube and Vimeo to host videos for their customers and employees. Families upload videos for their relatives and friends. People can play videos hosted by YouTube and Vimeo using almost any browser on any computer, as well as an iPad, iPhone, or iPod touch and many other smartphones and devices that offer YouTube and Vimeo. And, did I mention that they're free?

Facebook is the fastest-growing free-access social networking site as of this writing (it's also free), with more than half a billion active users worldwide. If you're one of them (as I am), you already know that you can upload photos to your personal profile — and you can do it from iPhoto (as I show in Chapter 6). You can also upload videos to your Facebook account from iMovie.

CNN iReport (http://ireport.cnn.com), also free, lets you upload news stories — the stories aren't edited, fact-checked, or screened, but the ones marked *CNN iReport* have been checked out by CNN producers and made a part of CNN news coverage.

To upload a video to YouTube, Facebook, Vimeo, or CNN iReport, follow these steps:

1. **Select the video project in the iMovie Project Library and choose Share➪YouTube, Share➪Facebook, Share➪Vimeo, or Share➪ CNN iReport.**

   The YouTube, Facebook, Vimeo, or CNN iReport dialog appears, as shown in Figure 11-4 for YouTube.

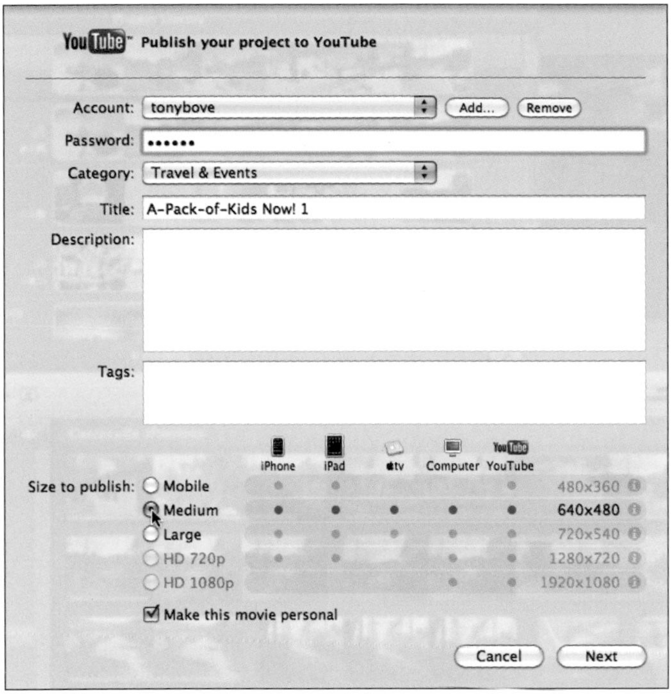

Figure 11-4: Upload the video to your YouTube account.

2. **If you have ever uploaded to YouTube, Facebook, Vimeo, or CNN iReport, your account may already be in the Account pop-up menu, and you can simply choose it; if you haven't already uploaded, you can add the account to the pop-up menu by clicking Add.**

   If you don't yet have a YouTube, Facebook, Vimeo, or CNN iReport account, go to the site first and create an account. After clicking Add, enter your account name, and type the password in the Password field.

3. **Fill out the Title and Description fields for YouTube, Facebook, Vimeo, or CNN iReport, and for YouTube, choose a category from the Category pop-up menu.**

4. **Add *tags* (search keywords) for your video in the Tags field to help people find your video when they search by keyword on the site.**

5. **Select a size to publish, using the size grid as a guide. (Medium works best for YouTube, Facebook, Vimeo, and CNN iReport.)**

6. **(Optional) If you don't want the video to be publicly available for viewing on YouTube, Facebook, or Vimeo, do the following:**

   - *YouTube:* Select the Make This Movie Personal option.

   - *Facebook:* Select Friends of Friends, Only Friends, or Only Me from the Viewable By pop-up menu.

   - *Vimeo:* Select My Contacts or Nobody Else from the Viewable By pop-up menu.

   You can always share a Facebook video to specific people on Facebook or copy the Web address (URL) for the video from the YouTube or Vimeo site and then send the URL by e-mail or post it on a Web page, to give people access to a personal or private video.

7. **Click Next to read the site's terms of service (TOS), and then click Publish to publish the video (or Cancel to cancel).**

   After you click to accept the terms of service offered by the site and click Publish, iMovie automatically uploads the video.

After the video has been uploaded, the Shared To pop-up menu appears on the title bar of the project and is set to the hosting site (YouTube, Vimeo, Facebook, or CNN iReport). The pop-up menu includes the Visit button, to go to the hosting site, and the Tell a Friend button, to send a notification (by e-mail) to other people to watch the video.

To remove versions of your video project from YouTube, Vimeo, Facebook, or CNN iReport, select the project and choose Share⇨Remove From and then pick the hosting site.

Using Videos with iLife Applications

iMovie lets you save a finished video to the Media Browser so that iDVD, iWeb, and GarageBand, and other Apple applications including Pages and Keynote, can find it and use it. You may want to include your movie in a DVD project or use iWeb to post video on your Web page or blog. You can also send the video directly to iDVD, as I describe in this section.

If you want to do more editing to the video with Final Cut Express or Final Cut Pro, Apple's professional video applications, you can export the video as a digital movie file, as I describe in "Exporting movie files," later in this chapter.

A casting call for the Media Browser

The Media Browser holds all your finished media elements, including your iPhoto photos and projects, and your iTunes library and GarageBand songs, so that other iLife applications can find them and use them. When you save your finished video project in the Media Browser, you can then use the entire video in other iLife applications, just like anything else in the Media Browser. You can post video on your Web page or blog with iWeb or burn a DVD with iDVD. GarageBand, Pages, Keynote, and other Apple applications (and even some third-party applications, such as Roxio Toast 10 Titanium) let you open the Media Browser to use them. You can even add a finished video as a clip to another video project in iMovie.

To save your video in the Media Browser, follow these steps:

1. **Select its project in the Project Library and choose Share⇨Media Browser.**

   A dialog appears, as shown in Figure 11-5, with a grid showing the video picture sizes that work with different devices.

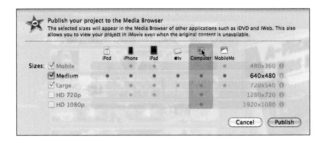

Figure 11-5: Select the video picture sizes.

2. **Select as many sizes as you want to create multiple versions of your video, or choose just the size you want for one version.**

   Click a target device for the video, such as Computer, and iMovie automatically selects all sizes that work with it.

   Sizes that have already been rendered are grayed out — iMovie doesn't have to render them again to share those versions.

3. **Click Publish to save the video in the Media Library (or Cancel to cancel).**

   After iMovie renders the video in the size or sizes you selected, an icon appears next to the project's name in the Project Library to indicate that the project has been rendered. If you make further edits to your project in iMovie after you save it to the Media Browser, the icon disappears and the title bar indicates that your project is out of date and needs to be rendered again. If you render your project again by saving it to the Media Browser, the previously rendered versions are deleted.

To remove versions of your video project from the Media Browser, select the project and choose Share⇨Remove From⇨Media Browser.

Readying a video podcast

Video podcasts are ideal for distributing university lectures, training sessions, or product demos, or for simply keeping people up-to-date with your latest videos. Apple's Podcast Producer 2 server-based solution simplifies the process of publishing video podcasts, automating details such as encoding the content into specific file formats and adding standard title frames and opening videos. You can set up and configure Podcast Producer and all its related services in a matter of minutes, whether you're setting up a single server or a cluster of servers.

For more information about Podcast Producer 2, see the site information at `www.apple.com/server/macosx/features/podcast-producer.html`.

After the podcast is complete, Podcast Producer 2 helps you easily and automatically publish it to a blog, to the video podcast section of the iTunes Store, or to the iTunes U section of the iTunes Store.

To share your completed iMovie project with Podcast Producer 2, follow these steps:

1. **Select the project in the Project Library and choose Share⇨Podcast Producer.**

   A dialog appears with a grid showing the video picture sizes that work with different devices.

2. **If you haven't used Podcast Producer 2, click the Configure button and specify the Podcast Producer 2 server name.**

3. **Select the size you want to use to create the video podcast.**

   Click the Podcast choice to see sizes that work well for video podcasts in iTunes.

4. **Click Publish to transfer the video to the Podcast Producer 2 server.**

Going directly to iDVD

Saving the video in the Media Browser lets iDVD grab the video, which is useful if you have an iDVD project in progress. But if you haven't started the iDVD project yet, sending the video directly to iDVD is faster and easier. Your video opens in a new iDVD project, and you're ready to burn a DVD disc.

To send your video directly to iDVD, select its project in the Project Library and choose Share⇨iDVD. iMovie immediately starts rendering the video in a DVD-compliant size (720 by 480 pixels for full screen) for the iDVD project. When iMovie is finished, iDVD appears with a new project and your video, ready to edit and burn as a DVD, as shown in Figure 11-6. Jump to Chapter 12 to learn how to use iDVD.

Figure 11-6: Send the video directly to iDVD.

Saving Video Files

To save a version of your video project, you can export it as a video file (or *movie* file) on any hard drive. The file can then be imported back into iMovie later or used with other applications that don't have a Media Browser interface, such as Mail to e-mail the file.

You can also save a video file with custom QuickTime settings for playing on just about any digital video player or computer, or for *streaming* over the Internet (transmitting in short bursts, which is enough to start playing the video while the computer receives more data).

Exporting movie files

When you export a project as a movie file, the file uses the same format as a video saved to your iTunes library or to the Media Browser. The benefit is that other applications that don't use the Media Browser can access it and you can copy it or move it using the Finder.

After exporting a movie file, you can choose File⇨Import⇨Movies to import the file back into iMovie as a source clip in the Event Library.

To export your video project as a movie file, follow these steps:

1. **Select the project and choose Share⇨Export Movie.**

   A dialog appears, as shown in Figure 11-7, with a grid showing the video picture sizes that work with different devices.

2. **Type a name for the movie in the Export As field.**

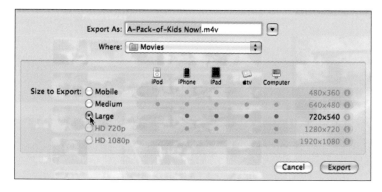

Figure 11-7: Save the video project as a movie file.

3. **Choose from the Where pop-up menu the location where you want to save the movie.**

4. **Select a size for the video picture.**

To display the compression method, frame rate, streaming rate, and file size for a particular picture size, move the pointer over the letter *i* next to the pixel dimensions for that size. (If these settings aren't to your liking or don't fit your needs, try using QuickTime settings, as I describe in the later section "Using QuickTime settings.")

5. **Click Export to save the file (or Cancel to cancel).**

After saving the file, you can use it with other applications or import it back into iMovie. If you picked a small enough picture size, you may even be able to e-mail the file.

Check the size of your file before e-mailing it. Movie files are large, and e-mail isn't meant for large files. Your e-mail server may limit the size of e-mail messages — mine has a limit of about 10MB. Larger files are bounced back to you.

Using QuickTime settings

Like a Hollywood agent who can get you any deal you want, Apple's QuickTime technology provides the settings you need in order to export your video into a format that you can widely distribute to computers, applications, servers, and players. QuickTime includes support for a collection of digital video file formats that offer many choices for quality, compression, picture size, and playback format.

To export your video project as a QuickTime file with control over settings, follow these steps:

1. **Select the project and choose Share⇨Export Using QuickTime.**

The Save Exported File As dialog appears, as shown in Figure 11-8.

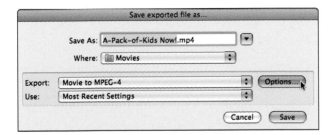

Figure 11-8: Save the video project as a file using custom QuickTime settings.

2. **Type a name in the Save As field, and then choose from the Where pop-up menu the location where you want to save the video file.**

3. **Choose a preset video compression format from the Export pop-up menu (such as Movie to MPEG-4, a standard format that's compatible with most computers, Internet servers, and digital video players).**

iMovie lets you export video files in a number of different formats, including 3G, AVI, DV Stream, and FLC, in addition to files in the MPEG-4 format, including MPEG-4 files encoded with the improved H.264 compression standard. H.264, also known as MPEG-4 AVC (Advanced Video Coding), offers significantly greater compression than the current MPEG-4 ASP (Advanced Simple Profile) standard and provides nearly DVD quality at less than 1 megabit per second, which makes it useful for wireless Internet connections, iPods, and iPhones. To pick H.264, first choose MPEG-4 from the Export pop-up menu (refer to Figure 11-8), click Options, and then choose H.264 from the Video Format pop-up menu. Other compression formats also offer multiple options: When saving as a QuickTime movie, you can choose compression formats such as H.264, MPEG-4 Video, Apple Intermediate Codec, DV/DVCPRO-NTSC, and others.

You can also choose to use the most recent transmission and streaming settings on the Use pop-up menu. However, if you want to see all possible settings and pick custom settings, click the Options button to see the settings for the compression format you chose from the Export pop-up menu.

You can export your video project as a Final Cut Pro XML Interchange Format file that you can then import into a Final Cut Pro project. Select the project and choose Share⇨Export Final Cut XML. The Export FCP XML dialog appears. Type a name in the Save As field, and then choose from the Where pop-up menu the location where you want to save the project. No Ken Burns or cropping effects are included, and all transitions are represented as cross-dissolves (which you can change in Final Cut Pro). Neither are titles, voice-overs or other types of audio recordings, sound effects, or music tracks included.

Part III
Burning Your Releases with iDVD

The 5th Wave   By Rich Tennant

RICHTENNANT

"Has the old media been delivered yet?"

*I*n Part III, you see how to use iDVD to organize a digital versatile disc (DVD) project and burn a disc of your videos and slideshows — for safe-keeping, to share with friends and family, or to create a master disc you can duplicate.

✔ Chapter 12 shows you what you can do with iDVD. You can use iDVD Magic to create a disc project quickly and easily with your videos and slideshows. This chapter also shows you how to create one from scratch and add your videos and slideshows.

✔ Chapter 13 describes how to customize an iDVD project to jazz up the disc's main menu, sub-menus, and buttons that viewers use to select the disc's content. You see how to change the back-grounds, add videos and slideshows to drop zones and buttons, and add music to the menus.

✔ Chapter 14 shows you how to preview the disc project, set up an autoplay video that starts when the disc is inserted in a DVD player or com-puter, and then do the deed: burn the DVD.

12

Creating a DVD Project

In This Chapter

▸ Using Magic iDVD to create a project

▸ Touring iDVD

▸ Creating a project from scratch

▸ Adding videos and slideshows with sound

▸ Creating a disc in one step

DVD, or *digital versatile disc,* is the medium of choice for movies, at least for the moment. (Though some people say that a DVD is a *digital videodisc,* I prefer to reserve the term for the older medium that has since bought the farm, along with the short-lived Betamax format for video, and music 8-track cartridges.) DVD can be used to play video, music, and slideshows, and some DVDs carry all three types on the same disc. DVD lets the viewer interact with the content by using menus to navigate the disc's movies, excerpts, photos, and multiple soundtracks.

This chapter introduces you to iDVD, which offers tools for creating DVD discs with menus and buttons for navigation. iDVD requires a Mac with an Apple SuperDrive, which is a DVD burner. Besides offering professionally designed menu themes with spectacular special effects, iDVD allows you to grab your photos from iPhoto, your videos from iMovie, and your music from GarageBand and your iTunes library.

iDVD

Create a New P

Open an Existi

Magic iDVD

OneStep DVD

What You Can Do with iDVD

Using iDVD, you can put videos on DVD, of course. But you can add several features to the DVD other than a menu with a button to play a video:

- ✔ Put photo slideshows on your DVD accompanied by music from GarageBand or your iTunes library. Read the section "Adding slideshows with music," later in this chapter.

- ✔ Add nifty menus animated with scenes from the videos and slideshows. See Chapter 13 for more about changing the theme background and drop zones for your DVD.

- ✔ Define buttons on a menu that can play short video clips and slideshows as well as link to submenus, slideshows, and different videos. See Chapter 13 for more about changing the theme buttons for your DVD.

- ✔ Add submenus and scene selection menus to your DVD so that viewers can jump to specific sections. See Chapter 13 for more about adding and customizing submenus.

DVD is a mass-produced medium, like audio CDs. The discs are *read-only* — they can't be modified in any way; only viewed. To create even a mass-produced DVD, you have to burn a *recordable* DVD (DVD-R) with the content. The DVD-R serves as a master to mass-produce the type of DVDs you see in stores. With iDVD, you can burn a DVD-R disc that you can then use in normal DVD players, and you can also use the DVD-R disc as a master to provide a service that mass-produces DVDs.

Saying that you can fit a lot of information on a DVD is an understatement, but video takes up a lot of disc space. Though single-layer recordable DVDs hold as much as 4.7GB of data, double-layer discs offer two layers, nearly doubling the amount of storage to 8.5GB You can fit as much as 90 minutes of video on a single-layer DVD-R disc using iDVD, including all still images and backgrounds. However, if you put more than 60 minutes of video on a single-layer DVD-R disc, the picture quality may suffer because iDVD uses stronger compression with a slower bit rate to fit more than 60 minutes, and both factors reduce overall picture quality. The best approach is to limit each single-layer DVD-R to 60 minutes. Also, keep in mind that the audio portion of the DVD takes up about 10MB per minute.

You get one chance with a DVD-R disc. After you burn video to it, you can't rewrite it. Gather everything you want to put on the disc beforehand so that you don't waste a disc.

Where you can play your DVD-R disc

The discs are *DVD-R* discs because they are a recordable format. DVD-R discs should play in all new DVD players.

I say *should* with some trepidation. If you purchased your DVD player after 2003, it's likely compatible with DVD-R discs. But some older players can't play DVD-R media, or can play them only marginally well, with picture artifacts, sound problems, or navigation problems.

In addition, most commercial DVDs have a *region code* that ties the DVD to specific regions of the world, as a measure of copy protection. Fortunately, you can play DVD-R discs created by iDVD in all regions and you don't have to specify a region code. But keep in mind that you must burn a different DVD-R disc for some countries: You must use the proper format (for

example, NTSC for the United States and PAL for Europe, although many PAL players also support NTSC), and your DVD can't hold more than one format. iDVD is already set to use the proper format for your region (depending on where you bought your Mac), but you can also change the format used by iDVD.

The Apple SuperDrive burns standard 4.7GB 2.0 General DVD-R media, which are playable in most standard DVD players and computer DVD-ROM drives, and double-layer (DVD+R DL) discs, which play in newer DVD players. You can burn a DVD-R or DVD+R disc once (recommended for all uses). A DVD-RW or DVD+RW disc can be burned more than once (RW stands for rewritable), but doesn't play in many consumer DVD players.

Making a Disc Like Magic

On most Macs, you find the iDVD icon in the Dock, but in any case you can find it in the Applications folder. Double-click the icon to open iDVD, and the dialog in Figure 12-1 appears.

You can create a new project without any help from iDVD, as I describe in the section "Creating a Project from Scratch," later in this chapter. But the quick-and-painless method to start a project is to let iDVD help you: The Magic iDVD feature lets you quickly apply a theme and assemble the disc's contents. You can then burn the result on disc or continue customizing, as I describe in Chapter 13.

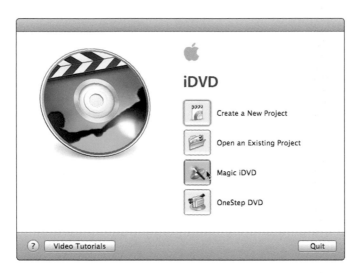

Figure 12-1: Start an iDVD project.

Just follow these steps to create a project like magic:

1. **Click Magic iDVD.**

   Magic iDVD creates a project and displays the Magic iDVD window, as shown in Figure 12-2.

2. **Enter the title of the DVD.**

   Type over the *My Great DVD* title with your own in the DVD Title field in the upper left corner of the Magic iDVD window.

3. **Choose a theme for your DVD project.**

   iDVD offers professional themes that you can use to create animated menus and submenus. The themes appear as thumbnails along the top of the Magic iDVD window in the Theme Browser (refer to Figure 12-2). Scroll the Theme Browser horizontally to see more themes, and click a thumbnail to select a theme. To see even more themes, click the 7.0 Themes pop-up menu and choose earlier versions of iDVD, or All to see all of them.

   A theme provides a design that integrates menu elements in a consistent way and makes navigation easier. iDVD lets you customize these themes, of course (as I describe in Chapter 13), so that you can make them unique for your project.

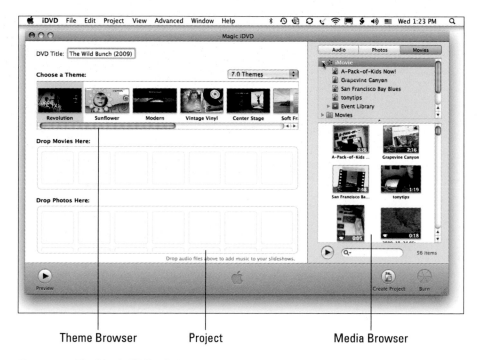

Theme Browser　　　　　Project　　　　　Media Browser

Figure 12-2: The Magic iDVD window.

4. **Select a content type from the Media Browser.**

   The Media Browser occupies the right side of the Magic iDVD window, with tabs for Audio, Photos, and Movies. Click Movies to see a list of your videos from iMovie and other (compatible) video files in your Movies folder (refer to Figure 12-2). Click the triangle next to iMovie or the Movies folder to browse individual videos. Thumbnails for the videos appear below the browser's list.

5. **Drag thumbnails of videos from the Media Browser to the Drop Movies Here area.**

   iDVD lets you drag finished iMovie projects that were prepared for sharing in the Media Browser (see Chapter 11 for details) as well as folders and digital video files in your Movies folder.

6. **(Optional) To include iPhoto slideshows, click the Photos tab of the Media Browser, browse the photo albums and events, and drag thumbnails of albums or events to the project, also shown in Figure 12-3.**

Figure 12-3: Drag an iPhoto event or album to the iDVD project.

You have access to your iPhoto events, photo albums, and some keepsakes such as photo books. Drag the album or keepsake name to include all photos in an album or a keepsake, or drag an event tile to include all photos of an event.

7. **(Optional) To add music or any recorded audio to your iPhoto slideshows from iTunes or GarageBand, click the Audio tab of the Media Browser, browse your iTunes library or GarageBand songs, and drag a song over each slideshow thumbnail in the project.**

   You have access to your iTunes library and GarageBand songs — click the triangle next to iTunes or GarageBand to browse individual songs. Drag the song on top of the set of photos you dragged over in Step 6. The thumbnail for the photos changes to include a Music icon to indicate that audio has been added to the slideshow.

8. **Click the Create Project (or Burn) button.**

   Magic iDVD can start your burn operation immediately if you click Burn, but if you want to preview the DVD's menus or modify anything, don't burn your disc yet — click Create Project to finish creating the project.

That's it! iDVD magically prepares the DVD of your dreams and displays the new project in the main iDVD window. Now is a good time to take a tour of that window.

Touring iDVD

The iDVD main window, shown in Figure 12-4, is the control panel for modifying your iDVD project, offering the following elements:

- ✔ **Viewer:** The Viewer shows the DVD project with animated menus in motion. Click the Motion button to turn motion on or off in the Viewer.

- ✔ **Motion playhead:** The motion playhead shows the animated menu playback on a timeline. You can drag the playhead to see the animation without having to turn on motion. Animated menus loop, and you can add a fade transition to either the beginning or end of the loop, or both, by clicking the check boxes at either end of the timeline.

- ✔ **Add and Info:** Click Add to add a button to a menu for navigating to a movie, submenu, or slideshow. Click Info to show the Inspector window for the project's DVD menu and drop zones.

Figure 12-4: The iDVD main window.

✔ **Drop zone and Drop Zone Editor:** Many themes offer sections of the main background for running movies and slideshows. Drop zones aren't links to movies — they show only part of the movie on your menu. You click the Drop Zone Editor button to open the Drop Zone Editor, which lets you fill, adjust, and rearrange drop zones, as I describe in Chapter 13.

✔ **Map view:** Map view provides a visual overview of your DVD project as a tree structure, showing the relationship of the main menu to submenus. Map view also lets you add an autoplay movie to a project that starts playing immediately when the DVD is inserted into the player, before the main menu appears. I unfold Map view in Chapter 13.

✔ **Motion:** Click the Motion button to turn off the motion in animated menus and buttons to make them easier to edit in the Viewer; click the button again to turn motion back on to see the animation.

✔ **Volume:** Drag the slider to control the computer's volume as you work in iDVD.

✔ **Preview:** Click the Preview button to preview the project. I give you a preview in Chapter 14 on how to use the Preview button and the preview's remote control.

✔ **Burn:** Click the Burn button to burn a DVD-R disc. See Chapter 14 for this hot topic.

✔ **Themes:** Click the Themes button to browse and select themes. A *theme* is a professionally designed combination of background elements, a music clip, and a button style. The DVD's main menu and submenus have typefaces and images that match, and so on. You can start with a theme and change it at any time as well as customize it, as I show in Chapter 13.

✔ **Buttons:** Click the Buttons button to browse and select button styles. A DVD's menu must offer buttons for viewers to use to play content and to access submenus. Without buttons, viewers couldn't make selections. I show you how to attach buttons to your menus (without a needle and thread) in Chapter 13.

✔ **Media:** Click the Media button to open the Media Browser, and then click one of these tabs:

   • **Audio:** Browse your iTunes library or GarageBand songs and add them to the DVD project to enhance a slideshow or play behind a menu or submenu. All the themes allow you to change the theme music for their menus.

   • **Photos:** Browse your iPhoto library and drag albums, events, and keepsakes to create slideshows, or drag single photos to add to drop zones in the background or to replace the background image.

  • **Movies:** Browse your iMovie videos and other video files in your
    Movies folder, and add them to your project (if they have been
    prepared for sharing, as I describe in Chapter 11). You can add a
    video with a button to play it, and also add videos to drop zones,
    as I describe in Chapter 13.

Creating a Project from Scratch

After you launch iDVD, the opening dialog appears (refer to Figure 12-1). To
create a new project, follow these steps:

1. **Click the Create a New Project button.**

   iDVD displays the Create Project dialog, as shown in Figure 12-5.

Figure 12-5: Create a new project.

2. **Replace the words *My Great DVD* in the Save As field with the title of
   your DVD, and choose from the Where pop-up menu a location on a
   hard drive to save it.**

3. **Define the video picture's aspect ratio.**

   Pick Standard for the 4:3 aspect ratio used in standard TV, or
   Widescreen for the 16:9 aspect ratio (used for HD and other formats).
   If none of the videos you're adding uses the widescreen format, you're
   probably better off with the standard format. You can change it at any
   time by choosing Project⇨Switch to Standard (4:3) or Project⇨
   Switch to Widescreen (16:9).

4. **Click OK to create the project.**

   iDVD opens its main window (refer to Figure 12-4). iDVD automatically
   picks the first theme (Revolution) and shows you the drop zone and
   other areas of the theme's main menu.

5. **On the right side of the main window, scroll the Theme Browser to see more themes, and click a theme to select it.**

   To see even more themes, click the 7.0 Themes pop-up menu and choose earlier versions of iDVD, or All to see all of them.

6. **To see the animation on the menu, click the Motion button.**

   You can also drag the motion playhead along the Motion timeline underneath the Viewer to see the animation.

Many iDVD themes use the widescreen aspect ratio. If your project is set to the standard aspect ratio and you pick a widescreen theme (or if your project is set to widescreen and you pick a standard theme), iDVD displays a dialog to choose whether to keep the project in its original format (click Keep) or switch to the theme's format (click Change).

Adding videos

To browse your videos, follow these steps:

1. **Click the Media button under the list of themes to switch from the Theme Browser to the Media Browser.**

2. **Click the Movies tab to see a list of your videos from iMovie and other video files in your Movies folder.**

3. **Click the triangle next to iMovie or the Movies folder to browse individual videos.**

Changing the format from NTSC or PAL

You may never have to do this, but if you need to create a DVD-R for a different country that uses a format other than the one iDVD is set up for, you can change the format. You're not being unpatriotic — spreading your culture abroad is a good thing.

NTSC is used in North America, Japan, and various non-European countries, and PAL is used in most European countries and in Brazil. Your Mac comes configured with iDVD set to the appropriate format for your region. But if you live in North America, for example, and you want to create a DVD-R for Europe, you can do this. You can't, however, mix formats on the same disc using iDVD.

Before adding media files to a project, choose iDVD➪Preferences, click the Projects tab, and select either NTSC or PAL for the Video Mode option.

To add a video selection to your DVD menu, choose Project⇨Add Movie or drag the video to any area of the menu in the Viewer that is *not* a drop zone. If dotted lines appear in the menu as you drag the video, move the pointer until the dotted lines disappear, and then let go to drop the video. (Dotted lines indicate a drop zone, which is part of the menu background. You can add videos to drop zones, as I describe in Chapter 13.)

A button appears on the menu for selecting the video, as shown in Figure 12-6. (I show you how to reposition and customize the button in Chapter 13.) To add more video selections to the DVD menu, simply drag more videos to the menu in the Viewer (although each theme has a maximum number of buttons that can appear on an individual menu — usually 6 or 12, including navigation buttons).

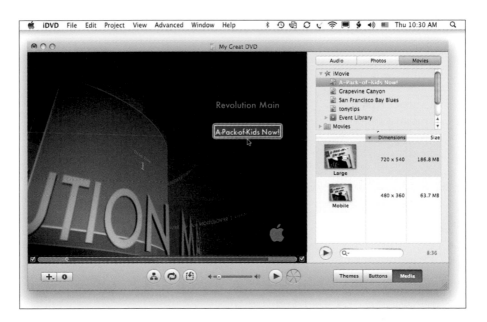

Figure 12-6: Drag a video and a button appears on the menu.

To change the button title, or to change the DVD title, click inside the title in the Viewer and then edit it, as shown in Figure 12-7. You can choose a different font, typeface (style), and size from the pop-up menus underneath the title.

iDVD is quite forgiving if you do things you don't like. You can undo just about every operation you perform, going backward. Just choose Edit⇨Undo for each consecutive operation to undo them.

Figure 12-7: Edit the title of the DVD.

You can save your iDVD project at any time by choosing File⇨Save. If you quit iDVD before saving a project, iDVD displays a warning dialog so that you can click Save to save the project.

Adding slideshows with music

Photo slideshows are reason enough to burn DVDs. You can show photos on your home TV or take a DVD to show your friends or relatives on their televisions. All they need is a DVD player. You can offer a complete slideshow on DVD with buttons for navigating the photos.

You can send an already completed slideshow from iPhoto directly to iDVD or create a custom slideshow in iDVD — drag photos (and video clips) one at a time or entire photo albums from the Media Browser. You can then rearrange photos, delete slides, or add more images from iPhoto using the iDVD Slideshow Editor, which offers tools for setting the slide duration, assigning transitions, and adding songs from your iTunes library.

TIP

If you created a slideshow in iPhoto, as I describe in Chapter 5, select the slideshow in iPhoto and select all thumbnails in the slideshow, and then choose Share⇨Send to iDVD. iPhoto prepares the slideshow for iDVD and then adds the slideshow to your project in iDVD automatically, or it opens iDVD and starts a new project if iDVD isn't already open. A new button appears with the title of the slideshow as it was in your iPhoto library. You can also send a keepsake, such as a photo book, to iDVD as a slideshow.

To create a slideshow in iDVD, follow these steps:

1. **Click the Add (+) button in the lower left corner of the iDVD window (refer to Figure 12-4), and choose Add Slideshow from the pop-up menu that appears (or choose Project⇨Add Slideshow).**

   A new button, named My Slideshow, appears on the menu shown in the Viewer.

2. **Double-click this button to open the Slideshow Editor (see Figure 12-8).**

   The Media Browser also switches automatically to the Photos tab.

Figure 12-8: Add photos and albums with the Slideshow Editor.

3. **Drag events, selected photos, or albums directly from the Media Browser into the Slideshow Editor in the order you want for your slideshow.**

   Arranging and rearranging is as easy as dragging to new positions the thumbnails of the photos in the Slideshow Editor, as shown in Figure 12-9. As you drag a thumbnail to a new position, the sequence opens up to make room for it.

   You can also view your slideshow as a list of slides by clicking the List View button. To see your slideshow as a grid of thumbnails, click the Grid View button.

4. **To add music to your slideshow, click the Audio tab in the Media Browser, browse GarageBand or your iTunes library for a song, and drag the song to the Audio well (the Speaker icon) in the Toolbar section of the Slideshow Editor, as shown in Figure 12-10.**

   The Audio well icon changes to show the type of audio file — for example, an MP3 icon for an MP3 file or an AIFF icon for an AIFF sound file.

Figure 12-9: Rearrange photos in the Slideshow Editor.

5. **To set the overall volume of the audio, drag the Slideshow Volume slider in the Toolbar section of the Slideshow Editor to the right for higher volume, or to the left for lower volume.**

You can set the Slide Duration pop-up menu in the Toolbar section of the Slideshow Editor to show each slide for a specific amount of time, which is usually set to 3 seconds. After adding sound or music, the Slide Duration pop-up menu changes to Fit to Audio, which matches the duration to the length of the song. You can change the pop-up menu to set the duration to 10 seconds or to 5, 3, or 1 second.

The Slideshow Editor displays the duration of the entire slideshow in the upper center border of its window (refer to Figure 12-8). You can switch the Slide Duration pop-up menu from Fit to Audio to, say, 10 seconds, and see what the duration of the slideshow would be. When set to Fit to Audio, the slideshow duration is very close if not the same as the song's duration.

6. **To set a transition between slides, choose one from the Transition pop-up menu in the Toolbar section of the Slideshow Editor.**

Some transitions, such as Reveal, can occur from different directions — click one of the four arrows in the circle next to the pop-up menu to indicate from which direction the transition should start.

Figure 12-10: Add music for the slideshow.

7. **To set the slideshow to play in a loop, or to add navigation controls or titles and descriptions, click the Settings button (with the Gear icon) in the Toolbar section of the Slideshow Editor.**

The Settings dialog appears, as shown in Figure 12-11, with these options:

- *Loop Slideshow* plays the slideshow continuously.

- *Display Navigation Arrows* places left and right arrows on each slide that viewers can use to manually control the slideshow with their DVD remotes.

- *Add Image Files to DVD-ROM* copies the individual image files to the data portion of the DVD-ROM in addition to the slideshow being placed on the video portion.

- *Show Titles and Comments* displays each photo's title and comment in the slideshow.

- *Duck Audio While Playing Movies* ensures that if the slideshow includes video clips with sound, the music or other type of audio you added to the slideshow plays at half-volume so that you can hear the video clip.

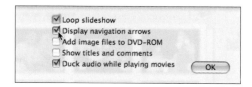

Figure 12-11: Change slideshow settings.

Transferring Video to Disc in One Step

If you have a videotape or cartridge that you want to burn to a DVD-R disc without editing, and without menus, you can transfer video directly from a digital video (DV) camcorder (a mini-DV or Digital-8 tape camcorder connected by FireWire) to a DVD-R disc in one step. The disc you burn starts playing the video automatically after you insert it into a DVD player.

If your camera records video in high definition (HD), you can't use the iDVD OneStep feature — use iMovie first, as I explain in Chapter 8.

iDVD records the disc in whichever video mode (NTSC or PAL) that's selected in your iDVD preferences. (Choose iDVD⇨Preferences and click the Projects tab to switch the video mode from NTSC to PAL or vice versa.) If your taped footage is in a different format, iDVD warns you before burning the disc.

Don't create a OneStep disc from your camcorder if you've already imported the video into iMovie. Creating a OneStep disc from the camcorder can take longer than simply burning an iDVD project to a disc, because the video needs to be captured to your hard drive from the camera first. If you've already captured the video on your hard drive using iMovie, you save a lot of time by adding the video to iDVD and burning a project. You can also choose File⇨OneStep DVD from Movie to create a OneStep disc from a video file on your hard drive.

To burn a OneStep disc, follow these steps:

1. **Turn on your camcorder and insert the tape or cartridge.**

2. **Connect the camcorder to your computer (as I describe in Chapter 8).**

3. **Switch your camcorder to VTR, VCR, or Play mode.**

4. **Open iDVD and click OneStep DVD (or choose File⇨OneStep DVD).**

5. **Insert a blank DVD-R disc into your computer's SuperDrive or external DVD burner when you're prompted to do so.**

   After rewinding the tape (if necessary), iDVD captures the video from the beginning.

   You can also set the tape in the camcorder to the point where you want to begin recording. Then, when you insert the blank DVD-R disc and the tape begins to rewind, press the Play button on your camcorder to stop rewinding. Video capturing starts and then stops automatically at the end of the tape or after ten seconds with no video. You can also manually stop capturing at any time by pressing the Stop button on your camcorder.

6. **When the process is complete, remove the DVD-R.**

   You may need to press the Media Eject key on your keyboard (if it has one) or hold down the F12 key.

You can also click Cancel to stop capturing video at any time and leave the DVD-R untouched. A dialog appears and lets you either cancel the entire OneStep DVD or stop capturing and begin burning with the video that was already captured.

13

Customizing DVD Menus and Buttons

In This Chapter

▶ Modifying themes

▶ Adding slideshows and videos to drop zones

▶ Fine-tuning motion menus and buttons

▶ Adding submenus

Commercial DVDs offer menus and buttons so that viewers can find and select content. But the menus and buttons don't stop there: They also help set up a mood, offer a preview, or try to capture your attention. Many of these menus resemble touch-screen kiosks, with buttons that play little videos and backgrounds that show animation and video clips. Movies and music videos are usually broken up into *chapters,* or scenes, that viewers can choose from a submenu to start watching.

Using iDVD, you can produce DVDs with menus and buttons that rival the commercial videos of Hollywood. The themes in iDVD do the work of supplying motion buttons and menu backgrounds, and you can customize them in iDVD uniquely for your DVD. Start with a theme and then customize it. You can change the music, change the background picture and text, change the buttons, and add your own videos and slideshows to drop zones in the background and to buttons, as I show you in this chapter.

Changing a Theme's Menus

In iDVD, a *theme* consists of a professionally designed combination of background elements and drop zones, a music clip, and a button style for arranging the main menu and submenus. A *theme family* is a collection of menu designs that work together to provide a unified appearance to submenus. The designs include typefaces and images to match the theme, and the text selections are set to readable font sizes and placed in areas that attract attention.

You can use a theme as is, replacing only the text for the menus and buttons to match the content you're putting on your DVD. You can also change various elements of the theme to make it unique for your DVD and then save your variant as a favorite to use with other DVD projects.

To choose the theme, follow these steps:

1. **Click the Themes button at the bottom of the iDVD window to show the Theme Browser.**

2. **Scroll down to see all themes. To see even more themes, click the 7.0 Themes pop-up menu and choose earlier versions of iDVD, or All to see all of them.**

3. **Click the triangle next to a theme to reveal all the submenu templates in the theme family.**

4. **Click the Main template to select the theme for your DVD's main menu, as shown in Figure 13-1.**

   If your project is set to the standard aspect ratio and you pick a widescreen theme (or if your project is set to widescreen and you pick a standard theme), iDVD displays a dialog so that you can choose whether to keep the project in its original format (click Keep) or switch to the theme's format (click Change).

   The theme you select replaces whichever theme was last displayed in the Viewer. A cool feature is that if you already dragged videos or slideshows to create buttons for the menu, the new theme uses the same buttons. In all themes, buttons automatically appear where they should, in the proper text font, button shape, and size.

 Most themes provide an animated main menu that loops. To see the animation, click the Motion button. You can also drag the motion playhead along the motion timeline underneath the Viewer to see the animation.

Figure 13-1: Select the Main theme for the DVD's main menu.

After you modify a menu, you can save the modified theme as a custom theme by choosing File⇨Save Theme As Favorite. The customized theme appears in the Theme Browser. Choose Favorites from the Theme Browser's pop-up menu to select the theme. You can use the custom theme for future projects in the same way as you use other themes.

Redecorating the background and text

Many themes let you change the background image of the theme while keeping the drop zones. For example, the Modern theme's Main template offers a plain background that's easy to replace.

To change the background of a theme, follow these steps:

1. **Click the Drop Zone Editor button underneath the Viewer (the icon with the arrow pointing into an open rectangle), as shown in Figure 13-2.**

   The Drop Zone Editor appears, with a well for each of the menu's drop zones (some themes have only one drop zone, and certain older themes have no drop zones) and the Menu well for the menu itself. The Theme Browser on the right side of the iDVD window switches to the Media Browser.

Figure 13-2: Open the Drop Zone Editor.

2. **In the Media Browser, click the Audio tab to browse your GarageBand songs or iTunes library, the Photos tab to browse your iPhoto library, or the Movies tab to browse your iMovie videos and video files in your Movies folder.**

3. **To change the background image of the menu, drag content to the Menu well.**

   For example, I can drag a photo from the Photos tab of the Media Browser to the Menu well in the Drop Zone Editor. You can just as easily add a video as a background by clicking the Movies tab and browsing to find your video, and then dragging the video to the Menu well — although with some themes, a video background may be too distracting.

4. **To change the title, click inside the title and then click the Info button in the lower left corner of the iDVD window to show the Text Info Window, as shown in Figure 13-3.**

   You may also want to change the button text, which I explain how to do in "Changing a Theme's Buttons," later in this chapter.

Figure 13-3: Change the title's text attributes, including color.

5. **Format the title text however you like using the options in the Text Info window.**

   The window includes the font, typeface, and size pop-up menus and buttons for left-aligned, centered, or right-aligned text. The window also includes the Shadow option for adding a drop shadow to the text, and a color tile showing the text color. Click the color tile to open the miniature Colors window (refer to Figure 13-3), and then click a color to change the text color or drag the slider to change the color's intensity (or both).

6. **Close the Colors mini-window by clicking its red dot in the upper left corner, and close the Text Info window by clicking the circled *x* in its upper left corner. To close the Drop Zone Editor, click the Drop Zone Editor button (the same one you used to open it).**

Dropping into the drop zones

Drop zones sound like places where military helicopters land, but *drop zones* in iDVD are sections of the menu background that can play videos and slideshows. You can also place a still image in a drop zone.

Drop zones aren't buttons — viewers of your DVD won't get anywhere by clicking them. Adding content to a drop zone is essentially a cool way to frame a movie or slideshow loop.

To add content to a drop zone, such as a single image or a video or slideshow to loop in the background, follow these steps:

1. **Click the Drop Zone Editor button underneath the Viewer (refer to Figure 13-2).**

   The Drop Zone Editor appears, with a well for each of the menu's drop zones.

   Though some themes have only one drop zone, others have multiple drop zones that appear at different times in the Viewer.

2. **Click the Motion button to turn on the animated menu, or drag the motion playhead to see the animation, so that you can see the other drop zones.**

   The Drop Zone Editor offers a well for each drop zone.

3. **To add a video to a drop zone, click the Movies tab to browse videos and then drag a video to the drop zone well in the Drop Zone Editor, as shown in Figure 13-4.**

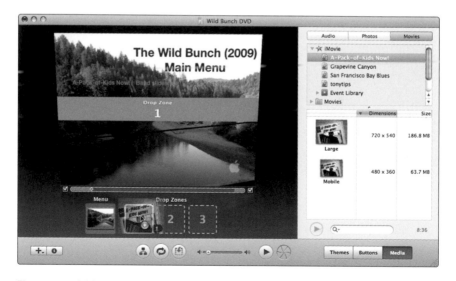

Figure 13-4: Add a video to a drop zone to loop in the background.

To control the duration of the drop zone's video, click the drop zone in the Viewer to see the Movie Start / End slider, shown in Figure 13-5, and drag either end to specify the start and end points.

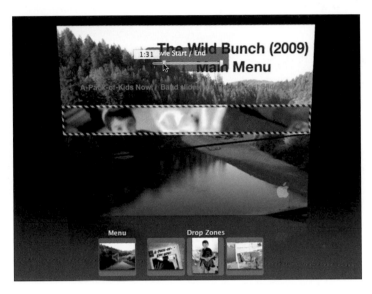

Figure 13-5: Adjust the start and end points of the video loop in the drop zone.

4. **To add one or more photos to a drop zone, click the Photos tab to browse photos and then drag a single photo, a set of selected photos, an album, or an event to the drop zone well.**

   If you dragged an event or album, you can see the photo slideshow by clicking the drop zone in the Viewer to see the Photos slider, as shown in Figure 13-6, and then dragging the slider to see the slides.

   To adjust the order in which the slides appear in the drop zone, click the Edit Order button to open the Drop Zone Photos Editor, as shown in Figure 13-4. You can then drag thumbnails of the photos to rearrange the slideshow.

5. **To remove an item from a drop zone, select the drop zone well in the Drop Zone Editor and press the Delete key.**

You can also Control-click (or right-click) the image, slideshow, or video in the drop zone and then select the Clear Drop Zone Contents option from the shortcut menu that appears — or simply drag it from the drop zone to a location outside the iDVD window.

Figure 13-6: View the slideshow in the drop zone.

Rockin' out the menu with music

In some themes, music or sounds play while the menu loops, but you probably will change the audio to a selection more in tune with your content.

To add a song (or to replace the song) for the menu, click the Drop Zone Editor button (refer to Figure 13-2) to show the Drop Zone Editor. Click the Audio tab to browse your GarageBand songs or iTunes library, and then drag a song to the menu well in the Drop Zone Editor.

The song plays in the background — at half volume — and repeats in a loop until the viewer clicks a button on the menu.

Adjusting the menu duration and volume

To control the menu music volume, and the duration of the looping menu, click anywhere on the menu in the Viewer (but not on any single element, such as a drop zone, title, or button), and then click the Info button in the lower left corner of the iDVD window. You see the Menu Info window, as shown in Figure 13-7.

Figure 13-7: Set the duration of the animated menu.

You can then drag the Loop Duration slider to set how long the animated menu plays before repeating in a loop. Drag the Menu Volume slider to adjust the volume of the menu's music.

Adding text to the menu

You can add plain old text to the DVD menu anywhere you like. You may want to add a copyright notice or some credits or another element to show viewers which menu they're looking at (such as Main Menu on the bottom). Whatever text you want to add, you can add it by choosing Project⇨Add Text. A place-holder with the words *Click to Edit* appears on the menu in the Viewer, as shown in Figure 13-8, and you can click the placeholder to edit the text. Click outside the text, and then click the text element again, to drag it into position on the menu.

Figure 13-8: Add text to the menu.

To change the text attributes, select the text element and then click the Info button in the lower left corner of the iDVD window to show the Text Info window for the text (refer to Figure 13-3).

Staying within the safety zone

When you edit titles, add text, and rearrange buttons on a DVD menu, keep in mind that these elements shouldn't be placed close to the edges of the picture area. You may want your DVD to play on standard-definition TVs, even though a growing segment of the population uses high-definition TVs and computers to show their DVDs. But the standard TV is the common denominator, and when you create DVD menus, you should keep all relevant information away from the edges of the picture.

Most analog TVs overscan the screen — the cathode-ray guns overshoot the margins of the screen to make sure that the screen is covered from edge to edge. As a result, you lose about 10 percent of the picture on each edge (sometimes less on the top and bottom, depending on the TV). If you place an element on the extreme edge of the picture, it may get cut off when viewed on this type of television. iDVD works around this limitation by defining the TV *safe area,* where all the action takes place — that area is, essentially, inside the edges of the picture, leaving at least a 10 percent margin around all sides.

iDVD themes follow the rules: All titles, buttons, and drop zones are within the TV safe area. But it doesn't hurt to check. If you add text, edit titles, move buttons, or otherwise customize the menu, you should check the TV safe area: Choose View⇨Show TV Safe Area. The gray-shaded border of the iDVD movie window is outside the safe area, and everything inside the border is inside the safe area, as shown in Figure 13-9.

You can move elements or reduce the font size of text to bring these elements safely inside the safe area. To turn off the safe area display, choose View⇨Hide TV Safe Area.

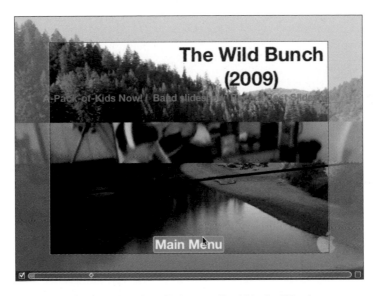

Figure 13-9: Check to see that all elements fit within the TV safe area.

Changing a Theme's Buttons

DVDs offer menus with buttons that viewers click to play movies and slideshows. Some iDVD themes offer text buttons, and some offer buttons, in shapes that can play miniature videos and slideshows. You can customize any button in any theme and create truly wacky combinations, if you want.

You already know how to create the buttons — simply drag the video or photos to the menu, as I describe in Chapter 12. You can also customize buttons, as you can just about everything else in iDVD, to your liking:

✓ **To change the button's text:** Click inside the text to highlight it, and then type new text. You can also change the button text attributes, just like the menu text and title, by clicking inside the text and choosing a different font, typeface (style), and size from the pop-up menus that appear underneath the text.

✓ **To rearrange buttons and move them to new positions:** Select and then drag buttons in the Viewer. As you move a button to a new position, a line appears, as shown in Figure 13-10, for snapping the button to an invisible grid. The grid is set by the theme's designer so that you can align the buttons perfectly. When the arrows appear in the line, the button is lined up both horizontally and vertically.

Figure 13-10: Drag to move a button's location and snap it to the invisible grid.

Some themes let you freely position the buttons where you want, and others snap the buttons to a grid when you drag them. To change the behavior of buttons when you drag them, click anywhere on the menu in the Viewer (but not any single element, such as a drop zone, title, or button), and then click the Info button in the lower left corner of the iDVD window to show the Menu Info window (refer to Figure 13-10). In the Buttons section near the bottom are two options: Snap to Grid and Free Positioning. You can move the buttons around the menu freely if you click the Free Positioning option, or move them to positions on an invisible grid (set by the theme's designer) by selecting the Snap to Grid option.

Activating a transition for a clicked button

Menu buttons are supposed to trigger the start of something: a video, a slide-show, or a submenu. You can also set the transition that occurs after the viewer clicks the button.

To be consistent, you may want to use the same transition for all buttons. You can select more than one button by holding down Shift while clicking the next button. After selecting multiple buttons, click the Info button in the lower left corner of the iDVD window to show the Button Info window, as shown in Figure 13-11.

Figure 13-11: Set the button transition and text attributes.

Choose a transition from the Transition pop-up menu. For many transitions, you can also choose a direction (such as from right to left) for the transition on the pop-up menu below the Transition menu.

You can also change the button text alignment, font, typeface (style), size, and color in the Button Info window and turn on the Shadow option to add a drop shadow to the button text.

Changing a button's appearance

To change the appearance of menu buttons, follow these steps:

1. **Select one or more buttons and then click the Buttons button under the Theme or Media Browser to show the Button Browser, as shown in Figure 13-12.**

   For themes that use text buttons, the Buttons Browser shows the text styles first.

2. **Select a text style (such as the squiggly underlining shown in Figure 13-12) for the button.**

3. **To see what the button looks like to a viewer of the DVD, click the Preview button under the Viewer.**

   The Preview window appears with the remote control, as shown in Figure 13-13.

Figure 13-12: Set a text style for a button.

4. **As you move the pointer over the button the way a viewer would, the button shows the new text button style (the squiggly underlining).**

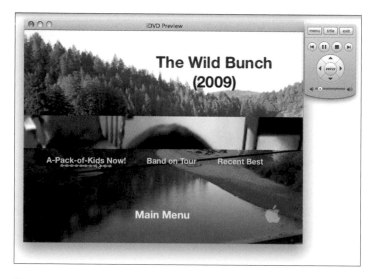

Figure 13-13: A preview of the menu with the button set to the new text style.

5. Click the Exit button in the remote control to return to the iDVD window.

For details on previewing and using the remote control, see Chapter 14.

You may want to experiment further. To try other button styles, choose a type of button from the pop-up menu at the top of the Buttons Browser — choose Bullets or Shapes for different bullet styles and shapes. If you prefer a button style that shows video or photos, choose Frames, Artistic, Rectangle, or Rounded.

For example, I chose a Rounded style that plays a looping video clip inside the selected button, and I already chose the TV-shaped Rounded styles for the other two buttons, which play looping slideshows. (See Figure 13-14.)

Figure 13-14: Adjust the starting point of a video playing in a button.

iDVD uses the first frame of the video selection as the button's image and loops the video for about 30-90 seconds (depending on the theme). To shorten the loop or change the starting image, select the button in the Viewer and click the button again (slowly so that you don't activate the video selection itself). The Movie slider appears above the button, as shown in Figure 13-14 — drag the slider to set a new starting point for the video loop. To use a still image rather than a looping video, click the Still Image option.

If you don't like the video or photo slideshow that iDVD chose for the button, you can change it by holding down the Command key while dragging another photo, set of photos, or video from the Media Browser to the thumbnail portion of the button. Note, however, that if you don't press the Command key as you drag a video or slideshow to the button, the new video or slideshow replaces the existing one as the media item the button links to.

Adding Submenus

Depending on which theme you choose, the menus in your iDVD project can hold either 6 or 12 buttons. But a menu can turn ugly with too many buttons. Where do you put all the good stuff — the individual scenes from the movie, the alternative version of the slideshow, the outtakes? You can put them behind a single button that opens a *submenu*. And, if you have lots of choices, your submenus can have buttons that open more submenus.

To add a submenu, click the Add (+) button in the lower left corner of the iDVD window and choose Add Submenu from the pop-up menu that appears (or choose Project⇨Add Submenu). A new button, named My Submenu (which, when clicked, leads to the submenu) appears on the menu shown in the Viewer. Click this button to highlight the text, and then type over the My Submenu wording to replace it with more appropriate wording (such as More Stuff), as shown in Figure 13-15. You can then customize the button as I describe in "Changing a Theme's Buttons," earlier in this chapter.

Figure 13-15: Change the text of the My Submenu button that appears.

Navigating the disc's map

To see a new submenu, click the Map view button under the Viewer (the icon with the flowchart). Map view, shown in Figure 13-16, displays a flowchart of your DVD project that shows the relationship of the main menu to submenus and content. The following points are handy to know as you work in Map view:

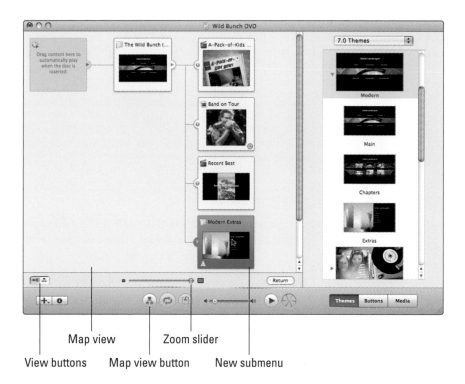

Figure 13-16: View the map of the project to select a submenu.

- ✔ **Change the orientation:** You can switch the flowchart from a horizontal orientation (refer to Figure 13-16) to a vertical orientation, and vice versa, by clicking the View buttons.

- ✔ **Zoom:** You can also zoom in to see the project menu thumbnails in more detail, or zoom out, by dragging the Zoom slider.

- ✔ **See submenus:** Click the triangle at the edge of (horizontal) or underneath (vertical) each thumbnail to display project submenus linked to it.

- ✔ **Remove menus:** You can even delete a menu and all its linked submenus and content in one fell swoop by selecting the menu thumbnail and then pressing Delete.

Making edits in Map view

You can edit project menus and submenus and content in Map view. Click once to select a menu, movie, or slideshow thumbnail, and then use commands to apply a change; for example, select a movie thumbnail and choose Advanced⇨Loop Movie, or select a menu thumbnail and choose Project⇨Autofill Drop Zones to fill them automatically, or Advanced⇨Reset Object To Theme Settings to reset the menu elements to match the theme. You can even select a menu thumbnail and choose Advanced⇨Apply Theme to Submenus to quickly apply the theme without visiting each submenu. To add a soundtrack to a menu or slideshow, drag an audio file from the Audio pane of the Media Browser to a menu or slideshow thumbnail.

Map view displays a little warning symbol whenever something goes awry with your DVD project.

Customizing submenus

To select the new submenu and customize it, click its "page" in Map view. Double-click the submenu "page" to see it and make changes to it in the Viewer.

You can then change the submenu title, as shown in Figure 13-17, by clicking inside the title and typing over it. You can also set the title's text attributes by choosing the font, typeface, and size from the pop-up menus that appear below the text.

You can use a different theme for each submenu. Though you can pick contrasting themes that boggle the mind and confuse everyone, using a different theme for a submenu may make sense if the submenu offers content that is entirely different from the content offered on the main menu.

Some themes offer drop zones on their submenu templates (such as the Modern theme's Extra template), as well as the capability to change the background and music. See "Dropping into the drop zones," earlier in this chapter.

After customizing the theme for the submenu, you can add the content selections that viewers will select when they reach the submenu. In Figure 13-18, I'm adding a slideshow to the submenu, using the same method as I describe in Chapter 12.

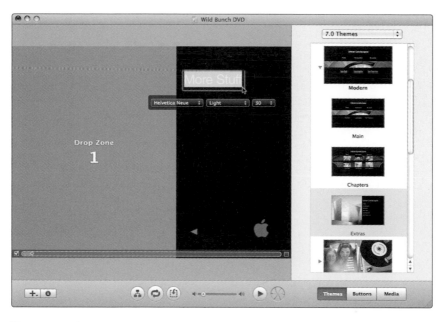

Figure 13-17: Change the title of the submenu.

Figure 13-18: Add media selections to the submenu.

Adding scene selection menus

Commercial videos are typically divided into scenes that viewers can select to start watching from. When you play a commercial DVD, the main menu usually offers a button to show a *scene selection* submenu that lets you choose a scene to start watching from. Long movies often have several scene selection menus to accommodate many scenes.

No matter how long your videos are, you can add chapter markers to them to mark their scenes. You can then use iDVD to create scene selection menus. You can define as many as 99 chapter markers in a video that's added to iDVD.

Using iMovie (and Final Cut Pro and Final Cut Express), you can create chapter markers in advance to divide a video into scenes, as I describe in Chapter 23.

If you add chapter markers to your iMovie video project and then add the video to an iDVD project, iDVD creates one or more scene selection submenus (depending on how many chapters you have marked in the video) to enable viewers to select individual scenes.

You can also add rudimentary chapter markers in iDVD. Follow these steps:

1. **Select the menu button for the video in the Viewer, and choose Advanced⇨Create Chapter Markers for Movie.**

   iDVD displays the dialog shown in Figure 13-19.

2. **Set the number of minutes in the video between chapter markers and click OK.**

Figure 13-19: Create markers for every five minutes of video.

After creating chapter markers for a video, or after you add a video that's already chapter-marked, iDVD automatically creates scene selection submenus for the video:

- ✓ **If the main menu or submenu you're adding the video to has no buttons,** iDVD puts two buttons on the menu: one to play the entire video and a Scene Selection button that links to the first scene selection submenu.

- ✓ **If the main menu or submenu already has one or more buttons, or if you already added the video to the project,** iDVD instead links the existing button to a submenu that offers the Play button to play the entire video and a Scene Selection button that links to the first scene selection submenu.

Each scene selection submenu has a Back button to return to the previous menu and a Forward button if your submenu needs to offer more than the limit of 6 selections (or 12, in certain themes). You can customize the scene selection submenus using the same methods I describe in this chapter.

Burning Down the Disc

*T*he entire point of using iDVD is to burn a DVD disc that can be played in any DVD player or used as a master for duplication. Discs you can burn using the Apple SuperDrive are named DVD-*R* because they're in a *recordable* format.

A SuperDrive built into a Mac after 2005 can also burn either single-layer or double-layer (DVD+R DL) discs. Though single-layer recordable DVDs hold as much as 4.7 gigabytes (GB) of data, double-layer discs offer two layers, nearly doubling the amount of storage to 8.5GB.

You can fit as much as two hours of video on a single-layer DVD-R disc, or four hours on a double-layer disc, using iDVD, including all still images, sounds, and backgrounds.

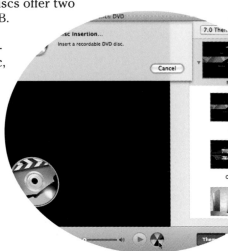

Previewing the DVD

You don't want to burn a disc with mistakes, because you can't redo or fix a DVD-R disc after you've burned it. To be on the safe side, use Preview mode in iDVD to preview the DVD menus and movie playback before you burn.

You can burn a DVD-R or DVD+R disc once (recommended for all uses). A DVD-RW or DVD+RW (*rewritable*) disc can be burned more than once, but doesn't play in many consumer-level DVD players.

Checking your movie's features

Before you burn your DVD, I recommend completing this checklist:

- **Make sure that all menus, drop zones, and buttons are animated the way you want.** Click the Motion button in the iDVD window to turn on motion, and then click on menus, drop zones, and buttons to make sure they work. Click the Motion button again to turn off motion. You can also drag the motion playhead along the motion timeline underneath the Viewer to see the animation.

  If you want to place a fade transition at the beginning of the animation loop, select the check box at the beginning of the motion timeline. If you want a transition at the end, select the check box at the end of the motion timeline. If you don't want a transition at either end, deselect the check box.

- **Check for warning symbols in Map view.** Click the Map View button under the Viewer (the Flowchart icon). Map view is useful for detecting problems *before* you burn. When iDVD has a problem, it displays a warning symbol (either a yellow Yield icon or a Red Stop sign icon) in the lower left corner of a menu or content thumbnail. Move the pointer over each symbol to read its warning message.

- **Preview your movie by using the remote control.** Make sure that the movie has no typos or mistakes and that the slideshow runs the way you want it to run. Chapters in a video should be accessible using the left and right arrows on the iDVD remote control. Ensure that you have the correct videos — you might be surprised by how often people forget to include one, and a typo on a DVD can haunt you forever. I explain how to preview using the remote control in the later section "Using Preview and the remote control."

See "Checking the Project Size and Status," later in this chapter, for more tips on making sure your movie is ready to burn.

Using Preview and the remote control

To see a preview of your project, click the Preview button at any time. iDVD provides a cute remote control panel on the display, shown in Figure 14-1, to simulate a physical remote control for a DVD player. When you're done, you can click either the Exit button on the remote control or the Preview button again.

Figure 14-1: Preview the disc project using the simulated remote control.

Like a remote control unit for a DVD player, the preview remote control in iDVD provides navigation, selection, and movie-playing buttons:

✔ **Arrow buttons:** Select a button on a menu. Press the left and right arrows to advance slides in a slideshow.

✔ **Enter button:** Activate a selected button.

✔ **Player buttons:** Play, pause, stop, fast-forward, or rewind the video.

✔ **Volume control:** Drag this slider to control the audio volume.

✔ **Menu button:** Return to the menu or submenu you just used.

✔ **Title button:** Return to the title menu (the first one).

✔ **Exit button:** Exit Preview mode and return to iDVD.

Testing DVD menus with the remote control is the best strategy because viewers may use a remote control to view the video on a commercial DVD player. However, you can also click the menus with the mouse.

Adding an Autoplay Video

An *autoplay* video clip or slideshow starts playing immediately after the DVD is inserted in a DVD player or computer, before showing the main menu.

For many reasons, you might want your DVD to start with a short autoplay clip or slideshow. You may want to show credits or a production company logo before showing the main menu, for example. Or, you may just want to introduce the DVD with a wacky video clip before displaying its even wackier menu. Whatever.

To add an autoplay video clip or slideshow, follow these steps:

1. **Click the Map View button under the Viewer (the Flowchart icon).**

   Map view, which I describe in more detail in Chapter 13, displays a flowchart of your DVD project. The first project thumbnail before the main menu in this flowchart is the blank Autoplay thumbnail for adding an autoplay clip or slideshow.

2. **Browse videos or slideshow photos in the Media Browser, as I describe in Chapter 12, and drag a video or a set of photos to the Autoplay thumbnail, as shown in Figure 14-2.**

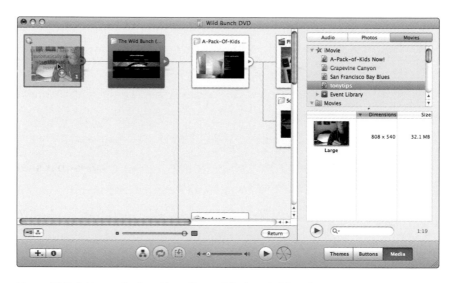

Figure 14-2: Add an autoplay video clip or slideshow in Map view.

Videos with chapter markers can be navigated by pressing the Next or Previous buttons on the remote control.

If you added a slideshow or a single photo, you can double-click the Autoplay thumbnail to open the Slideshow Editor. (For details on using the Slideshow Editor, see Chapter 12.)

3. To turn on looping, click the Autoplay project icon and then choose Advanced⇨Loop Movie or Advanced⇨Loop Slideshow.

You might want to burn a DVD with only an autoplay video or slideshow: If you set the autoplay content to loop, it plays continuously, like a kiosk, with no need for menus. Creating a project with just an autoplay video or slideshow can be useful for presentations that require little or no viewer interaction.

Checking the Project Size and Status

While you were sleeping (if you left iDVD running), or even while you were designing menus, submenus, and buttons, iDVD has been silently *compressing* and *encoding* your project for the DVD format. Compressing and encoding a video of any length takes a considerable amount of time. Fortunately, you can continue working in iDVD while the encoding process continues.

If you prefer to have iDVD do nothing else except encode the rest of your project, choose Advanced⇨Encode in Background so that the check mark is removed (to turn off background encoding). To turn on background encoding again, choose Advanced⇨Encode in Background again.

As you're working on your project, monitor its size to ensure that everything will fit on a DVD-R. To check the size of your project and the status of the encoding process, and to change the quality of the encoding and compression, choose Project⇨Project Info. The Project Info window appears, as shown in Figure 14-3, with encoding and compression progress bars for every media element in your project. When the progress bar shows Done, the media element is ready.

As you peruse the Project Info window, this information is handy to know:

 ✓ **Project size:** The total size of your project (in minutes and in megabytes or gigabytes) appears below the Capacity meter on the far right side. This meter uses color bands to show how much of a project's total size is occupied by the different elements in the project. The numbers below the DVD-ROM, Slideshows, Menus, and Movies labels specify the number of megabytes each category uses. You can click these amounts to toggle them to show how many of these items are in your project and how many tracks they use — an iDVD project is limited to 99 tracks.

✓ **Encoding method and quality:** The amount of space your project occupies depends on the quality setting you choose for the encoding-and-compressing process. To change the quality setting, choose Best Performance, High Quality, or Professional Quality from the Encoding pop-up menu in the Project Info window. The Capacity meter changes to reflect the new setting — and the white arrow in the Capacity meter points to a color band showing the estimated quality of your burned DVD. Green indicates the highest quality. (The color band is entirely green if you select the Best Performance encoding setting.)

You can set the encoding quality for all projects in advance by choosing iDVD⇨Preferences, clicking the Projects tab, and then choosing Best Performance, High Quality, or Professional Quality from the Encoding pop-up menu.

Figure 14-3: Check the project size and encoding progress or change encoding settings.

✔ **Aspect ratio:** The Project Info window also lets you choose the video picture aspect ratio from the Aspect Ratio pop-up menu (which I describe in Chapter 12) and the type of DVD-R disc from the DVD Type pop-up menu.

✔ **Status of media elements:** The media elements in your project appear in the Media area of the Project Info window (refer to Figure 14-3), along with the path to their locations on your hard disk or elsewhere. If you see no table in the Media area, click the triangle to show it. A check mark in the Status column tells you that the media element is present and accounted for.

If you moved the file from its original location, you can see at a glance that it's missing — a missing check mark indicates that iDVD can't find it.

Close your iDVD project before renaming or moving any source files. When you open the iDVD project again, a warning dialog tells you that one or more files is missing and asks you to find the missing items. Click Find File, and then browse your hard drive and select the missing file. If other missing files are in the same location, iDVD finds them automatically.

Saving and Archiving a Project

You can save an iDVD project at any time by choosing File➪Save. If you quit iDVD before saving a project, iDVD displays a warning dialog so that you can click Save to save the project.

However, you may want to either save the iDVD project with all its elements in an archive on another hard drive or move it to another computer. The *archive* process creates a copy of your project, keeping all its elements together and linked within the project file. To archive a project, choose File➪Archive Project and select a destination folder on your hard drive.

You can also save a *disc image* of the project — a file formatted as a finished DVD but not yet burned to a disc. To create a disc image, choose File➪Save As Disc Image. The elements are encoded and compressed into the DVD format so that you can play the disc image on your computer as though it were a DVD by double-clicking the disc image icon. You can move the disc image to another computer or hard drive, but you can't edit using iDVD. When you're ready to burn the disc image to a DVD, you can use Disk Utility in Mac OS X.

iDVD also lets you save a project as a `VIDEO_TS` folder, which you can use on your computer with software such as VLC media player or the DVD Player application supplied with Mac OS X. Choose File➪Save As VIDEO_TS Folder.

The process is similar to saving a disc image and takes about the same amount of time.

Adding Files to the Disc's DVD-ROM

In addition to using iDVD to show videos and slideshows, you can use it to back up project archives and to put nearly any digital file on the DVD-ROM portion (the part not accessible with a DVD player) of the DVD-R. You *first* set up iDVD to add the project files or other files to the DVD-ROM portion and *then* burn the disc.

You may not want the recipients of your DVD-R (or a DVD created from it, if you plan to make multiple copies) to be able to access these files — which they can do using a computer. But if you want to archive the files associated with a DVD-R project, you can add them to the disc. By including photos, slideshows, and video files in the DVD-ROM portion of the disc, you make it possible for viewers to download them, which is useful if you want viewers to be able to print photos.

To prepare iDVD to add the photos of a slideshow to the DVD-ROM portion of the disc, open the Slideshow Editor as I describe in Chapter 12 and select the Add Image Files to DVD-ROM option. To set iDVD to always add photos automatically, choose iDVD⇨Preferences, click Slideshow, and then select the Always Add Original Photos to DVD-ROM Contents option.

 The photos added to the DVD-ROM portion of the disc have the same resolution and quality as the originals. The added photos aren't scaled to fit the DVD window, as are their counterparts in the slideshow. The reason is so that viewers can download photos that print well. In fact, if you add Raw images from iPhoto to your slideshow, iDVD places JPEG files of the images in the slideshow and adds the original Raw images to the DVD-ROM contents.

To prepare iDVD to add any type of folders or files to the DVD-ROM portion of the disc, choose Advanced⇨Edit DVD-ROM Contents. The DVD-ROM Contents window appears, as shown in Figure 14-4.

You can click the New Folder button to create a new folder and click the Add Files button to add a file or folder, or you can simply drag files or folders to the DVD-ROM Contents window. After you burn the disc, these files and folders show up in the DVD-ROM portion of it.

Figure 14-4: Add files and folders to the DVD-ROM portion of the soon-to-be-burned disc.

Burning and Testing the DVD

As part of your Mac system, your SuperDrive laser is always ready to burn media.

Burning a DVD takes a lot of processing power and can tie up your computer for a while. Before you start burning a disc, consider closing all other open projects and any open applications that place demands on the system. Then let the computer do its thing with the SuperDrive. If you're burning a disc on a laptop, be sure that the laptop is plugged into a power outlet and avoid moving it while the drive is burning the disc.

Don't press the Media Eject button on the keyboard while a burn operation is in process or else you'll ruin the disc.

To burn your project to DVD, follow these steps:

1. **Click the Burn button underneath the Viewer.**

   The Burn button starts pulsating, and its icon is replaced with the Radioactivity symbol. (Apple at least has a sense of humor.) A dialog appears and asks you to either insert a disc or click Cancel, as shown in Figure 14-5. This is your failsafe point.

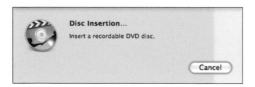

Figure 14-5: Burn, baby, burn!

2. Insert a blank DVD-R disc to start the process.

You may want to take a break now — iDVD burns the new DVD-R while displaying a progress bar indicating the number of minutes required for the preparation, processing, and burning operations.

At the end of this process, iDVD spits out your newly burned DVD-R disc and displays a message asking whether you want to burn another one just like it.

3. Insert another blank disc or click Done to finish the operation.

Although you may be tempted to fire off a dozen more discs for your friends, test the first disc before making duplicates. You can always open iDVD and burn another one later.

Testing the disc

The best way to test a newly burned DVD-R disc is to pop it right back into your SuperDrive or a similar DVD-R drive on your Mac. The disc should play just like any commercial DVD title.

The DVD Player application, supplied with every Mac that has a DVD drive, provides a simulated remote control for controlling playback. DVD Player also offers the capability to play the DVD in a window of (depending on your display) half, normal, or maximum size by choosing options from the Video menu.

You can also double-click the disc's icon in the Finder to see the contents of the DVD-ROM portion of the DVD-R disc. You can copy the folders and files to a hard disk by using the Finder.

After you test the DVD-R disc on a Mac, test the DVD with a commercial DVD player. If the disc works on the Mac but not on the commercial player, the player and DVD-R discs may have a compatibility problem.

That's it! You can now call yourself a DVD author, and DVD is now an important part of your iLife.

Troubleshooting DVD problems

I created my first DVD-R with videos, music, sounds, and lots of files copied to the DVD-ROM portion. The newly burned DVD-R worked perfectly the first time. (How often does that happen with new technology?) If you're not as lucky, check out the solutions to the common issues in this list:

✔ **The disc won't burn.**

 Solution: Perhaps you have a bum disc. (It happens.) Try another one, and get a refund if the newer one works.

✔ **iDVD can't find all the media files.**

 Solution: This problem happens often, especially if you move or delete the source files for the media. Copy the files back into the hard drive in their proper places, and import the media into the project again. See the earlier section "Checking the Project Size and Status" for details.

✔ **The DVD-R won't play on my DVD player.**

 Solution: If this problem happens to you, try the DVD-R disc in your Mac. If it works fine there, the disc is burned properly. Your DVD player probably doesn't play DVD-R discs. Try another blank DVD-R, and make sure to turn off all virus protection, automatic update, and automated backup software. Disconnect from the Internet and close all applications. Then start iDVD again to burn the disc.

Part IV
Getting Out-a-Site with iWeb

The 5th Wave — By Rich Tennant

"You know, I've asked you a dozen times NOT to animate the torches on our Web site."

*P*art IV is all about using iWeb to design and create a Web site with professionally designed pages using photos and slideshows from iPhoto, songs from GarageBand and iTunes, and video clips from the iMovie.

✔ In Chapter 15, you see what iWeb can do, what you need to host your Web pages, and how to pick a theme and template for each Web page, change the image and text place-holders, and add hyperlinks.

✔ Chapter 16 describes how to customize your Web page elements; add videos, songs, and slideshows; create a blog; and add widgets to your pages such as Google Maps and AdSense ads, YouTube videos, and news feeds.

✔ Chapter 17 shows you how to manage your site pages and publish your Web site using MobileMe or publish it to another hosting service.

15

Creating a Web Site

In This Chapter

▶ Finding out what iWeb can do

▶ What you need for hosting a Web site

▶ Choosing a theme and templates for pages

▶ Changing image and text placeholders

▶ Adding hyperlinks

*I*f you could advertise yourself, your travels, your projects, or your business on a highway billboard, how would you design that billboard?

That's what the first page of your Web site represents, from a design perspective: a billboard on the information highway. People may glance at yours as they surf by, and if it looks professional, they may linger a bit longer to see what you're offering. Chances are good that if you put too much text on your billboard in a small font with no photos or graphics, people won't spend the time to stop and read it. If you offer an excellent design or one with eye-catching images, people might spend more time looking at it.

iWeb helps you organize your Web site to make it more attractive and easy to navigate. It provides professionally designed themes and templates for Web pages so that you don't have to be a designer to create a well-designed site with a compelling first page.

Of course, a Web site is not a billboard — it's more like a front door to a miniature world of content and services. You might use a Web site's front page to link to other pages that offer content, for example. Or, you may want to keep a *blog* (or Web *log*), which is a journal of your activities or a collection of your writings that can also include images and videos. Perhaps you want to show photo albums as a portfolio of your work or a record of your travels. You might want to add a map to show your location, the location of your business, or other locations, or put other interactive widgets (code fragments) on your Web page to show news feeds or videos from YouTube or other useful functions. You may want to separate your personal life from your business and create two sites. iWeb can easily manage multiple sites.

Even if you have no idea what blogs and widgets are but you're sure that you need them, you're in luck: iWeb makes it painless to add them and use them. This chapter explains what you need in order to create a Web site and what you can do with iWeb. I walk you through the steps of creating a Web page with text and graphics, photos and slideshows, video clips, and links to other Web pages and sites.

What You Can Do with iWeb

iWeb is Web site design, made easy. Just consider these features:

- **Simplified publishing:** You can create Web pages and then publish your Web site without having to consult a Web genius. And, iWeb connects directly to MobileMe to publish your Web site, or you can publish it on almost any other host's server.

- **Easy-to-use themes:** iWeb is supplied with professional-looking themes that do all the design work for you. You can cut the time it takes to design your Web pages by choosing a theme and then adding content. Every theme is supplied with fonts, backgrounds, and colors that give your pages a consistent look throughout your site. Every theme also comes with ready-made templates for the typical pages you find on a Web site — such as the Welcome page, the About Me page, and pages for photo albums, movies, blogs, and podcasts. You can create as many pages as you need, and iWeb automatically creates navigation menus for every page.

- **Built-in multimedia tools and widgets:** Put together graphical Web pages with photos and slideshows from iPhoto, songs from GarageBand and iTunes, and video clips from iMovie. You can even resize and rotate images as you add them. Use iWeb to add a blog that visitors can add comments to, and interactive widgets that offer functions such as Google Maps, Google AdSense ads, feeds that deliver news from your favorite sources, and a YouTube video player. You can even have iWeb take a photo using the iSight camera and place the photo immediately on the Web page.

✔ **Many ways to link content:** Hyperlinks form the backbone of the Web, enabling visitors to click and follow a link to any other Web page. Using iWeb, linking is a simple drag-and-drop affair: Drag a page's link from Safari directly into your Web page. You can also add links to objects such as images, and links are included in widgets such as Google AdSense. Add an image that links to your MobileMe Gallery. You can pick the album to use as a slideshow within the image or use a video in the MobileMe Gallery to play a video within the image.

✔ **Quick site updates:** After initially publishing a site, iWeb uploads only your changes when you publish again. And, you can easily notify Facebook friends when you update your site by using iWeb to link your site to your Facebook account so that your updates are noted in your Facebook profile.

What You Need to Create a Site

If you use MobileMe, you already have everything you need in order to publish a public Web site, including space on the MobileMe server. (You need to put Web pages on a Web server, which is typically hosted by a service such as MobileMe.) iWeb uses your MobileMe account information from System Preferences to publish the site.

You can get a free trial MobileMe subscription (at www.me.com) and then subscribe when the trial period expires. During the trial period, and as a full MobileMe member, you can publish your site and anyone with a Web browser can view the site.

You don't have to use MobileMe. You can publish your Web site using any Web hosting service that offers the File Transfer Protocol (FTP) for transferring files. iWeb supports FTP so that you can transfer your Web pages directly to an existing site at a hosting service. All you need to do is set up the site in advance and obtain the necessary FTP address, username, and password to transfer files.

If you don't publish your site using MobileMe, you don't benefit from the advanced features of iWeb: protected passwords, hit counter, enhanced slideshows, blog searches, and comments about your blog, podcast, and photos.

Touring iWeb

You create a Web site by designing its pages, filling in the elements for each page, and then publishing the pages as a complete site. After that, you can edit the pages at any time and then update your site with the new pages. I walk you through the steps of starting iWeb for the first time, designing a Web page, and filling in some page elements in "Designing a Web Site," later in this chapter.

After you've designed a few pages, the iWeb window looks similar to the one shown in Figure 15-1, and offers the elements described in this list:

Figure 15-1: The iWeb window and tools.

✔ **Sidebar:** The titles of sites and their pages appear in the Sidebar. Click a page title to display the page in the Canvas. Click the triangle next to a Blog or Podcast title to show or hide page titles within the blog or podcast, or the triangle next to the Site title to show or hide page titles in a site.

✔ **Canvas:** The Web page appears here. You can select elements to change and text to type over or edit. You also drag elements from the Media Browser to the Canvas to place them on a Web page. The Canvas is separated into regions for the navigation bar (which contains the navigation menu), the header at the top of the page, the footer at the bottom of the page, and the page body between the header and the footer.

✔ **Navigation menu:** All pages in the site are placed as links on this menu. Visitors click these links to navigate to different pages in the site.

✔ **Toolbar:** The tool buttons and controls appear on the toolbar.

✔ **Show/Hide Media:** Click the Show Media button to open the Media Browser and then click these tabs:

- *Audio:* Browse your iTunes library or GarageBand songs and add them to your Web page.

- *Photos:* Browse your iPhoto library and drag albums, events, and keepsakes to Photo Album pages, or drag single photos to replace placeholder images or add them to pages.

- *Movies:* Browse your iMovie videos and other video files in your Movies folder, and add them to Movies or Photo Album pages.

- *Widgets:* Browse widgets that are available in iWeb to place on your pages, such as Google Maps and YouTube. *Widgets* are fragments of HTML (HyperText Markup Language) code that usually also include JavaScript code. You can add your own fragment of HTML code by choosing the HTML Snippet widget.

iWeb is quite forgiving if you do things you don't like. You can undo just about every operation you perform, going backward. Just choose Edit➪Undo for each consecutive operation to undo it.

You can save your iWeb sites and pages at any time by choosing File➪Save. If you quit iWeb before saving, iWeb displays a warning dialog so that you can click Save to save the sites and pages. iWeb doesn't save the Web pages and page elements separately. All the information iWeb needs in order to create your Web site is saved in a file named Domain and located in your user folder's Library folder, at this location:

```
your user folder/Library/Application Support/iWeb
```

The Domain file consists of links to your media files and the information needed to re-create the Web pages. When you publish your site, iWeb gathers all media elements, assembles the pages, and copies them to the Web server at MobileMe (or your hosting service), as I describe in Chapter 17. You can also "publish" your Web site pages to a folder on your hard drive — which is useful if you have a Web server on your computer or your computer has Web Sharing turned on or you want to edit the HTML files before copying the pages to your Web server or hosting service. See Chapter 17 for details on publishing your site to a folder on your hard drive.

Designing a Web Site

On most Macs, you find the iWeb icon in the Dock, but in any case you can find it in the Applications folder. Double-click the icon to open iWeb. If this is the first time you're using iWeb, the dialog shown in Figure 15-2 appears. If it doesn't, the last Web page you were working on appears.

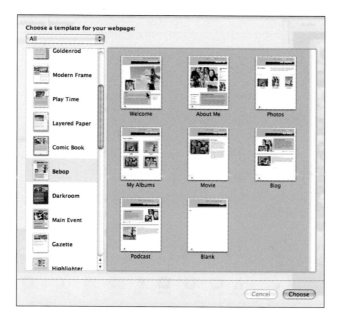

Figure 15-2: Choose a theme for your Web site.

A theme defines the look of your site. Every theme offers templates designed for a specific purpose, such as a blog, a podcast, or a photo album. Each time you add a new Web page, you choose the page's template. You can change the theme and template for a page at any time.

Choosing a theme and page template

Theme thumbnails appear in a column along the left side of the opening dialog (refer to Figure 15-2). Select a theme to see the templates for that theme on the right side of the dialog.

If you decide later to change the theme for a page, just select the page in the Sidebar (refer to Figure 15-1), click the Theme button on the toolbar, and choose a new theme from the pop-up menu.

Every theme offers these templates for different types of Web pages:

- ✔ **Welcome:** Offers one or more images and some welcoming text. Think of it as the first page or "billboard" for your site.

- ✔ **About Me:** Helps you easily create the typical About Me or About Us (or About This Company) page you find on Web sites that explains who you are, with photos and text.

- ✔ **Photos:** Includes a grid that automatically sizes and positions each photo as you add it, and provides for each photo a placeholder caption that you can easily replace with your own caption. This template also offers a Play Slideshow button that visitors can click to view the photos in a slideshow.

- ✔ **My Albums:** Lets you easily add photo or video albums. It creates an index page of images that a visitor can move the pointer over to see a mini-slideshow or video, or click to see the entire photo or video album. iWeb places on the page a smaller version of the first album photo for a photo album. For a video album, iWeb places the first frame inside a poster frame.

  If you have photo or video albums that you placed on Photos or Movies pages, you can create a My Albums page to organize a single index for all your albums so that visitors don't see a confusing navigation menu. Instead, they can click a single link for the My Albums page to see all your photo and video albums.

- ✔ **Movie:** Offers a video placeholder that includes player controls. All you need to do is drag a video and change the page text, and you're done.

- ✔ **Blog:** Shows the most recent entry first in a journal of entries, followed by previous entries. This template offers a layout with Previous and Next buttons to jump from one blog entry to another, and lets you add new entries to your blog, delete entries, and maintain an archive. It also enables visitors to click a button to add your blog's Really Simple Syndication (RSS) feed to their RSS readers and browsers. All you have to do is change its name from Our Blog to one that suits you, change the placeholder image, and start blogging.

✔ **Podcast:** Similar to a blog, except that each "entry" is an MP3 audio file or MPEG-4 video file, and you can subscribe to a podcast via the iTunes Store. This template offers a layout similar to the Blog template, with Previous and Next buttons to jump from one podcast episode to another, and lets you add new episodes to your podcast, delete episodes, and maintain an archive. It also enables visitors to click a button to subscribe to your podcast in iTunes, or to subscribe to the RSS feed of your podcast. All you have to do is change its name from Our Podcasts to one that suits you, change the placeholder image, and start podcasting.

✔ **Blank:** Nearly blank but still offers the theme graphics and text placeholders so that you can quickly modify the text. You can then drag media elements to the blank page and arrange the elements in any layout you want.

Choose a template to create a page. After you choose a template, the page appears in the iWeb Canvas, as shown in Figure 15-3. You can then change the page's placeholder text and images.

Figure 15-3: Choose the Welcome template for a welcome page.

As you create pages, you don't need to add links for visitors to navigate them within your site — iWeb automatically adds a navigation menu (refer to Figure 15-1) for all pages you create in your site.

Changing text and images

One key way that you can make an iWeb template your own space on the Web is by adding your own text and images. Here's how:

✔ **To change the placeholder text on the Web page,** click the text block in the Canvas, and then type over it (as I'm doing with the Welcome place-holder text shown in Figure 15-3). You can change all placeholder text blocks by scrolling the page in the Canvas to see them and then clicking them to type over them, as shown in Figure 15-4.

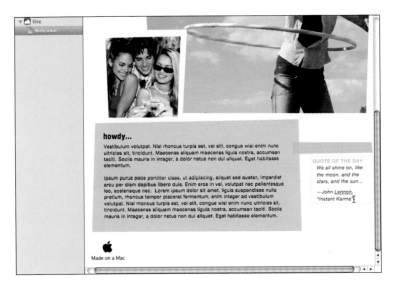

Figure 15-4: Click on and then type over the text block to change its text.

✔ **To change the placeholder images on the page,** click the Photos tab in the upper right corner of the iWeb window to show the Photos pane of the Media Browser. (You may have to click the Show Media button first.) You can then browse your iPhoto library, as shown in Figure 15-5 — you can browse events, photo albums, and certain keepsakes such as photo books. To change the placeholder to a photo, drag the photo from the Media Browser to the placeholder image in the Canvas.

You can also drag a photo from the Finder or from iPhoto itself over a placeholder image in the Canvas to replace the image.

After dragging photos to the Canvas, you can edit them as described in this list:

Figure 15-5: Drag a photo from the Media Browser to a placeholder image to change it.

- ✔ **Crop:** Click the photo to crop it for the frame — the cropping slider appears, as shown in Figure 15-6, and you can drag the slider to zoom in to the photo and show more detail, or zoom out to show more of the entire picture.

- ✔ **Resize:** Click a photo so that selection handles appear, and then drag the selection handles to resize it.

- ✔ **Rotate:** Select the photo and then click the Rotate tool on the toolbar.

- ✔ **Overlap:** You can even adjust the way two images overlap on the page. Click one of the images in the Canvas, and then click the Edit Mask button underneath the Cropping slider (refer to Figure 15-6). Selection handles appear on the mask, which defines how the images overlap. Drag a selection handle to change the shape of the mask and thereby change the shape of the overlap.

You can also adjust the brightness, contrast, saturation, and other attributes of photos, as well as the attributes of text blocks — I show you how in Chapter 16.

Figure 15-6: Crop the photo in the frame by dragging the slider.

Adding hyperlinks

A *hyperlink* is a piece of text or an object that links to another Web page in the same site or another site. iWeb makes it easy to add a hyperlink by dragging one directly from your browser, typing it directly into a text block, or using the Link Inspector. You can also drag the title of a different page in your site from the Sidebar to the page in the Canvas to create a hyperlink to the other page.

To drag a link from your browser, follow these steps:

1. **Open Safari to browse the Web page.**

   The *URL* (Uniform Resource Locator), which is the global address of the Web page on the Internet, appears on the address bar at the top of Safari.

2. **Drag the URL to a text block or image in the Canvas, as shown in Figure 15-7 (or to any open place on the page).**

   • To add the link within existing text, drag the object to the point in the text where you want the link to appear. iWeb automatically creates the hyperlink using the page's title. You can edit the text hyperlink directly on the page by clicking inside it and retyping (or using the Delete key).

• If you drag the URL to an image or another object, the object takes on the hyperlink so that visitors can click it like any other hyperlink. An object that is a hyperlink has a blue arrow in its lower right corner, but don't worry — the arrows don't appear on your published Web site.

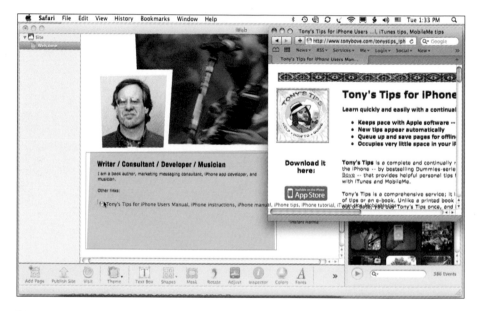

Figure 15-7: Add a text hyperlink directly to a page by dragging its URL from Safari.

You can also type a URL directly into a text block on a page. iWeb recognizes the URL and turns it into a hyperlink.

To turn a piece of text into a hyperlink, or to add a hyperlink to an object, follow these steps:

1. **Select the text or object on the page, and click Inspector on the Toolbar at the bottom of the iWeb window (or choose View➪Show Inspector).**

   The Inspector window appears with buttons along the top.

2. **Click the Link Inspector button (the curled arrow) in the upper right corner of the Inspector window.**

3. **Click the Hyperlink tab at the top (if it isn't already selected), as shown in Figure 15-8.**

Link Inspector button

Inspector window

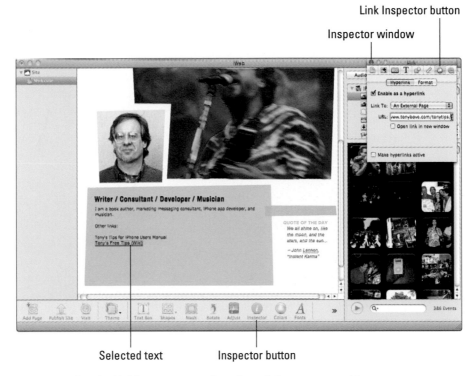

Selected text   Inspector button

Figure 15-8: Use the Link Inspector to assign a hyperlink to text or an object.

4. **Select the Enable as a Hyperlink option in the Link Inspector, and then choose the type of link from the Link pop-up menu:**

   - *One of My Pages:* A page in the same site (created by iWeb). After selecting One of My Pages, you can then choose the page from the Page pop-up menu that appears underneath.

   - *An External Page:* A page on another Web site. After selecting An External Page, you can type the URL in the URL field and, if you want, select the Open Link in New Window option to open the external page in a separate browser window.

   - *A File:* A file on your site or hard drive. When a visitor clicks this link, the file downloads to the visitor's computer. After selecting A File, you can browse the same directory or a subdirectory to select the file. When you publish the site, linked files in the same directory or subdirectory are copied to the site.

Part IV: Getting Out-a-Site with iWeb

• *An Email Message:* An e-mail message containing the email address and subject you specify. After selecting An Email Message, you can fill in the e-mail address for the To field (where the message is sent when the visitor clicks the hyperlink) and the subject in the Subject field.

You can add hyperlinks that open songs, audiobooks, videos, and podcasts in the iTunes Store — the links take visitors there so that they can preview and download the content. To add hyperlinks to songs that are already in your iTunes library so that they open in the iTunes Store, drag an iTunes playlist from the Audio pane of the Media Browser to a position or text block on the page in the Canvas. You can also open iTunes and drag a playlist directly from your library to the Canvas in the iWeb window or drag content directly from an iTunes Store page to the Canvas. To see how to add the audio file to a Web page so that visitors can play it, see Chapter 16.

Testing and formatting links

Links on the page in the iWeb Canvas aren't active, which makes them easy to edit without accidentally activating them and going off to another site. If you want to test your links, you can turn them on in the Link Inspector by clicking the Make Hyperlinks Active option.

You can also use the Link Inspector window to format a text hyperlink by choosing colors for the normal, rollover, and visited states. Select the hyperlink text on the page in the Canvas, and then click Format tab in the Link Inspector, as shown in Figure 15-9.

Figure 15-9: Change the colors of the text hyperlink.

In the Format pane of the Link Inspector, you can choose a color for each state of the hyperlink:

✔ **Normal:** The text color for hyperlinks before they're clicked

✔ **Rollover:** The text color of hyperlinks when visitors move the pointer over them

✔ **Visited:** The text color *after* a visitor has clicked the hyperlink, to show that the link has already been visited

✔ **Disabled:** The text color of a hyperlink that can't be clicked (because it doesn't work)

The Format pane settings apply to only the hyperlink you selected. If you want to use these settings for all new hyperlinks you create on the page in the Canvas, click the Use for New Links on Page button (refer to Figure 15-9).

Renaming pages

iWeb starts you off with generic page names, such as Welcome, About Me, Photos, Movies, and Blog. When you create a page, the page name is automatically added to the navigation menu on the other pages of the site (as well as on the new page). When a visitor lands on the page, the page name appears at the top of the visitor's browser window.

You will probably want to rename these pages so that they more closely match your content. To rename a page, double-click the name in the Sidebar and type the new name, as shown in Figure 15-10.

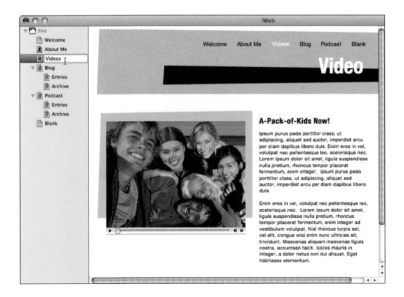

Figure 15-10: Change the Web page name.

After you change the page name, the name on the navigation menu changes automatically on all site pages.

You can also change the name of the site itself — see Chapter 17.

16

Customizing Your Pages

*T*he Web has been around for more than two decades. People expect Web sites to be not only tastefully designed and informative but also entertaining. Even button-down suit-and-tie sites need to capture attention, and educational sites can't afford to lose their audience with boring pages. As philosopher Marshall McLuhan, who coined the terms "the medium is the message" and "global village," pointed out, "Anyone who tries to make a distinction between education and entertainment doesn't know the first thing about either."

You have an arsenal of entertaining, informative, educational, and even business-oriented Web site tools at your fingertips. iWeb themes are already set up with templates for pages that can contain entire photo albums, movies, blogs, and podcasts.

This chapter explains how to customize your Web pages and page elements. You can quickly assemble graphical Web pages with photos and slideshows from iPhoto, songs from GarageBand and iTunes, and video clips from iMovie. Using iWeb, you can add a blog where visitors can comment, and interactive widgets in iWeb offer functions as diverse as Google Maps to put a map on your page, Google AdSense to put ads on your page (and earn revenue), feeds that deliver news from your favorite sources, and even a YouTube video player.

Adding and Modifying Page Elements

The themes provide excellent template designs for pages, but they're *your* pages, and you can do what you want with them. After replacing the text on the page with your own text, as I explain in Chapter 15, you may want to change the text attributes; move, resize, or delete text boxes; and adjust photos or add other page elements to fit your content.

You can also change the theme for any page of your Web site without affecting the theme used for other pages. Click a page title in the Sidebar to display the page in the Canvas, click the Themes button on the toolbar, and then select a theme.

Changing the layout

Every iWeb page template has text boxes for the header, title, body text, and footer. The header appears at the top of the page and starts with placeholder text, such as My Blog or Welcome to My Site. The Title box is usually just above the Body box, and the Footer box appears at the bottom of the page. You can change virtually any element in this layout, and as you do so, the following pointers can help you make the page your own:

- **Tinker with text boxes:** As you replace the placeholder text in any of these boxes and add more text, the box grows to accommodate the text. You can see the region boundaries of these text boxes by choosing View⇨Show Layout. You can drag any boundary to resize the text box, as shown in Figure 16-1.

  To delete any text box or page element, select it and press the Delete key.

- **Rearrange page elements:** You can also drag any page element to any position on the page. To align page elements on the page, select two or more elements and choose Arrange⇨Align Objects, and then choose Left, Center, Right, Top, Middle, or Bottom.

  To distribute page elements across the page horizontally, or down the page vertically, select two or more elements and choose Arrange⇨Distribute Objects⇨Horizontally or Arrange⇨Distribute Objects⇨Vertically.

  If the page element you selected is obscured by another page element, such as a graphical image, select the other element and choose Arrange⇨Send Backward (or Control-click and choose Send Backward) so that the other element is sent backward in the layout, behind other objects. To send the element *all* the way to the background, behind *all* other objects, choose Arrange⇨Send to Back (or Control-click and choose Send to Back). To bring the object forward again so that you can see it, choose Arrange⇨Bring Forward (or Control-click and choose Bring Forward). To bring the object all the way up in front of the other objects, choose — you guessed it — Arrange⇨Bring to Front (or Control-click and choose Bring to Front).

✓ **Color the background:** When changing the page background, you can choose Color Fill, Gradient Fill, Image Fill, or Tinted Image Fill from the Page Background pop-up menu and then choose a color from the color swatch, a starting and ending color and angle for a gradient fill, or an image from your hard drive.

✓ **Revise the Mac branding in the footer:** Most themes include the *Made on a Mac* logo in the Footer box at the bottom of every page template — you can select and then delete the logo (if you want) by pressing the Delete key or choosing Edit⇨Delete. (You delete the logo in the same basic manner as you delete any text box or page element.)

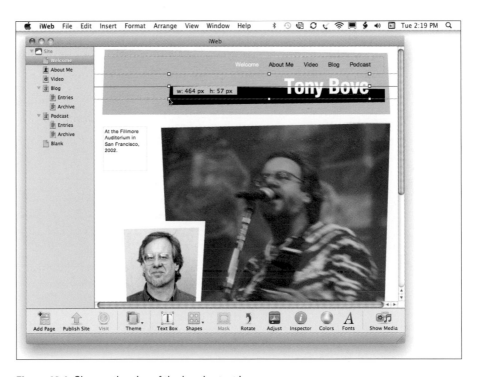

Figure 16-1: Change the size of the header text box.

You can also choose Insert➪Button➪Made on a Mac to remove the logo from the footer, and choose it again to add the logo *back* to the footer.

✔ **Fill in the footer:** To add text to the footer, first add a text box (see "Adding a text box," later in this chapter), and then press Command as you drag the text box from the body of the page to the footer. You can also drag photos and movies and other objects to the footer, just as you can to other areas of the page — though if you drag a photo or movie, the picture size may shrink to fit into the footer space.

✔ **Size the header and footer:** You can set the minimum height of the Header or Footer box by clicking the Inspector button on the tool-bar to open the Inspector window, clicking the leftmost button (Page Inspector) at the top of the Inspector window, and clicking the Layout tab, as shown in Figure 16-2. The Layout pane lets you change the height of the header or footer, the height and width of the page content, the fill for the page background, and the fill for the browser background (behind your Web page).

To add a header or footer to a page that doesn't have one, increase its height (in the Layout pane of the Page Inspector) to a value greater than zero; to remove the header or footer, decrease its height to zero.

Figure 16-2: Change the page layout attributes.

Changing the navigation menu

The page templates for themes include a navigation menu with links to other pages in the Web site. The navigation menu is created automatically on every page, with links to some or all of the other pages. The size (depth) of the navigation menu depends on the number of links.

When you add a page to the site, a link to the page is automatically added to the navigation menu. But you can choose, on a page-by-page basis, whether the newly added page should be included in the navigation menu or removed. For example, you may have more pages than you want to include in the navigation menu (which in some templates can hold only about six to eight links without growing too large), and use custom navigation elements for those pages.

To remove a page link from the navigation menu, follow these steps:

1. **Select the newly added page in the Sidebar.**

2. **Click the Inspector button to open the Inspector window, and click the leftmost button (Page Inspector) at the top to show the Page Inspector pane (refer to Figure 16-2).**

3. **Click the Page tab in the Page Inspector pane, as shown in Figure 16-3, to show the Page options.**

4. **Turn off the Include Page in Navigation Menu option.**

You don't have to put the navigation menu on every page — you may want to use custom navigation elements on some pages. To remove the navigation menu from a page so that the page doesn't show the menu, select the page in the Sidebar, follow Steps 2–3 above, and then turn off the Display Navigation Menu option.

Figure 16-3: Turn the navigation menu on or off.

If you change a page's name (see Chapter 15 for details on renaming pages), iWeb also changes the link in the navigation menus on the pages where the menus appear.

Setting text attributes

When you want to change font attributes of text on an iWeb page, the Font panel is your destination. How you get to the Font panel depends on the text you want to change. To change

✏ **The font attributes of an entire box of text:** Click the text box once. You can then click the Fonts button on the toolbar (or choose Format➪Font➪Show Fonts) to open the Font panel, where you can change the font, typeface, and point size, as shown in Figure 16-4.

✏ **The font attributes of a selection of text:** Double-click the text box, and then drag across the text to make a selection. Then click the Fonts button to change the font. You can also change the text color by clicking the third button (it has the letter *T* and a color tile) along the top of the Font panel to open the color picker, as shown in Figure 16-5.

Figure 16-4: Change the font for the selected text box.

Figure 16-5: Change the text color for the selected text inside the box.

The Font panel (see the left side of Figure 16-6, a little later in this section) lets you set the font family, such as Times New Roman or Verdana; its type-face, such as regular or italic; and its point size. You can click the first button along the top of the panel to set an underline or double underline (or to change the color of the underline). Click the second button along the top of the panel to set a strikethrough or double-strikethrough in the text. If you've ever used a word processor, all these options should be familiar to you. The collections feature of the Font panel may be new to you, though, especially if you're new to designing Web pages.

✔ **Fonts are organized into collections,** such as Web (which are fonts that work well on the Web), PDF (fonts that work well in PDF files), Chinese, Japanese, or Korean. On the Web, using collections of fonts is standard practice because not every visitor to your site has access to the same fonts installed on your Mac. The first font in the group is your first font choice, and your visitors' Web browsers check the list of fonts you specify until they find a match. PDFs are more similar to pictures, so which-ever font you choose is displayed on visitors' computers. However, some fonts still display better in PDFs than do others.

✔ **You can create your own collections.** Click the plus (+) sign to add a new collection, or select a collection and click the minus (−) sign to remove it. Click the Gear button to access the pop-up menu (refer to the left side of Figure 16-6) that lets you save the current font family, typeface, and size as a favorite, to show a preview, or to change the text color, for example.

When you want to change attributes of paragraphs and lines of text on an iWeb page, the Text Inspector is your destination. To unveil the attributes options in the Text Inspector, follow these steps:

1. **Select a text box (or a portion of the text within a box), just as you do to open the Font panel.**

2. **Click the Inspector button on the toolbar to bring up the Inspector window.**

3. **Click the T button at the top of the window, shown in the center of Figure 16-6, to open the Text Inspector.**

4. **Click the Text tab to show text attributes.**

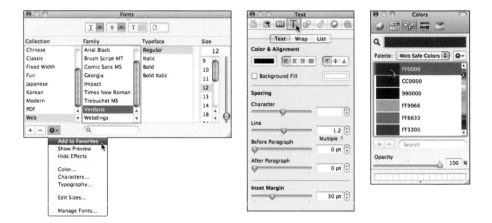

Figure 16-6: Save your favorite font settings (left), set more attributes (center), and specify the color (right).

In the Text Inspector, you find the options described in this list:

- **Color:** You can change the color of the selected text by clicking the color tile to show the color picker panel. The color picker panel (see the right side of Figure 16-6) offers buttons along the top to choose a model for picking colors — a color wheel, color sliders, color palettes, image palettes, and crayons. I picked the Color Palettes model on the right side of Figure 16-6 so that I could choose a palette such as Web Safe Colors (colors that look basically the same in just about all Web browsers).

- **Alignment**: You can change the selected text box's paragraph alignment by clicking one of the alignment buttons (left, centered, right, or justified). You can also click the up-arrow, two-arrows, or down-arrow button to align text to the top, middle, or bottom of a text box or shape, respectively. You can colorize the background behind the text — click the Background Fill option and click the color tile next to the option to bring up the color picker window.

✓ **Spacing:** You can change paragraph character, line, before paragraph, and after paragraph spacing by dragging the sliders or clicking the up or down arrows for specific amounts.

✓ **Inset Margin:** You can define an inset margin, which is the space around the text in a text box or shape.

Click the Wrap tab in the Text Inspector to wrap text around an object (such as a graphical image or photo) and set the wrap spacing. Click the List tab to set text to become a bulleted or numbered list.

Adding a text box

To add a new text box to your page, click the Text Box button on the toolbar. A blank square appears in the middle of the page — choose View➪Show Layout to see its boundaries. Drag the blank square to a position on the page, and the pixel dimensions of the box appear as you drag. One or more purple guidelines appear as you drag the text box, to help you place it so that it's aligned with other objects. You can also resize the text box by dragging one of its boundaries; holding down the Shift key while dragging constrains the resizing to the box's original proportions.

Now all you need to do is type some text into the empty box, as shown in Figure 16-7.

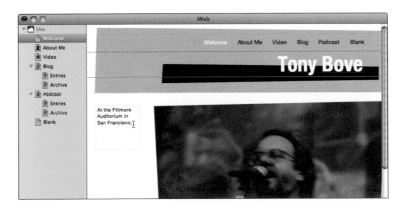

Figure 16-7: Enter text into the empty box.

Adding a graphical element

iWeb comes supplied with shape graphics you can add to a page, and you can add photos and graphics of your own.

To add a snazzy shape element to your page, follow these steps:

1. **Click the Shapes button on the toolbar.**

   A pop-up menu appears, showing various shapes (arrows, geometric shapes, and comic-book quote bubbles, for example).

2. **Choose a shape.**

   I picked the comic-book quote bubble. (You can also choose Insert⇨ Shape⇨Quote Bubble to insert that shape — all shapes are available on the Shape submenu.)

3. **(Optional) To modify your selected shape, click the Inspector button on the toolbar to open the Inspector window, and then click the Graphic Inspector button (the circle-in-a-square icon at the top of the Inspector window).**

The Graphic Inspector lets you change attributes such as the ones described in this list:

- **Stroke line thickness**

- **Shadow color and angle as well as its offset, blur, and opacity:** (*Opacity* determines how transparent your graphic is, or whether it's even transparent.)

- **Opacity of the graphical element against other objects behind it:** For example, I set the Opacity of the speech bubble graphic to 85 percent.

- **Background fill of the element:** Use the Graphic Inspector's Fill pop-up menu to choose Color Fill, Gradient Fill, Advanced Gradient Fill, Image Fill, or Tinted Image Fill. You can then choose a color from the color tile, a starting color and an ending color and an angle for a gradient or an advanced gradient fill, or an image from your hard drive.

- **Size, rotation, and position of the graphical element:** The Metrics Inspector is your tool for each of these tasks. Click the Ruler button at the top of the Inspector window, as shown in Figure 16-8.

  - In the Size section, the width and height of the element can be adjusted by using the up and down arrows. Click the Constrain Proportions option if you want to adjust the size without stretching or distorting the image.

- The Metrics Inspector also lets you position the element precisely on the page with X and Y coordinates in the Position section.

- And, as I show you in Figure 16-8, you can rotate the element to any angle by dragging to turn the Rotate knob. You can also flip the element horizontally or vertically by using the Flip buttons in the Rotate section.

Figure 16-8: Rotate the graphical element on the page. (The photo of me with Mickey Hart was taken by Jay Blakesberg.)

After adding the graphical element, you can easily add a text box on top by clicking the Text Box button on the toolbar and dragging the element into position. (See "Adding a text box," earlier in this chapter.) You can then enter text into the box

You can place a graphical image or photo anywhere on the page where there's no placeholder graphic. (You can select the placeholder and press Delete to delete it if it's in your way.) To insert a graphical image or photo in a standard iWeb page (as opposed to the Photos or My Albums pages discussed later in this chapter), drag its file from the Finder to the iWeb page.

You can also drag a photo or an image into the middle of a text box. These *floating* objects are inserted within text and pushed along as the text grows. You can wrap text only around floating objects — see the second Tip paragraph, about wrapping text, in the earlier section "Setting text attributes."

Adding a hit counter

A *hit counter* isn't for counting the misdeeds of Murder, Incorporated but, rather, for counting and displaying the number of visits to your Web page. To use the iWeb hit counter, you have to publish your site using MobileMe, which I describe in Chapter 17.

To add the hit counter, choose Insert➪Button➪Hit Counter. The hit counter appears in the footer in an appropriate position based on the page template, as shown in Figure 16-9, but you can also click it and then drag to move it to a new position.

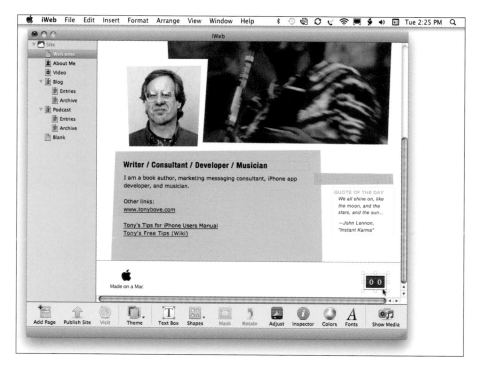

Figure 16-9: Add a hit counter to the footer.

When you publish the site using MobileMe, as I describe in Chapter 17, the hit counter is activated.

Choose Insert➪Button➪Hit Counter again if you want to remove the counter from the page. If you want to reset the counter to zero, remove the counter and then publish the page without it. After publishing, restore the hit counter to the page and publish your page again.

See the section in Chapter 23 about adding an Email Me button to set up a button so that people who visit your page can automatically e-mail you.

Paging Multimedia

Photos and photo albums are the pride and joy of a personal Web site, and iWeb makes it as easy as point-and-click to add a photo album complete with thumbnail images, navigation, and slideshow buttons. Movies are also just a click away — you can add a movie that includes player controls, and you can set the poster frame for the movie's link on the page. You can even add a song or any type of audio file to a Web page so that visitors can click it and listen.

Publishing a Web site carries with it certain responsibilities. Chief among them is not violating anyone else's copyrights with regard to photos, videos, and songs or audio files. (YouTube is a special case that I explain in "Adding Widgets," later in this chapter.) Be certain that you own the copyright and other rights to the material you're posting, or that you obtained all necessary permissions. You've been warned.

Every theme offers a Photos page template for adding photos, a Movies page template for adding movies, and a My Albums page template to create an index page for multiple photo and movie albums.

It's not like you're restricted to adding photos and movies only to the Photos and Movies pages — you can add photos and movies to *any* page by simply dragging them to the page. However, if you want the photos and movies to be automatically added to a My Albums page, they must appear on a Photos or Movies page created from a theme's template.

Adding photos to a Photos page

Every theme offers a Photos page template that uses a grid for automatically sizing and positioning photos as you add them and provides a placeholder caption for each photo. The Photos page also includes a Play Slideshow button that visitors can click to view your photos in a slideshow.

To add a Photos page, follow these steps:

1. Click the Add Page button on the toolbar, or choose File⇨New Page.

The theme chooser appears , as shown in Figure 16-10 (See Chapter 15 for details on themes and page templates.)

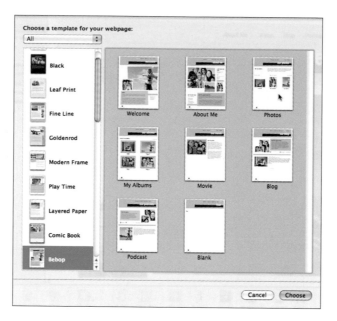

Figure 16-10: Select the Photos page template.

2. **Select a theme from the list on the left and Photos from the page templates on the right, and then click Choose.**

   The new page appears with placeholder photos aligned to a grid.

3. **If the Media Browser isn't open, click Show Media on the toolbar and then click Photos.**

   The Photos browser appears on the right side, as shown in Figure 16-11, with your iPhoto library. (See Chapter 1 for iPhoto info.)

4. **Choose the event or album that contains the photos you want to add.**

   Thumbnails for the event or album appear along the bottom of the Media Browser.

5. **Select thumbnails at the bottom of the Media Browser for the photos you want to add, or select the album name or event title if you're adding the entire album or event.**

   You can select an entire album or event or select thumbnails of the photos you want to add. To select multiple thumbnails in a range, click the first one and Shift-click the last one. To select multiple thumbnails that aren't next to each other, click the first one and Command-click the rest.

Figure 16-11: Drag a photo or an entire album to the page.

6. **Drag and drop the album, event, or photo thumbnails on the photo grid of the Photos page (refer to Figure 16-11).**

   A blue line appears around the photo grid when you drag the photos over it. When you drop the photos, they replace the existing placeholder graphics.

   If you drag only one photo, all extra placeholders in the photo grid disappear. This is a feature, not a bug — iWeb assumes that you want only the photos you've dragged. The next photo you drag is automatically formatted and aligned to the grid like the first one, using the same style and size.

7. **(Optional) Click the placeholder text below each photo and type a caption.**

After dragging your photos to the Photos page, you can drag them to rearrange their order on the page.

When you click a photo on the Photos page, a Photo Grid window appears, as shown on the left side of Figure 16-12.

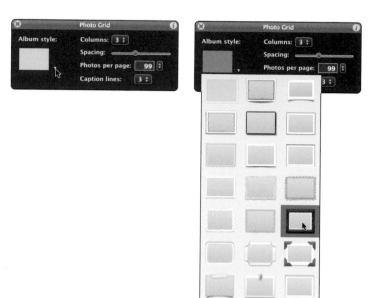

Figure 16-12: Specify a frame and other settings in the Photo Grid window.

Here's what you can do in the Photo Grid window:

- **Change the style and organization of page elements:** Click Album Style to see a pop-up menu of frame styles for all photos on the page, as I do on the right side of in Figure 16-10. You can also change the number of columns and the number of lines for each caption. (Choose 0 for no caption.)

- **Set the Photos per Page option:** The default setting is 99 photos. If you set the Photos per Page option to be lower than the number of photos you've added to the photo grid, iWeb divides the photo grid into multiple pages for your photos and adds page numbers and navigation arrows.

Visitors to your Photos page see an album of photos arranged and framed, just as I show you in Figure 16-13. One great feature of iWeb's Photos page is that when a visitor clicks a photo, the photo automatically appears enlarged, along with a row of thumbnails for other photos along the top and buttons for downloading the photo, navigating more thumbnails, playing a slideshow, and returning to the album page. You don't have to do anything to make these controls appear — iWeb does it all.

Figure 16-13: What the visitor sees before clicking a photo.

If you're placing large, high-quality JPEG images in your iWeb pages and you want to automatically reduce their file sizes with further compression and optimization before publishing them on your site, choose iWeb⊅Preferences and turn on the Optimize Images on Import option. It reduces the size of images you place on your pages by as much as 60 percent.

Adding videos to a Movie page

Every theme offers a Movie page template that offers a placeholder for a video and video playback controls. To add a Movie page and place your video on it, follow these steps:

1. **Click the Add Page button on the toolbar, or choose File⊅New Page.**

   The theme chooser appears (refer to Figure 16-10).

2. **Select a theme from the list on the left and Movie from the page templates on the right, and then click Choose.**

   The new page appears with a placeholder video.

3. **If the Media Browser isn't open, click Show Media on the toolbar and then click Movies.**

The Movies Browser appears on the right side with your iMovie projects that were saved to the Media Browser (see Chapter 11 for details on using videos with iLife applications) and video files in your Movies folder.

4. Choose a video to add.

You can click the Play button at the bottom of the Media Browser to preview the selected video, as I do in Figure 16-14 — I also renamed the Movie page to *Video* in the title. (Apple calls them *movies,* though much of the world refers to them as *videos.*)

5. Drag and drop the video on the placeholder in the Movie page.

After you drop the video, it replaces the existing placeholder video.

6. (Optional) Click the placeholder text below the video and type a caption.

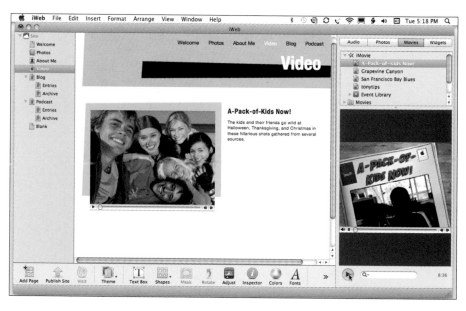

Figure 16-14: Preview the video in the Media Browser before adding it to the Movie page (the renamed Video page).

Adding a My Albums page for photos and videos

Every theme also offers a My Albums page template, which creates a page that acts like a folder for Photos and Movie pages. Each photo album appears on the My Albums page with one of the album's photos as the link. Each video appears on the page with its poster frame as the link. Page visitors can click the photo to view the Photos page with the album or click the poster frame to watch the video. Even cooler — when a visitor moves the pointer across a photo on the My Albums page, the visitor sees a miniature slideshow.

To add a My Albums page, click the Add Page button on the toolbar or choose File↪New Page. In the theme chooser that appears (refer to Figure 16-10), select a theme from the list on the left and My Albums from the page templates on the right, and then click Choose. The new page appears with a placeholder for adding a photo album.

Organizing all your Photos and Movie pages under My Albums

You can set up the My Albums page to be a submenu for all content on your Photos and Movie pages. All you need to do is organize your Photos and Movie pages so that they're within the My Albums page in the Sidebar. iWeb automatically updates the navigation menu bar so that you have a My Albums link rather than a clutter of multiple links to photo and video pages.

To organize your existing Photos and Movie pages so that they're inside the My Albums page, follow these steps:

1. **Drag your Photos and Movie pages to the My Albums page in the Sidebar, as I do in Figure 16-15.**

   The My Albums page opens like a folder in the Sidebar so that you can place the Photos and Movie pages inside.

Figure 16-15: Drag the Photos page inside the My Albums page (which acts like a folder).

2. **In the Sidebar, drag pages up or down to rearrange the order.**

   The order in which they appear underneath the My Albums page determines the order in which their photo and video links appear on the My Albums page.

   The My Albums page name in the Sidebar opens and closes like a folder — click the triangle next to My Albums to open or close it.

3. **(Optional) Rename the My Albums page (My Stuff or Shows, for example), just as you rename any page.**

   The new name appears on the navigation menu bar.

After dragging your Photos and Movie pages inside the My Albums page, select the My Albums page — it should look similar to Figure 16-16. If you have multiple Photos and Movie pages inside the My Albums page, all of them are represented on the My Albums page — the first photo appears for a photo album, and the poster frame appears for a video.

Figure 16-16: Drag a photo album directly to your My Albums page.

Customizing a My Albums page

To switch the photo for a photo album, simply rearrange the Photos page to put the photo you want first, as I describe in "Adding photos to a Photos page," earlier in this chapter. (In the later section "Refreshing the content on your My Albums page," I show you how to set the poster frame.)

Click a photo album on the My Albums page to open the Media Index window, shown in Figure 16-17. You can change the layout and format of the My Albums page, including the number of columns and column spacing. You can also choose from the Album Animation pop-up menu a transition effect between photos in a slideshow. Deselect the Show Title option to make the titles disappear. You can turn off the number of photos below each photo album title by deselecting the Show Number option.

Figure 16-17: Click a photo album for the Media Index window.

Refreshing the content on your My Albums page

You can drag more photo albums and videos directly to the My Albums page (refer to Figure 16-16). After you drag a photo album to the My Albums page, iWeb automatically creates a new Photos page for the album, as shown in Figure 16-18.

If you want to allow page visitors to subscribe to an RSS feed of the My Albums page — to update them on additions and modifications — turn on the Allow Subscribe option. The Subscribe button appears on the right side of the My Albums page above the photos (refer to Figure 16-16). I explain RSS feeds in "Entering Blog Heaven," later in this chapter.

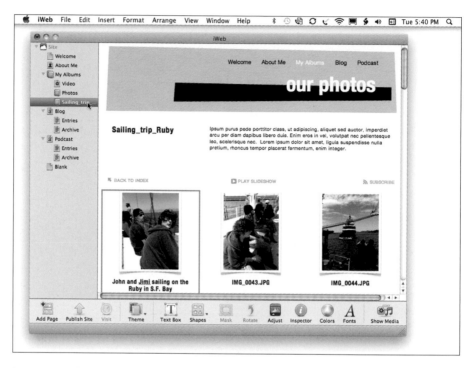

Figure 16-18: The Photos page for the photo album is automatically created.

Adjusting photos and slideshows

You can regain some of the detail lost in a photo by using the Adjust tool and then adjusting the Brightness, Contrast, and Saturation sliders. These sliders show the effects of changes immediately. Follow these steps:

1. **Select a photo on a page and click the Adjust button on the toolbar.**

   The Adjust Image window appears on top of the page, as shown in Figure 16-19.

2. **Try clicking the Enhance button to see whether the automatic adjustment works best.**

3. **To make further adjustments, drag the sliders left or right to make changes.**

   You can bring out some details in photos taken in poor lighting conditions by adjusting the Brightness and Contrast sliders. You use the sliders to make incremental adjustments: Drag each slider gradually until you see the effect you want, or click anywhere along the slider bar to jump directly to a setting.

Figure 16-19: Adjust a photo's brightness, contrast, saturation, and other settings.

4. **If you don't like all the changes you made, you can click the Reset Image button at the bottom of the Adjust Image window to reset the sliders to their original settings.**

5. **To finish making adjustments, click the circled *x* in the upper left corner.**

Visitors to your site can download photos from a photo album on a Photos page, though you may want to control the size of the photos they download or set the size to None to disallow downloading. Follow these steps to choose settings:

1. **Select a photo on a Photos page and click the Inspector button on the toolbar.**

2. **Click the Photos Inspector button (second from the left at the top of the Inspector window), as shown on the left side of Figure 16-20.**

3. **You can then select a size (or None) from the Photo Download Size pop-up menu.**

Figure 16-20: Change settings for a photo album (left), slideshow (center), and video (right).

The Photos Inspector is also where you control settings for the features described in this list:

✔ **Subscribing via RSS:** You can turn on the Allow Visitors to Subscribe option, which allows visitors to subscribe to an RSS feed of the Photos page. (A Subscribe button appears on the top of the page.) I explain RSS feeds in "Entering Blog Heaven," later in this chapter.

✔ **Photo comments:** If you want to allow visitors to leave comments attached to your photos in the album, turn on the Allow Comments option (refer to the left side of Figure 16-20). If you allow comments, you can also allow attachments so that visitors can upload pictures attached to your photo. You can also turn on or off the Display Comment Indicator option.

✔ **Slideshows:** Click the Slideshow tab in the Photos Inspector, as I do in the center of Figure 16-20, to enable the Slideshow button for the Photos page so that visitors can play a slideshow of the photo album. Don't forget to choose a transition between slides on the Transitions pop-up menu. Turn on the Show Reflection option for a nice reflection of the image during the show, and turn on the Show Captions option to show captions with each image. Turn on the Full Screen option to allow visitors to click the Full Screen button to see the slideshow in full-screen view.

Adjusting video

To adjust a video, select the video on a Movie page, click the Inspector button on the toolbar, and then click the Q (for QuickTime) icon in the upper right corner of the Inspector window, as I do on the right side of Figure 16-20, in the earlier section "Adjusting photos and slideshows." Here's a look at the options you can set:

✔ **Start and stop frames of the video:** Drag the left corner (start) or the right corner (stop), or both — you can see the video frames on the page as you drag.

✔ **Poster frame:** Drag the Poster Frame slider to the frame you want.

✔ **Movie controller:** Turn on the Show Movie Controller option to display the movie controller underneath the video (or turn off the option to remove the controller).

✔ **Autoplay:** The Autoplay option starts playing the video as soon as the visitor visits the Movie page, and the Loop option makes the video loop continuously after the visitor starts playing it — combining Autoplay with Loop produces a kiosk-like, never-ending video. You should turn off the Show Movie Controller option if you want the video to play just like a kiosk.

Adding audio files

If you're a musician with songs, a book author with audio versions of your chapters, or anyone who simply wants to play sounds or voice-overs on your Web page, you'll like the iWeb audio feature. You can add a song or an audio file to any page of your Web site so that visitors can listen to it while visiting the page.

Your page automatically includes audio controls that visitors can use to play, rewind, fast-forward, and scrub over the audio and to change the volume. You can add an image (or a text box with text) about the song or audio file. You can even drag multiple audio files to a single page.

To add an audio file to a page, follow these steps:

1. **Select the page in the Sidebar on the left side of the iWeb window.**

2. **If the Media Browser isn't open, click the Show Media button on the toolbar and then click the Audio button.**

   The Audio Browser appears. You can select audio files from your Music folder, including GarageBand compositions and iTunes songs, audio podcasts, and audiobooks.

3. **Drag one or more audio files from the Audio Browser to the page.**

   You can drag a single audio file to a media placeholder or drag one or more audio files to an empty area of the page. An image placeholder, with audio controls, appears on the page for each audio file. (If you dragged a single file to a media placeholder, the new image placeholder replaces it.) You can then add an image to each placeholder.

4. **(Optional) Resize the image placeholder for each audio file by dragging its boundaries.**

   Drag any boundary to resize the image placeholder. Hold down the Shift key to resize the placeholder in the same proportions. You can also drag the placeholder to another position on the page.

5. **Drag an image for the image placeholder, as shown in Figure 16-21.**

Figure 16-21: Drag an image for the audio file.

To add links to songs in your iTunes library without adding the audio files, drag a playlist from the Media Browser or iTunes to the page. Links to songs appear on the page and take visitors to the iTunes Store, where they can preview and purchase the songs. You can also drag a song or an album from the iTunes Store to the page, which is useful if you have music to sell or you want to show a playlist of music that you don't own.

To see the name of an audio file you've added to a page, select the image placeholder for the audio file, click the Inspector button on the toolbar, and then click the Metrics Inspector button. The name of the file appears at the top of the Metrics Inspector.

Entering Blog Heaven

A *blog* resembles a diary in reverse: The first entry a visitor reads is the most recent, followed by previous entries. That makes a blog an open-ended diary that's never completed because you continue adding entries as you go along. Your blog may not be as interesting to the wide public as *The Basketball Diaries* or *Diary of a Mad Black Woman,* or as useful for setting public policy as *The Journals of Lewis and Clark,* but personal blogs have gained a large following (such as *Kahlee's Blog: Never Give a Cheerleader a Keyboard* and *Will Blog for Cake*). Many professional news sites (such as *TechCrunch* and *Daily Kos*) began as the personal blogs of enterprising individuals.

A *podcast* is a blog that plays an audio or a video. Podcasts are similar to syndicated radio and TV shows, except that people can download podcasts into iTunes and play them at their convenience on their computers and on iPods or iPhones. Podcasts are also segmented into *episodes,* which are similar to blog entries — the first is the most recent.

Putting on the RSS

Although visitors can visit a blog's Web page, they can also (or instead) subscribe to a blog's RSS feed. The standard format Really Simple Syndication (RSS) is designed for publishing frequently updated works. By *subscribe,* I mean that you can access blog entries using a browser's RSS reader or an RSS widget that appears on another Web page. (See the later section "Incorporating Widgets" for more about RSS widgets.)

Podcasts work the same way: Though visitors can download each episode manually, they can also download new episodes automatically by way of a subscription. Visitors can use iTunes to subscribe to your podcast so that it shows up in their iTunes Podcasts panes with new episodes downloaded automatically.

That's what RSS widgets, RSS readers, and iTunes do — check RSS feeds for new entries. The process is similar to a magazine subscription that's updated with a new issue every month or so. You don't have to register or fill out a form, and you don't have to provide an e-mail address or any other information.

Though a blog consists mostly of text and graphics (with hyperlinks, of course), a podcast can be anything from a single song to a commentary-hosted radio show. Podcasts are saved in the MP3 format and can be used with any media player, device, or application that supports MP3, including an iPod or iPhone.

iWeb publishes an RSS feed of your blog and podcast. RSS feeds are typically linked to a button labeled RSS or Subscribe — iWeb supplies a Subscribe button on Blog, Podcast, Photos, and Movie pages that visitors can click to subscribe to your feeds. Visitors using a feed reader, an aggregator application, or a browser plug-in can automatically check RSS-enabled Web pages and display updated blog entries and podcasts. RSS is supported directly by many Web browsers, including Apple Safari for Mac OS X.

Birth of a blog

To create a blog, follow these steps:

1. **Click the Add Page button on the toolbar, or choose File➪New Page.**

   The theme chooser appears (refer to Figure 16-10).

2. **Select a theme from the list on the left and Blog from the page templates on the right, and then click Choose.**

   The first blog entry appears with the current date, as shown in Figure 16-22. iWeb also creates the Entries and Archive pages in the Sidebar inside the Blog page, which acts like a folder.

3. **Double-click the `our blog` placeholder text to replace the blog's header with your own.**

Figure 16-22: A blog is born.

After you set up your blog in iWeb, you can add entries to your blog and edit them as described in this list:

- ✔ **Adding multimedia:** Most themes offer a Blog page with a media placeholder — you can drag an image, an audio file, or a movie to this media placeholder to enhance your blog. Drag images from the Photo Browser to the media placeholders in the entries (or delete the placeholders if you don't need them).

- ✔ **Adding a new blog entry:** Click the Entries page in the Sidebar. Visitors don't see this page — you use it to edit your blog entries. The theme is supplied with two placeholder entries, as shown in Figure 16-23. You can edit these entries by selecting each one in the Title list and making changes in the entry below the list. To add a new entry, click the Add Entry button.

  After you publish your blog, the Blog page contains excerpts (the opening text) from your most recent blog entries. Visitors can click the Read More button to see the whole entry.

- ✔ **Deleting an entry:** Select the entry in the Title list and click the Delete Entry button.

Figure 16-23: Edit an existing blog entry.

✔ **Editing titles:** To edit the entry title, double-click the text box (as I do in Figure 16-23) and type a new title; do the same for the body text of the entry.

✔ **Changing the date and time of a blog entry:** Click the date above the entry, as shown in Figure 16-24. A calendar appears for selecting a date, or you can click the arrows next to the month, day, and year to select a date. You can also set the time and change the date format on the pop-up menu.

✔ **Editing the layout of an entry:** You can change the placement of elements in a blog entry, the space between elements, the size of any photos, and other settings by clicking the blog entry on the Blog page to open the Blog Summary window, shown on the left side of Figure 16-25. The Photo Proportion pop-up menu lets you change the orientation to Square, Portrait, Landscape, or Original.

Figure 16-24: Change the date of an entry.

To change the number of excerpts shown, the excerpt length on the Blog page, or other RSS-related settings, click the *i* in the upper right corner of the Blog Summary window to bring up the Blog & Podcast Inspector window (refer to the right side of Figure 16-25). (You can also reach this window by clicking the Inspector button on the toolbar and clicking the RSS button at the top of the Inspector window.) Be sure to turn on the Display Search Field option to give your visitors a Search field on the Blog page for searching for a phrase throughout your entries.

Figure 16-25: Change blog layout settings (left) and RSS settings (right).

If you publish your site using MobileMe (as I describe in Chapter 17), you can turn on the Allow Comments option to allow visitors to leave comments on each blog entry. If you also turn on the Allow attachments option, visitors can attach files (such as photos) to their comments. To prevent automated programs from posting spam as blog comments, anyone who posts a comment is first required to type a displayed word.

The Archive page contains all your entries sorted by date, including those that don't appear on the main Blog page — but the Blog pages include a link to the archive so that your visitors can find it.

Setting up a podcast

Podcasts are easy to set up. For one thing, they're just like blogs, and for another, you set them up the same way as you do a blog in iWeb. The only difference is that you choose a Podcast page template and drag an audio file or a video file to the media placeholder.

To set up a podcast, follow these steps:

1. **Click the Add Page button on the toolbar, or choose File⇨New Page.**

    The theme chooser appears (refer to Figure 16-10).

2. **Select a theme from the list on the left and Podcast from the page templates on the right, and then click Choose.**

    The first podcast episode appears with the current date. iWeb also creates the Entries and Archive pages in the Sidebar inside the Podcast page, which acts like the Blog page.

3. **Double-click the** `our podcast` **placeholder text to replace the podcast header with your own.**

The Podcast page contains excerpts (the opening text) from your most recent episodes. To add a new episode, follow these steps:

1. **Click the Entries page in the Sidebar under Podcast.**

2. **If this is your first entry, select the first entry (a dummy entry supplied by iWeb) in the Title list; if not, click the Add Entry button to add a new entry.**

3. **To edit the title of the entry for the episode, double-click the text box and type a new title.**

4. **Click in the body text of the entry to edit the episode's text.**

5. **If your podcast episode is an MP3 audio file, drag it from the Audio Browser to the media placeholder in the entry, as I do in Figure 16-26; if it's a video file, drag it from the Movies Browser to the placeholder.**

6. **(Optional) Drag an image from the Photo Browser to the media place-holder to include an image.**

7. **(Optional) To change the date of an episode, click the date above the entry and, in the calendar that appears, select a date, just like a blog (refer to Figure 16-24).**

Dragging a podcast file

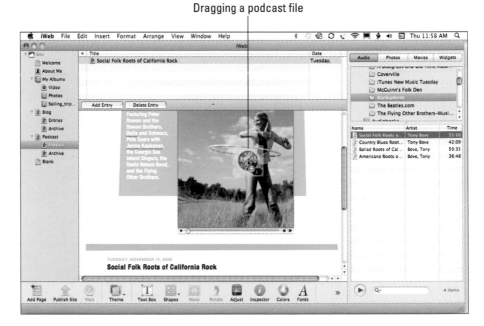

Figure 16-26: Drag an audio file to the placeholder in a podcast episode entry.

8. (Optional) To change the placement of elements in the episode, the space between elements, and all other settings associated with a typical blog entry, click the episode on the Podcast page to bring up the Blog Summary window (refer to Figure 16-25).

9. To change the RSS-related settings for a podcast, click the *i* in the upper right corner of the Blog Summary window to bring up the Blog & Podcast Inspector window, and then click the Podcast tab at the top, as shown in Figure 16-27.

10. Add the artist and contact e-mail, and set podcast options (refer to Figure 16-27).

Type a name for the series artist (the podcast producer or featured artist), add the contact e-mail address for the podcast, and select the Allow Podcast in iTunes Store option so that your podcast appears in the store. You also need to choose Clean, Explicit, or None from the Parental Advisory pop-up menu. You can also change the settings for each episode: the artist, the parental advisory, and the option to allow the episode in the store. The Duration field is filled in by iWeb when you save your project.

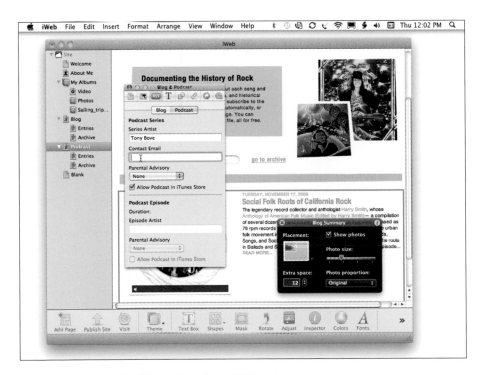

Figure 16-27: Specify the RSS settings for publishing the podcast.

To delete an episode, select its entry in the Title list and click the Delete Entry button — just like a blog.

Incorporating Widgets

Widgets are snippets of code (available on other sites) that you can add to your Web page. (The word *widget* is a deliberately invented word meant to suggest *gadget,* but I remember an old James Garner movie, *The Wheeler Dealers,* that introduced a fictional company named "Universal Widgets.")

iWeb offers a few widgets that let you add RSS feeds, iSight photos and videos, a countdown timer, a Google map, and YouTube videos. If you're familiar with the HyperText Markup Language (HTML), you can also manually add HTML code snippets to your site as widgets.

Adding a widget to your page is simplicity itself: If the Media Browser isn't open, click Show Media on the toolbar and then click Widgets in the upper right corner. The Widgets Browser appears on the right side, as shown in Figure 16-28. Drag a widget, such as YouTube, to the Canvas and place it anywhere on a page. You can then resize the widget's area by dragging its boundaries. If you're connected to the Internet, the widget starts working immediately.

Figure 16-28: Drag the YouTube widget and enter the URL of the video.

After selecting the widget, its property window appears so that you can set up the widget with your information. For example, I entered the URL for the YouTube video in the YouTube widget's property window (refer to Figure 16-28). I then turned on the Show Related Videos option so that related videos appear as thumbnails for visitors to check out.

The settings in the property window that appears above the widget depends on the widget you select. For example, if you drag a Google AdSense widget to place Google ads on your site, you can change the size of the widget from the Select Ad Format pop-up menu, and its color in the Select Ad Color menu.

Before using the Google AdSense widget, choose File⇨Set Up Google AdSense to set up a Google AdSense account or use an existing one. (Be sure to connect to the Internet if your Mac isn't already connected.) Supply an e-mail address and a zip code or phone number for an existing account and click Submit, or click Create A New Account and follow the instructions.

Maps are just as easy to add to your page as other widgets. Drag the Google Maps widget, enter your address in the Address field, and click Apply. The map changes to the address you entered. You can drag the map's boundaries to change its size.

To enter HTML code into your page, drag the HTML Snippet widget. You can then enter the code into the HTML Snippet window (or paste it into the window after copying it from another site).

Managing and Publishing Your Site

In This Chapter

▶ Rearranging, deleting, and renaming pages

▶ Creating multiple sites

▶ Publishing your site with MobileMe or FTP

▶ Updating your Facebook profile

▶ Updating and protecting your site

The *New Yorker* journalist A. J. Liebling pointed out the hypocrisy of a free press in the 1930s: "Freedom of the press is guaranteed only to those who own one." The World Wide Web now brings a printing press to your door, mostly for free (except for the service fee from the hosting service, such as MobileMe). The major cost of publishing a Web site is putting it together, which is what Chapter 15 and Chapter 16 are all about.

After iWeb helps you put together a Web site, the moment of truth arrives for you to publish it. This chapter shows you how to set up your site for publishing by way of MobileMe or another hosting service. You also find out how to rearrange pages for navigation, delete pages, rename the site, and protect it from invaders.

On Becoming a Webmaster

In days of old, when the Web was young, the Webmaster needed to be versed in the intricacies of HTML and experienced in using many different tools to assemble and organize all the pages, graphics, video files, and widgets for a Web site. Images needed to be scaled, compressed, and stored in their own folder before being linked to the page with complex hyperlinks; video needed to be rendered at lower resolutions and uploaded separately; the code for navigation buttons on all the pages needed to be modified with every new or renamed page. Widgets interfered with page loading, and webmasters worked overtime to keep their newly formed blogs from being infiltrated by nefarious hackers and spam kings.

Now a Webmaster can focus more on the marketing of a site, because tools such as iWeb work like magic to keep sites well managed and organized. iWeb not only handles the work of maintaining hyperlinks and navigation menus behind the scenes but also takes care of scaling and compressing images and videos without forcing you to maintain a separate set of files and folders on your hard drive. When you publish your site, iWeb gathers all its media elements and assembles its pages and then copies all these elements to the Web server at MobileMe (or your hosting service). You can still "publish" your Web site pages to a folder on your hard drive — which is useful if you have a Web server on your computer or your computer has Web Sharing turned on or you want to edit the HTML files before copying the pages to your Web server or hosting service.

As a result of iWeb's magic, you can rename and rearrange pages without having to fix the navigation, and even rename the site without having to fix innumerable hyperlinks.

Publishing page and site changes

You will most likely want to update your Web site frequently. If you have a blog or podcast, you will probably want to add new material regularly — perhaps even daily. If you rearrange, rename, or delete pages, iWeb needs to record those changes on your hosted site.

To make your changes and new content public on the Internet, you publish your site again from iWeb, as I describe in the later section "Publishing Your Site." You can choose to publish only the changes to your site or publish the entire site. Publishing only changes is faster than publishing an entire site — all the pages you changed since the last time you published are published again, keeping it a mirror image of the one you have in iWeb. However, you need to publish your *entire* site again if your site's navigation menu changed (because of rearranging or renaming or deleting pages).

Rearranging pages for navigation

iWeb automatically puts a navigation menu bar on every page of your Web site for visitors to click to go to other pages. When you add a new page, iWeb automatically adds a link for it to the navigation menu bar. You can change the order of links on the menu by rearranging the pages in the Sidebar. The navigation menu is automatically updated to reflect the new organization. Note, however, that your My Albums, Blog, and Podcast pages must still keep their pages underneath them so that they work correctly. See Chapter 16 for details about these page types.

The first page in the Sidebar below the site name is your Web site's home page — the first page that visitors see. To make a different page the home page, drag it to the top of the list, just below the site name.

You may have pages that you don't want to include in the navigation bar — for example, if you have too many pages to fit in the navigation bar, you could create other links to those pages. To remove a page link from the navigation bar so that it doesn't appear in the other pages' navigation menus, select the page in the Sidebar, click the Inspector button on the toolbar to open the Inspector window, click the leftmost button (Page Inspector) at the top the Inspector window, and then click the Page tab of the Page Inspector. You can then turn off the Include Page in Navigation Menu option for the selected page so that it's removed from the navigation menus.

After rearranging pages in iWeb, you need to publish from iWeb to show those changes on the Internet.

Creating multiple sites

You can create more than one site in iWeb, and manage and publish multiple sites. Choose File➪New Site to create a new site, which appears below the first site in the Sidebar (also known as the *start site*). The template chooser appears so that you can create a new page for the site.

After you have created a new site, you can rename it (see the later section "Renaming a page or site"), create more pages inside it, and link to a new site from the first site by dragging the new site name from the Sidebar directly to a page in the first site. You can also set the new site's publishing settings by clicking the site name in the Sidebar — see "Publishing Your Site," later in this chapter, for details on changing site publishing settings.

Deleting pages and sites

You can delete a page or an entire site by selecting it in the Sidebar and pressing the Delete key or choosing Edit⇨Delete (which becomes Delete Page, Delete My Albums Page, Delete Blog, Delete Site, and so on, depending on the type of page you select).

The page is automatically removed from its site's navigation menu, and the page itself is permanently deleted — unless you immediately choose Edit⇨Undo Delete. (The photos, videos, and audio files you linked to the page aren't changed, but the text, graphic elements, and widgets you added to the page are gone.)

An iWeb site must contain at least one page, so if you try to delete the only page in a site, the Template Chooser appears so that you can create a new page.

If you already published a site to the Internet (hosted by MobileMe or another service), deleting the site or one of its pages in iWeb doesn't immediately delete the element from the Internet. The site or page is removed from the Internet the next time you publish using iWeb.

If you delete a published page or site and don't republish the page or site with the same name, visitors who try to visit the page or site by typing the URL or using a bookmark see the cryptic message that the page or site couldn't be found.

Renaming a page or site

Renaming a site or even a page is tricky. The best time to do it — regardless of whether you use iWeb or another tool — is *before* you publish your site and tell others about it. The reason is that your site's name and page name appear in the URL for the site. (A *URL* is the address a visitor types, or bookmarks, to reach a site).

For example, iWeb gives your site the default name Site when you create it. When you publish the first site (the first one listed in the Sidebar) using the default name, the iWeb creates the following URL for the Web site on MobileMe:

    http://web.me.com/YourMemberName

If you rename the site name before publishing it, or if you create more sites, iWeb gives you this URL for the first and subsequent sites on MobileMe:

    http://web.me.com/YourMemberName/SiteName

(If you continue using the default name Site for the first site and Site 2 and Site 3 for subsequent sites, iWeb adds an underscore, as in Site_2, Site_3, and so on, before using it as the *SiteName* for the URL.)

You can quite easily rename the site: Double-click the name in the Sidebar and type the new name. But if you publish a site and later rename it, previously created links to your site (such as bookmarks created by your visitors) don't work.

The same statement is true of pages within the site: The page name appears in the URL for that page, and visitors can see the page name displayed at the top of their browser windows. Renaming pages after you've published the site may require that you notify visitors to change their bookmarks.

Publishing Your Site

Your Web site doesn't exist as a true Web site until you publish it on the World Wide Web. Also, the changes you make in iWeb *after* publishing your site don't take effect on your site until you publish the site again.

If you have a MobileMe subscription, you can publish one or more sites using MobileMe.

You can also publish one or more sites to a third-party hosting service using FTP (File Transfer Protocol), which is built into iWeb, whether or not you have a MobileMe subscription. Most people use this option to publish into their own domains that are already set up for them.

As a backup, or to use your Mac as a Web server for your site, you can publish one or more sites to a folder. You can then turn on Web sharing or use Web server software on your Mac.

If you create more than one site in iWeb, you can publish each one separately, to whichever host you want — some to MobileMe and others to a different hosting service using FTP.

To publish a site, select the site in the Sidebar, set the site's publishing settings as I describe in the next few sections, and click the Publish Site button on the toolbar. (You can also choose File➪Publish Entire Site.) To publish only the changed pages of a site, choose File➪Publish Site Changes. Publishing only the changes is faster than publishing your entire site. However, you need to publish your *entire* site again if its navigation menu changed (because of rearranging or renaming or deleting pages).

Sites and pages that have been published are blue in the iWeb Sidebar, and sites and pages that have changed (even slightly) are red so that you can see whether a site needs to be published.

Going MobileMe

For one-click publishing, try MobileMe. You get all the advanced features of iWeb: password protection, hit counter, enhanced slideshows, blog searching, and visitor comments on your blog, podcast, and photos.

When you publish one or more sites using MobileMe, iWeb generates a URL for the site in the format `http://web.me.com/`*YourMemberName*. (See the earlier section "Renaming a page or site" for details.) To set up your own domain name using MobileMe, see the later section "Setting up your own domain."

Be sure that your site and pages are named the way you want *before* publishing them the first time. Click the site's name in the Sidebar. The Site Publishing Settings window appears, as shown in Figure 17-1. You can change your site's name (if you want) and set the Publish To pop-up menu to MobileMe, if it isn't set already.

Figure 17-1: Set the publishing settings for the site.

You can also add your e-mail address for the Email Me button. (See Chapter 23 for details on adding it.) MobileMe offers password protection, which I cover in "Protecting Your Site," later in this chapter, and the ability to notify your Facebook friends, which I describe in "Notifying Facebook," later in this chapter.

One-click publishing

If you have a MobileMe account and are already logged in to it, you can publish one or more sites to MobileMe the first time by selecting the site in the Sidebar and clicking the Publish Site button on the toolbar. (You can also choose File⇨Publish Entire Site.) To publish only the changed pages of a site, choose File⇨Publish Site Changes.

Before iWeb publishes the site, it displays a warning about content rights — be sure that you own the copyrights and other rights or have the necessary permissions. Click Continue, and iWeb displays a message telling you that publishing will continue in the background as you work in iWeb. Don't quit iWeb until publishing finishes.

Depending on how large your site is, it can take several minutes to publish. When finished, iWeb displays a message that your site has been published, as shown in Figure 17-2, and you can click Visit Site Now to go to the site in your Web browser, as I do in Figure 17-3.

Figure 17-2: Visit the site after publishing.

Click the Announce button (refer to Figure 17-2) to create an e-mail message in Mail that's ready to address and send — the message includes the text and link you can use to notify people about your Web site.

Setting up your own domain

So you want to be king of your own domain? You don't like web.me.com and your MobileMe username as the base URL for your sites? You can choose your own domain name to use with MobileMe (such as www.tonybove.com, which is what I use).

Figure 17-3: The Welcome page for the site appears on the Web.

You need to register your own domain name first (visit an accredited domain name registrar on the Internet and register the name) before you can set it up using MobileMe and use it as the URL for one or more sites you create with iWeb. You are still publishing to MobileMe, but using your domain name as an alias.

To help you use your registered domain name, MobileMe guides you through the process of changing the CNAME for your registered domain to `web. me.com` — but you must first ensure that your registrar allows it. Some domain registrars require you to contact them first, before making this kind of CNAME adjustment. Contact your domain registrar for more information.

If you can't enable MobileMe to change your CNAME or can't change it yourself, you can still publish to your own domain, as long as it's hosted by a service provider — see the later section "Using another service (the FTP method)."

To continue setting up your own domain with MobileMe, follow these steps.

1. **Choose File⇨Set Up Personal Domain on MobileMe.**

   The MobileMe login window appears in your browser.

2. **Type your account name and password and click Log In.**

   The Personal Domain window appears, as shown in Figure 17-4.

3. **Click the Add Domain button, enter your personal domain name in the Domain Name and Confirm Domain text fields, and then click Continue.**

4. **Follow the instructions to go to the Web site of your registrar (use a separate browser window) and enter your "www" CNAME.**

   The CNAME for your domain is web.me.com. Be careful when you enter the domain name, because some registrars require a period at the end of it, as in "web.me.com."

5. **Return to the MobileMe window and click Done.**

   It may take as long as 48 hours for your registered domain to begin pointing to your MobileMe site.

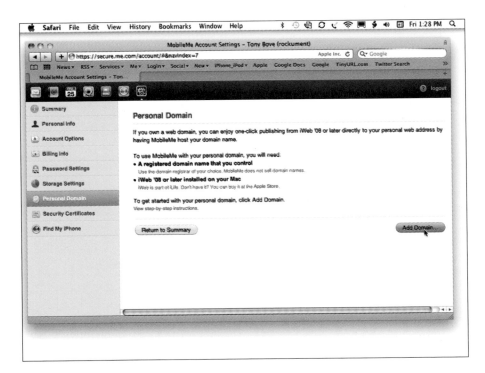

Figure 17-4: Add your personal domain to MobileMe.

After setting your domain name, publishing to MobileMe publishes directly to this domain name and provides all the features of a MobileMe-hosted site.

Using another service (the FTP method)

Using a third-party service is often a requirement — and may be an advantage over MobileMe, depending on the services provided. You can choose your own domain name, and you may be able to use databases and turn on features such as visitor tracking for each page (depending on the service). You may prefer a blogging system such as WordPress (offered by many services), or you may have other needs that only a third-party service can provide.

The File Transfer Protocol (FTP) has been in use since the late 1970s, and iWeb uses it to enable you to publish your iWeb site to any service that supports FTP for the domain you've established at that service. I have never met a service that didn't support FTP, so this method is probably the most universal for uploading a site.

Before publishing your site, you need to set up FTP. Follow these steps:

1. **Click the site's name in the Sidebar.**

   The Site Publishing Settings window appears (refer to Figure 17-1).

2. **Choose FTP Server from the Publish To pop-up menu, as shown in Figure 17-5.**

3. **Change your site's name, if you want.**

4. **Add your e-mail address if you want an Email Me button to appear in your site.**

   See Chapter 23 for details on adding this button.

5. **(Optional) Notify your Facebook friends about the new site or site update, which I describe in "Notifying Facebook," later in this chapter.**

6. **Fill in the FTP Server Settings (refer to Figure 17-5).**

   The Server address usually begins with `ftp.` but you must check first with your service provider.

7. **Enter the username and password you use for the service provider, and enter in the Directory/Path field any special directory or path for the site.**

Figure 17-5: Set the publishing settings for using FTP.

8. **If your service provider offers the options of FTP with Implicit SSL, FTP with TLS/SSL, or STP (which sounds like a faster, well-oiled version), choose it from the Protocol pop-up menu.**

   Otherwise, leave the pop-up menu set to normal FTP.

9. **If your service provider requires that you use a specific port number, enter the number in the Port field.**

   Otherwise, leave the port number set to its default value.

10. **Enter the Web site's domain name or root for the URL of your site in the Website URL section's URL field (refer to Figure 17-5).**

11. **Test your FTP connection by clicking Test Connection, which can save time spent debugging any site publishing issues.**

After entering your FTP server settings and Web site URL, you can publish the site by clicking the Publish Site button on the toolbar. (You can also choose File⇨Publish Entire Site or choose File⇨Publish Site Changes to publish only the changes.)

Publishing to a folder on your hard drive

You can also "publish" your iWeb site to a folder on your hard drive —
which is useful for making a backup of the site as an archive or serving the
site yourself on your Mac with Web server software or by turning on Web
Sharing. Publishing to a folder can also be useful if you want to edit the HTML
files before copying the pages to a Web server or hosting service.

To publish your site to a folder, follow these steps:

1. **Click the site's name in the Sidebar.**

   The Site Publishing Settings window appears (refer to Figure 17-1).

2. **Choose Local Folder from the Publish To pop-up menu, as shown in
   Figure 17-6.**

3. **Change your site's name, if you want.**

4. **Add your e-mail address for the Email Me button. (See Chapter 23 for
   details on adding this button.)**

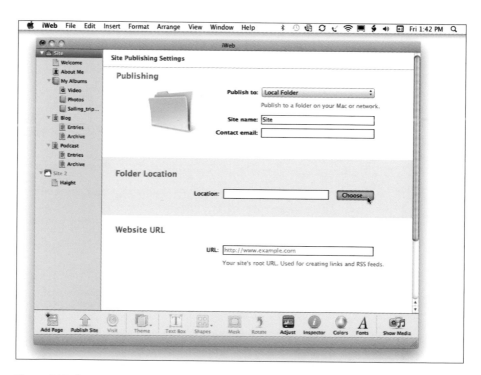

Figure 17-6: Set the publishing settings for using a local folder.

5. **Type the Web site's domain name or root for the URL of your site in the Website URL section's URL field (refer to Figure 17-6).**

6. **Click the Choose button to choose a folder for the Location field.**

Notifying Facebook

The fastest way to build traffic to your new site is to notify people directly, and Facebook is currently the most popular social media site. If you publish your site using MobileMe or FTP, you can automatically update your profile with a notice about your new site or site update, and anyone who can see your profile can click a link to go directly to your site.

Before publishing your site, click the site's name in the Sidebar. The Site Publishing Settings window appears (refer to Figure 17-1). You can then scroll the Site Publishing Settings window to the Facebook section at the bottom, as shown in Figure 17-7. Turn on the Update My Facebook Profile When I Publish This Site option.

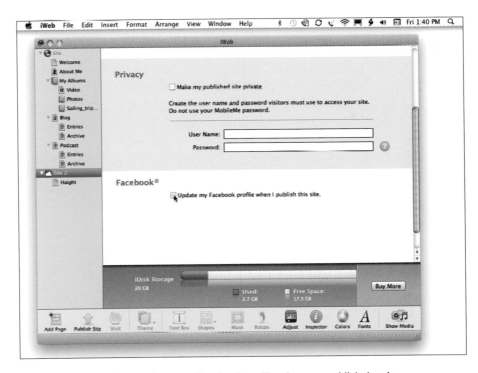

Figure 17-7: Set iWeb to update your Facebook profile when you publish the site.

After you click the Facebook option, a dialog appears for logging in to your Facebook account or creating a new one. Enter your e-mail address and password for your Facebook account and click Login, or click Sign Up for Facebook and follow the instructions to set up an account.

Protecting Your Site

Remember that anyone who has access to the Internet can visit your site. I recommend never putting sensitive information on a Web site. However, you may want to protect a site in order to charge admission to it or to collaborate on a project but keep it private to the world. Small companies may want to set up a private site to exchange information among employees. You can set a site to be private if you use MobileMe to publish it. You can set a username and password so that visitors have to type both before entering the site.

To password-protect a site, follow these steps:

1. **Select the site's name in the Sidebar before publishing it.**

   The Site Publishing Settings window appears (refer to Figure 17-1).

2. **Scroll the Site Publishing Settings window to the Privacy section at the bottom (refer to Figure 17-7).**

3. **Turn on the Make My Published Site Private option, and then enter a username and password for visitors to enter the private site.**

   If you don't enter a username and password, the site is truly private — only you can access it via iWeb!

Part V
Playing in the GarageBand

The 5th Wave   By Rich Tennant

"Composing with this software is so much like composing with a band. Even the drum preset launches late and is usually a little buggy."

*1*n Part V, you rock out with GarageBand to create songs, podcast episodes, or even iPhone ringtones. You can then use these songs in other projects, such as iWeb sites and iMovie soundtracks.

- ✓ In Chapter 18 you see what GarageBand can do and how to play your instrument, start a jam with the Magic Band, and explore the GarageBand window.

- ✓ Chapter 19 gets you plugging and playing with everything you need, from microphones and USB keyboards to electric guitar connections and audio interfaces.

- ✓ In Chapter 20, you get your mojo working with a new project, creating tracks and setting up track instruments and special effects, including all the simulated amplifier settings and pedals you could ever want.

- ✓ Chapter 21 shows you how to arrange tracks, work with track regions in the timeline, record into a cycle region to overdub or overlay instruments, and make podcast episodes.

- ✓ Chapter 22 describes how to control volume and panning for each track, set the master track controls to get the best mix, and share your creation with the world by way of iTunes or by exporting it.

18

What You Can Do with GarageBand

*N*othing moves you quite like a song. Making music is a tradition in every culture on the planet and serves as a global language that everyone recognizes and understands. Blind Lemon Jefferson wrote songs more than a century ago, traveled the dusty countryside singing and playing the blues, and died penniless, but one of his songs was included in a probe that's heading out of our solar system. The man's music will live on forever. Your music can, too.

GarageBand can get you started as a musician, if you're not one already. It offers extensive Learn to Play lessons that walk you through the basic techniques of playing guitar and piano. You can also purchase and download guitar and piano lessons from famous artists.

GarageBand also turns your Mac into a home recording studio. You can use the program's royalty-free loops for your songs, perform with software instruments that are built into GarageBand, and add recordings of real instruments to the mix, if you want — you can even plug in a guitar and use the built-in GarageBand amplifier simulators. You can record studio-quality music, as its name implies, in your garage or home or wherever else you use your Mac — even at your favorite coffeehouse.

Performing and recording have come a long way since the Beatles played live acoustic instruments in a Liverpool back yard and the Kingsmen practiced "Louie, Louie" in their garages in Oregon. GarageBand is ready for the do-it-yourself-in-a-garage attitude — it brings some basic functions of a Pro Tools setup down to the level of the rank amateur who's rocking out for the fun of it or the professional musician eager to make a demo without having to pay for a recording studio. GarageBand is for those of us who prefer working in garages, at least in spirit.

You can even compose on the fly with nothing more than a laptop, or add a keyboard, hook up an electric guitar, or connect a microphone and record anything (such as vocals). Record a podcast episode quickly and then add the episode to your Web site with iWeb. In fact, everything you create in GarageBand can be used with other iLife applications, such as iPhoto, for slideshows, iMovie for soundtracks, iDVD for menu music, and iWeb to add music to your Web site. Your songs and ringtones can also be transferred directly to iTunes and used in your iPod or iPhone.

Jamming with the Magic GarageBand

Are you ready to kick out the jams with Magic GarageBand? (No, not Captain Beefheart's Magic Band — that's from another time and another place.) The Magic GarageBand feature sets up a band for you and plays a song so that you can play along with it. It's a fun way to practice, sing along, and mix and match tracks to create your own songs. You can assign instruments and styles for the positions of guitarist, bassist, drummer, and keyboard player or shuffle instrument selections randomly to try new ideas with your band. You don't need any real-life instruments or playing ability — you can use the Mac keyboard to play along or sing along using the built-in microphone. After rehearsing, click the red Record button to record your contribution.

If you have a real instrument, such as a USB keyboard, guitar, or microphone, you can connect it to your Mac, as I describe in Chapter 19.

Follow these steps to get started with Magic GarageBand:

1. **After starting GarageBand, click Magic GarageBand in the dialog shown in Figure 18-1.**

2. **Click a Genre icon on the right side of the dialog (refer to Figure 18-1), and click the Preview button in the Genre icon to hear a song preview representing that genre.**

Figure 18-1: Select a genre for the Magic GarageBand.

3. **While the genre is still selected (or after clicking another Genre icon), click Choose to pick the selected genre.**

   The stage appears on your screen, as shown in Figure 18-2, with My Instrument highlighted front and center on the stage and a pop-up bubble with controls for muting, soloing, and controlling the instrument's volume. See the later section "Tuning your instrument" for help setting up the instrument you want to play.

4. **To play the song, click the Play button (the triangle) in the lower center part of the window, next to the red Record button.**

   See the later section "Playing in the band" for details about playing your chosen song.

Tuning your instrument

When you play with the Magic GarageBand, your instrument can be the keyboard, the internal mic, or a live instrument you have lying around the house.

Figure 18-2: The stage is set for the Magic GarageBand and your instrument.

Follow these steps to use the keyboard:

1. **Click the My Instrument pop-up menu on the lower left side of the window, as shown in Figure 18-3.**

2. **Choose Keyboard to use the Mac keyboard as your source.**

3. **After selecting Keyboard as your source, click the Tuner button (with the Tuning Fork icon) next to your source selection.**

   Like magic, piano keys appear in a row across the bottom of the stage, as shown in Figure 18-4, with their equivalent keys on the Mac keyboard (A, S, D, E, F, and so on — not musical notes but, rather, the keys on your Mac keyboard).

4. **Click the piano keys to play notes or type on the Mac keyboard and press several keys at a time to play chords, as I do in Figure 18-4.**

Figure 18-3: Select a source (Keyboard) for My Instrument.

Figure 18-4: Play the Mac keyboard to simulate a piano.

If you brought your axe (guitar or other live instrument) to this gig, read about connecting audio equipment first, in Chapter 19. Then follow these steps, which also work if you want to sing or play into the internal mic:

1. **Click the My Instrument pop-up menu on the lower left side of the window.**

2. **Choose Line In if you plan to play an instrument, or choose Internal Mic.**

3. **Connect your instrument as I describe in Chapter 19 (Skip this step if you selected Internal Mic).**

   You can connect anything from a guitar, keyboard, or special microphone to that electric sitar you have sitting in a closet.

4. **Click the Tuner button to get in tune.**

   A tuner that appears across the bottom of the stage shows you the key you're playing or singing in.

5. **Use the tuner to tune your instrument or adjust your singing accordingly.**

   You know you're in tune when a musical note appears in the center of the tuner.

Playing in the band

Daybreak may not appear on the land while you're playing with this band, but click the Play button to start the song and then start playing along on the Mac keyboard. The following tips point out handy features you can use as you play along:

- **Play just a snippet.** If you want to play along with just one segment of the song (a *snippet,* if you're a music industry professional) and repeat that snippet endlessly, click the segment in the timeline below the stage and the piano keys so that the snippet turns yellow, as shown in Figure 18-5. (I selected the Intro snippet.) Note also that the Snippet/Entire Song switch at the bottom of the window is set to Snippet. (It was set by default to Entire Song.) Click the Play button and the snippet then plays repeatedly.

- **Change instruments.** Move the pointer around the stage to highlight other instruments. As you click an instrument on the stage, a set of alternative instruments appear below the stage, as shown in Figure 18-6 for the Melody guitar instrument. Click a different instrument, and then click Play to see what it sounds like with the rest of the band during the song.

Figure 18-5: Play along with just a snippet of the song.

Figure 18-6: Alternatives for the Melody guitar.

✔ **Mute an instrument or adjust its volume.** To mute an instrument so that you can hear all the others, click the instrument and then click the triangle in the pop-up bubble to see the instrument's controls, as shown in Figure 18-7. Click the Mute button (with the Speaker icon) to mute the instrument and hear the rest of the band, as I do in Figure 18-7 (The instrument appears darkened.) You can also drag the slider to adjust the instrument volume.

✔ **Request a solo.** To hear the instrument solo, without the rest of the band, click the Solo button (with the Headphone icon) to hear only that instrument, as I do in Figure 18-8 — after substituting a Mellotron for the organ by clicking the organ and then clicking the Mellotron in the alternative selections below the stage.

✔ **Mix everything up a bit.** Click the stage, away from any instrument, and the Shuffle Instruments and Start Over buttons appear. Click Shuffle Instruments to change all instruments in the band to random alternatives — you can continue clicking Shuffle Instruments to see different combinations.

✔ **Jump to the original settings.** If you don't like all the changes you made, click the stage and then click Start Over.

Figure 18-7: Mute this instrument and hear the rest of the band.

Click Start Over to start over with the genre selection's original instruments, but be aware that this action also resets the Magic GarageBand and any settings or recordings you just made (unless you saved your recording in GarageBand, as I describe in the later section "Recording the show").

Recording the show

When you're ready to record a performance with the instrument you chose for My Instrument along with the Magic GarageBand, follow these steps:

1. **Click the red Record button, and then start playing along.**

   Just like a bandleader counting off time, GarageBand plays metronome clicks and displays numbers on the green strip under the stage (as in 1-2-3-4 for 4/4 time) for exactly one full measure before starting to play the song and enable recording — so that you can prepare to perform along with the beat. The green strip turns red as you record, and the volume level of the instrument appears in the instrument's bubble (see Figure 18-9).

Figure 18-8: Hear this instrument by itself (solo) without the rest of the band.

Figure 18-9: Recording a take.

2. To stop recording at any time, click the red Record button again.

The song continues playing but your recording stops.

3. To continue recording from any point as the song plays, click the red Record button.

As the song continues playing, you can play along and record.

4. To stop playback and record another take from the beginning, click the Play button (or press the spacebar), and then click the red Record button.

After clicking the Play button or pressing the spacebar, playback stops. After you click the red Record button, the metronome's countdown begins again (refer to Step 1). You can stop the playback and start recording take after take — GarageBand saves every one.

You should repeat Step 4 and record as many takes as you can, because GarageBand can save each one and let you choose the one you want. One Grammy award-winning producer I've worked with in a sound studio with my band says that he always likes to record 16 takes of a song. That way, he has 16 different versions to choose from and can use the best parts of each track.

5. **When you're finished, click the Open in GarageBand button in the lower right corner of the window (refer to Figure 18-9).**

   The main GarageBand window appears, with separate tracks for each Magic GarageBand instruments. I save that discussion for later in this chapter — see the section "Welcome to the Machine: The GarageBand Main Window" to find out all about the features of the GarageBand window. To continue working on your new project, see Chapter 19.

 To switch genres in Magic GarageBand, click the Change Genre button in the lower left corner of the Magic GarageBand window (refer to Figure 18-9). The genres appear in the window, and the Open in GarageBand button in the lower right corner changes to the Audition button. Click a genre, and then click Audition.

Careful with That Axe, Eugene

Bill Payne, the keyboard player, composer, and founder of Little Feat, once told me that the way you build confidence as a musician is to give yourself an advantage. If you're starting out learning how to play an instrument such as guitar or piano, you can find no better advantage than to have a competent musician help you. The Pink Floyd guitarist who co-wrote "Careful with That Axe, Eugene" had previously taken guitar lessons from the founder of the band, and he did so well that he eventually replaced the founder. You may not be so lucky, but you can take piano or guitar lessons from the likes of Norah Jones, John Legend, John Fogerty, or Sting, or from a host of other artists at the GarageBand Lesson Store.

GarageBand's Learn to Play lessons help you easily learn the basic techniques of playing guitar and piano, and the Lesson Store lets you purchase and download guitar lessons, piano lessons, and special artist lessons to learn songs from the artists who created them. GarageBand includes two basic lessons for guitar (Intro to Guitar and Chord Trainer) and one for piano (Intro to Piano). For example, Intro to Guitar covers the basic principles, including hand position, tuning, and technique. You can play along with the lesson, turn on the GarageBand metronome to keep within the beat, slow down the lesson so that you can figure out how to play it, and record your instrument as you play along. GarageBand even tells you how well you're playing by displaying colored notes, a progress bar, and a performance meter.

Buying lessons in the Lesson Store

You can also download additional, free basic lessons and purchase artist lessons. In the GarageBand dialog, click Lesson Store, and then select Guitar Lessons, Piano Lessons, or Artist Lessons on the right side of the window. The Lessons Browser appears on the right side of the window — click a lesson type (such as Basic Guitar), and a list of lessons appears for that type. Click the Download button for a lesson to download it, or click Download All to download all lessons of that type. Back and forward arrows appear in the upper left corner of the Lessons Browser to browse the previous or next pages.

You need an iTunes or Apple Store account to download lessons. If this is your first time, click the Account button in the upper right corner of the GarageBand Lessons Browser. If you already have an Apple Store or iTunes account, sign in with your ID and password. If you don't, click Create Apple ID Now, and the Create Apple ID window appears. You can fill in your name and e-mail address and create a password. Click the Continue button, and then follow the instructions to establish your account.

Taking guitar and piano lessons

If you want to take lessons in GarageBand, follow these steps:

1. **After starting GarageBand, click Learn to Play in the dialog shown earlier in this chapter, in Figure 18-1.**

   The basic lessons installed on your Mac appear on the right side of the window.

2. **Select the lesson you want to open, and then click Choose.**

   The lesson opens in full-screen view, as shown in Figure 18-10, where you see the items described in this list:

   - A video window in the upper part of the window showing the teacher and the chapter menu (showing your Learn and Play chapter choices)

   - An animated fret board (for guitar lessons) or keyboard (for piano lessons) in the lower part of the window

   - A control bar below the animated instrument, which includes controls to play the lesson, turn on the metronome and the cycle region, slow down the lesson, and record your instrument as you play along

   - Buttons in the upper right corner for selecting the glossary of musical terms, the tuner (to help you tune your guitar), the Mixer screen, and the Setup screen.

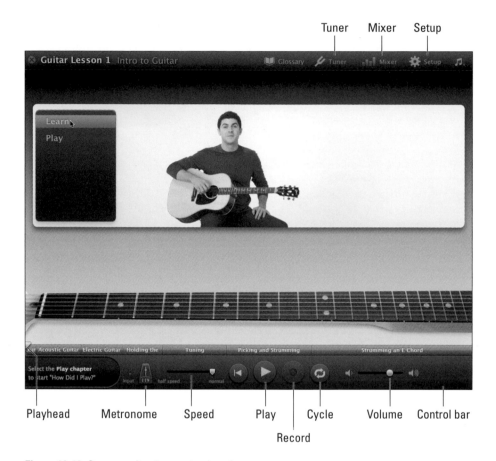

Figure 18-10: Open a guitar lesson to play along.

3. **Choose a chapter on the left side of the video window — either the Learn chapter to learn how to play or the Play chapter to play along.**

   Each Learn to Play lesson includes two chapters: Learn and Play. In the Learn chapter, the teacher shows you how to play the song, including details about techniques or special tunings. In the Play chapter, you can play along with the teacher and choose one or more sections to practice.

   Artist lessons for purchase (see the nearby sidebar "Buying lessons in the Lesson Store") may also include a Story chapter with information about the song and the artist, and other lessons you can purchase include Simple and Advanced chapters.

4. **To play the Learn chapter, click the CD-style Play button on the control bar or press the spacebar.**

   The playhead above the control bar (refer to Figure 18-10) shows the section of the lesson that's playing to switch to another section, click the section on the control bar. Click the Cycle button before clicking a section to play it repeatedly.

5. **To stop, click the Play button again or press the spacebar again.**

6. **To leave full-screen view and return to the GarageBand opening dialog, press the Esc key on the Mac keyboard or click the circled *x* in the upper left corner of the screen.**

   You can return to the same spot in the lesson by choosing the lesson again (refer to Step 2).

Setting up your guitar or keyboard

You can play your own guitar or piano along with the lesson. GarageBand is set up by default to enable you to play an acoustic guitar or a piano (or to sing) using the internal microphone. Using a USB-based keyboard is easy: Just plug it into the USB connection on your Mac (see Chapter 19 for details on connecting keyboards).

To hook your electric axe to the Mac, first click Setup in the upper right corner of the lesson screen to show the Setup window (see Figure 18-11), where you can set your input device. Choose Line-In from the Input Device pop-up menu to connect an electric guitar or external microphone, as I do in Figure 18-11.

If you're playing an electric guitar through an amplifier and using the internal microphone to record it, choose Monitor Off to avoid feedback. If your guitar is connected to the audio input port of a Mac or an audio interface, or if you're listening to GarageBand using headphones rather than speakers, choose Monitor On.

The Setup screen (click Setup in the upper right corner of the main lesson screen) also lets you specify the notation used to display chords, the Voice Over language, the display of subtitles, and the Top-Down Fretboard View and Left-Handed Guitar display options.

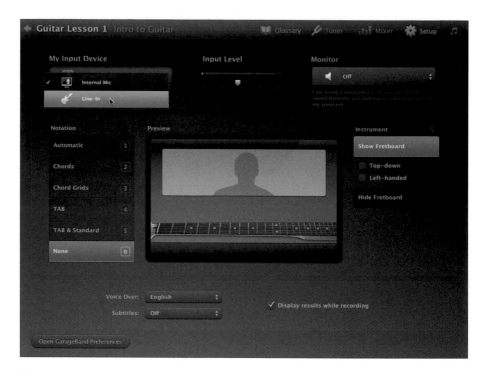

Figure 18-11: Set the input to Line-In for an electric guitar.

Recording takes with the teacher

While playing along with a lesson, you can record your contribution. Before you start recording, check out the tools for setting the metronome and using the tuner:

- **Metronome:** The GarageBand metronome plays an audible click for each beat of the measure, not recorded with the music, to help you keep time while playing your instrument. And, just like a bandleader counting 1-2-3-4 to prepare the band to begin a song, GarageBand plays the metronome clicks exactly one full measure before starting to record, so that you can prepare to perform along with the beat. You can turn the metronome on and off by clicking the Metronome button in the bottom row of buttons on the lesson screen (refer to Figure 18-10).

- **Tuner:** To tune your guitar before playing along, click the Tuner button (refer to Figure 18-10). The screen fills with a tuner that shows you which key you're playing when you pluck a string. (You can pluck a string on the animated fret board by clicking it.)

When you're ready to start recording, follow these steps:

1. **Choose Play from the chapter menu (refer to Figure 18-10).**

2. **(Optional) If you want to record multiple takes of your instrument while playing along with a lesson, click the Cycle button on the control bar (refer to Figure 18-10).**

3. **Click the section you want to record in, or move the playhead to the point where you want to start recording.**

4. **Click the red Record button on the control bar (refer to Figure 18-12) and start playing.**

5. **To stop recording, click the red Record button again.**

GarageBand displays a performance meter (showing 8% in Figure 18-12 — not good, but I'm just starting out on guitar) as well as notes on the guitar's fretboard or piano keyboard. Mistakes and missed notes appear in red. After completing a recording of playing along with the song in the lesson, click the History button in the lower right corner to see a progress chart.

Figure 18-12: Play along with the lesson.

Tweaking the mix

If that guitar solo is too fast, drag the Speed slider, located on the control bar next to the metronome (refer to Figure 18-10), to the left to slow down the lesson to make it easier to learn or practice. (You're just changing the tempo, which I describe in Chapter 20.) To speed up the solo again, drag the Speed slider to the right.

Can't hear the instrument or the band behind the teacher? You can change the mix of the teacher's voice and instrument, your own instrument, and the instruments in the backing band. Click Mixer in the upper right corner of the lesson screen (refer to Figure 18-10) to show a mixer overlaying the lesson, with a set of controls for each track, including a Mute button, Solo button, and Volume slider. Here's how it works:

- **To silence a track,** click its Mute button (with a Speaker icon).

- **To hear a track by itself,** click its Solo button (with the Headphone icon).

- **To close the mixer,** click Mixer in the upper right corner of the window, or click any part of the lesson window outside the mixer.

Welcome to the Machine: The GarageBand Main Window

If you just arrived in this section after recording your contribution with the Magic GarageBand, click your instrument's track, which includes a yellow badge showing the number of takes, and click the badge to choose a take, as I do in Figure 18-13.

In addition to opening a Magic GarageBand performance in GarageBand, you can create a project from scratch: Choose New Project from the GarageBand opening dialog (refer to Figure 18-1). To open an existing project, choose Recent Projects and then select a project that appears on the right side of the dialog.

The GarageBand window has controls that look like they belong in an expensive sound studio — round knobs, tiny sliders, and horizontal tracks with waveforms representing music. Click the Open Eye icon (to the left of the *i* icon in the lower right corner) to see the built-in prerecorded loops you can use in your songs, which I described in Chapter 21.

Track headers   Level meter

Mute   Volume   Curves

Solo   Pan   Playhead   Timeline   Beat ruler   Track region

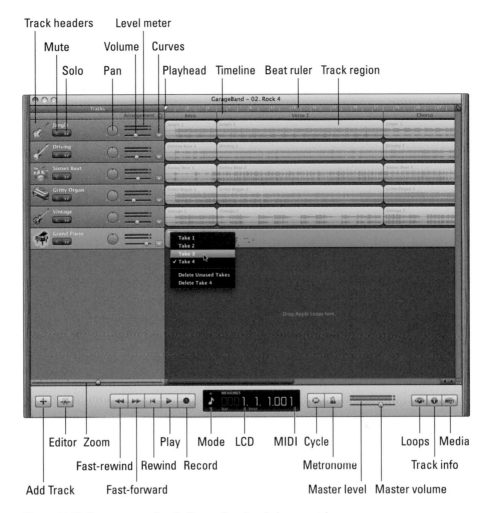

Editor Zoom   Play   Mode   LCD   MIDI Cycle   Loops | Media

Fast-rewind | Rewind Record   Metronome   Track info

Add Track   Fast-forward   Master level Master volume

Figure 18-13: Open your project in GarageBand and choose a take.

Each instrument or vocal performance is recorded in a separate track in GarageBand. A *track* stores the audio information in a way that makes it easy to isolate and change that audio information without affecting other instrument or vocal tracks. You can add tracks and change the instrument and effects for each track.

The GarageBand window is a recording studio and mixing console all in one window (refer to Figure 18-13):

- **Track headers:** A track contains the music from a single instrument or set of instruments. Each track has a header that shows the instrument icon and name, and several buttons:

  - **Mute** (with the speaker icon): Mutes the track.

  - **Solo** (with the headphone icon): Lets you hear only that track.

  - **Curves** (triangle): Opens automation curves for Track Volume, Track Pan, and automated mixing settings, all of which I describe in Chapter 22.

  - **Pan** (wheel): Adjusts the left-right placement of the track in the stereo field. Drag counter-clockwise to pan to the left channel, and drag clockwise to pan to the right. The wheel's white dot indicates the position. See Chapter 22 for mixing tips.

  - **Volume** (slider): Adjusts the track's volume.

  - **Level meter**: Shows the track's volume level as you record and play.

- **Timeline and beat ruler:** The timeline area of the GarageBand window contains the track information — in this area, you record instruments, add loops, and arrange recorded regions. The timeline area also offers a beat ruler with a playhead that you can drag to different locations within the song; you can also use the ruler to align regions to beats and measures.

- **Playhead:** The playhead shows the point where playback starts if you click the Play button, or the playback point in the song after clicking Play. You can move the playhead to start playing the project at a different point or select a point in a track region. When you cut or copy a track region and then paste it into a track, the pasted region appears at the playhead position in the track.

- **Track region:** The track's audio information appears as a region within a track, with its duration measured by the timeline beat ruler. A *region* is a colored area in a track that indicates the duration of a section of audio in the timeline. The region shows a waveform representing a Real

Instrument sound or a set of notes representing a Software Instrument sound. (See Chapter 20 for more about instruments.) You click inside a track before recording an instrument to create a region, and you drag loops into tracks to create loop regions. You can drag the regions within the track to arrange the music.

✔ **Zoom slider:** Use this slider to zoom into the timeline for a closer view of the regions at a particular time in the song.

✔ **Add Track and Editor buttons:** You can add a new track below the selected track by clicking the Add Track button (the + icon) or click the Editor button (the scissors cutting an audio wave icon) to show or hide the Track Editor. I show you how to add tracks in Chapter 20, and how to use the Track Editor in Chapter 22.

✔ **Loops, Track Info, and Media buttons:** Click the Loop Browser button (the Open Eye icon) to show or hide the Loop Browser, the Track Info button (the *i* icon) to show or hide track information, or the Media button (Filmstrip, Photo, and Audio icon) to show or hide the Media Browser. I show you how to use the Track Info feature in Chapter 20, and the Loop and Media Browsers in Chapter 21.

✔ **Transport controls:** Control recording and playback by using these buttons:

- **Fast-rewind and Fast-forward:** Moves the playhead quickly backward or forward in the song.

- **Rewind:** Moves the playhead back to the beginning of the song.

- **Play:** Starts playing at the point of the playhead. (You can also use the spacebar on your computer keyboard as a substitute for the Play button.) Play an entire song by clicking the Back-to-Beginning button to move the playhead back to the beginning of the song and then clicking the Play button or pressing the spacebar to start playback.

- **Record** (red dot): Starts or stops recording.

- **Cycle:** Plays the entire song or a cycle region repeatedly as a loop. (I describe cycle regions in Chapter 21.)

- **Metronome:** Whether on or off, its audible clicks aren't recorded.

✓ **LCD:** This indicator tells you the playhead position, and the MIDI indicator (a tiny green light) flashes when you're playing a MIDI instrument. (See Chapter 19 to learn about MIDI.) Click the Mode icon on the left side of the LCD to switch to one of these modes:

- **Measures:** Shows the playhead position in musical time (using musical measures, beats, and ticks)

- **Time:** Shows the playhead position in absolute time (hours, minutes, seconds, fractions of a second)

- **Chord:** Shows chord symbols when you play a software instrument.

- **Tuner:** Shows a tuner you can use to tune a guitar on either an Electric Guitar or Real Instrument track.

- **Project:** Lets you choose a different key and time signature for the project, and change the project tempo.

✓ **Master volume slider and level meter:** The master volume slider controls the overall volume of all tracks. The level meter shows you whether clipping is occurring. You can find out more about using these controls in Chapter 22.

You can also drag the playhead in the timeline to a specific region or time in the song and then click the Play button or press the spacebar to play from that point in the song to the end.

Getting Ready for the Gig

In This Chapter

▶ Using the onscreen keyboard and Music Typing

▶ Connecting a guitar, keyboard, microphone, or other instrument

▶ Using the line-in connection

▶ Using the internal microphone

▶ Setting up an audio interface

*M*usic and musical instruments change with the times and with the technologies that become available. Ancient people used brass, animal horn, bone, ivory, and even gold to make musical instruments — the oldest known lyre is Sumerian and made of gold, with gold and silver strings. In the 16th century, many instruments were made of wood, and by the 18th century, the technologies of woodworking and metalworking made the modern piano possible. By the 19th century, Adolphe Sax was so brazen as to combine a wind instrument and a brass horn to invent the instrument that now bears his name, the saxophone. It's not surprising that the technology of electricity, and eventually of the microprocessor, would lead to another change in musical instruments and music with synthesizers and computer-created music.

Yet musicians swear by their favorite instruments. No matter how you change the settings of a Software Instrument defined in GarageBand to sound like a slide guitar, you can't get the true sound of a slide guitar unless you play one. Professional musicians treat their favorite instruments like members of their families. "It's been through three wives," Waylon Jennings remarked about his Telecaster guitar. "To me, a guitar is kind of like a woman. You don't know why you like 'em, but you do."

GarageBand is more than accommodating to musicians who want to record using their own instruments — the software can simulate various amplifiers that would cost you a fortune to assemble yourself. For example, you can get the distorted guitar sound of early The Kinks records (as in "You Really Got Me") without having to do what guitarist Dave Davies of that band had to do to create that sound — slash the speaker in his amplifier. GarageBand offers virtual amps for Arena Rock, British Invasion, Clean Jazz, and other types. As I describe in this chapter, you can connect an electric instrument, such as your favorite guitar, or connect a microphone (or use the Mac's built-in microphone) to record acoustic instruments as well as vocals, using GarageBand's Real Instrument settings and effects for real instruments.

What You Need Backstage

A minimalist artist needs very little material to make art; and so it is with music. You can do any of the following, all with no additional equipment or software:

- Jam with the Magic GarageBand, as I show you in Chapter 18.
- Deploy royalty-free GarageBand loops, which I describe in Chapter 21.
- Play your Mac like a piano or an organ by using the onscreen keyboard, as I describe in "Using Your Mac As an Instrument," later in this chapter.
- Record vocals directly through your Mac's internal microphone, as I show you in "Using Line-In or the Internal Mic," later in this chapter.

GarageBand is part of the iLife set, which includes iPhoto, iMovie, iWeb, and iDVD, so you can use your GarageBand compositions with these applications. Because you also get iTunes with your Mac, you can use that service to download songs from the iTunes Store or rip CDs, and you can export songs you create in GarageBand to your iTunes library.

Assuming that you already have a properly configured Mac running the newest version of OS X, you still need enough space available on your hard drive to create multiple tracks for songs. The amount of space you need depends on how complex the song is, which types of instruments you use (real or software, as described in Chapter 20), and how long the song is. Each track extends from the beginning to the end of a song, so if you have lots of tracks in a song, the song occupies more space.

For example, a four-minute song with two Real Instrument tracks takes up 90MB. Each minute of stereo audio recorded into GarageBand from a Real Instrument uses about 10MB of space. The audio isn't compressed as it is in iTunes, because you're still working on the song and you need the highest level of quality.

The minimalist approach (no gear)

If you have nothing but GarageBand and your Mac for making music, you can create a song by using the tools and features described in this list:

- **Your computer keyboard and the onscreen keyboard:** You're probably already aware that digital synthesizers can sound like nearly any type of real-life instrument (as well as a good many imaginary ones). Your Mac can sound like a digital synthesizer with GarageBand's Software Instruments — you can perform live with the Mac using the onscreen Keyboard and Musical Typing keyboard, as I show in "Using Your Mac As an Instrument," later in this chapter.

- **Prerecorded loops:** Keith Richards of the Rolling Stones says that you need to know only three chords to make rock 'n' roll, but with GarageBand you don't even need to know that much. You can construct songs, even if you have no musical ability, using prerecorded loops like building blocks to create songs, as I demonstrate in Chapter 21. You can then stretch and compress these loops, repeat them, and even edit some of them to play exactly the notes you want.

- **The internal mic:** As for singing and playing acoustic instruments, you can use the Mac's built-in microphone if you have no other choice. It picks up sound from the room, so be aware that your recording might sound like just what it is — a recording made in a room with a single microphone.

Going to the max (guitars, keyboards, and microphones)

If you have an instrument or a microphone or another type of recording gear, you can use it with GarageBand. Here's a look at how you might record some common types of instruments and vocals with your Mac, the GarageBand software, and other gear:

- **USB MIDI keyboard:** You can connect a USB keyboard directly to your Mac, as I describe in "Connecting a USB MIDI Keyboard," later in this chapter (where I also explain MIDI). Use headphones or speakers connected to your Mac for high-quality stereo playback; headphones are best for *monitoring* a recording — hearing yourself play along with the music.

- **Electric instruments, such as electric guitars:** You can also connect an electric instrument, such as your favorite Stratocaster guitar.

- **Acoustic instruments and vocals:** Use a microphone to record acoustic instruments as well as vocals, using settings and effects designed for real instruments — named, appropriately, *Real Instruments*.

Before you plug your Stratocaster into the back of your laptop, know the limitations of input. Computers are typically set up for playing and recording audio on home stereos. However, instruments are typically set up to plug into amplifiers, using different connectors and input levels than for a home stereo. You can bridge this gap with a professional-quality *audio interface* that lets you plug in a microphone or an electric guitar or another electric instrument and control the volume level of the input. (See "Using an Audio Interface," later in this chapter.)

If your electric instrument or amplifier offers line-level output (for connecting to a home stereo), you don't need the audio interface — you can connect the line-level output directly into your Mac's Line-In connection (as I show in "Using Line-In or the Internal Mic," later in this chapter). Line-level microphones are available that can record professional-quality vocals. I play harmonica using a microphone connected directly to an iMac Line-In connection, and you can also record other acoustic instruments without electric pickups using an external microphone.

Let's get it straight from the start: GarageBand is not a professional recording tool, any more than your garage is a professional sound studio. For example, to create the best sound quality from an electric guitar with the widest frequency range, you might consider using a real amplifier *before* sending the signal into the computer for recording. You have to use a high-quality microphone with the amplifier, and perhaps phantom power, a compressor, and other items. For vocals, you need a silent vocal booth. If you "go cheap" on any of these components in the chain, you might as well be playing a $200 guitar over a $50 pocket amp.

The point is that GarageBand is more suited for rehearsal and composition using a real instrument than for recording a real instrument with studio quality. You can also use GarageBand to simulate effects and amplifier settings while performing live. And, there's always a chance that whatever you record will transcend any limitations of the process — you don't care that "Strawberry Fields" by the Beatles was recorded on a four-track tape machine with substantial generational loss, do you?

Using Your Mac As an Instrument

GarageBand includes an onscreen music keyboard, which you can use to record as a Software Instrument: Just choose Window⊅Keyboard. To use the keyboard, click the piano keys, as shown at the top of Figure 19-1.

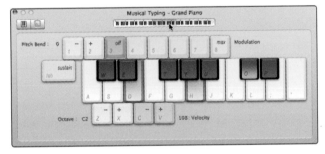

Figure 19-1: Click the keys (top) or type on the Mac keyboard (bottom).

As you play, follow these handy tips:

- ✐ **To simulate playing the piano keys harder or softer,** click lower in a white or black key to play the note harder, and click higher in the key to play the note softer.

- ✐ **To move the onscreen music keyboard** to any location on your screen, click in the space between the keys and the side of the keyboard and drag it.

- ✐ **To expand the keyboard,** increasing the number of keys that are shown, drag the expansion triangle in the lower right edge of the keyboard.

- ✐ **To change the range of notes you can play,** click the small triangles to the left or right of the keys — the left one lowers the keys by an octave, and the right one raises them an octave. You can also click the thumbnail of the piano keyboard above the keys to select an octave. By expanding the keyboard and changing its range of notes, you can play every note you could possibly hear.

The onscreen music keyboard is primitive, but you can use it to experiment with different instrument sounds and effects. Still, you may find it difficult to play by clicking the pointer, and you can't play more than one note at a time. To play several notes at a time (as in a chord) from your Mac keyboard, click the Musical Typing button (the A Key icon) in the upper left corner of the onscreen keyboard or choose Window⇨Musical Typing.

The Musical Typing onscreen keyboard lets you do both: Click keys or use the Mac's alphanumeric keyboard. You can press several keys at a time on the Mac keyboard to play chords. Here's how the Mac keyboard works:

- The keys in the second row (A to single quote) are the white piano keys in a 1½ octave range from C through F.

- The keys in the third row (W, E, T, Y, U, O, and P) are the black piano keys (sharps and flats).

- Press Z to move down an octave, or X to move up an octave.

- Press C to lower the velocity level, or V to raise it. (The velocity level determines how hard or fast the keys are pressed — acoustic pianos are velocity-sensitive.)

- To add pitch bend to notes you play (that is, to adjust the pitch of a note in the range of plus or minus one tone), press 1 to lower the pitch or 2 to raise it.

- To sustain notes you play, hold down the Tab key — notes are sustained for as long as you hold down the Tab key.

- To add modulation to notes you play, press 4 through 8 to add increasing amounts of modulation or press 3 to turn off modulation.

Connecting a USB MIDI Keyboard

The international *Musical Instrument Digital Interface (MIDI)* standard specifies how musical instruments with microprocessors can communicate with other microprocessor-controlled instruments or devices. The first synthesizer to "speak MIDI" was the Sequential Prophet 600 in 1983, played by some of the greatest keyboard players in jazz and rock.

MIDI communicates performance information, not the audio waveform — each note you play is converted to an instruction, which, like the holes on a piano roll for a player piano, tells the synthesizer which note to play. A MIDI device can also register how hard you played the note (how much pressure you applied to the key of a keyboard) or how quickly you released it (or took your finger off the key), and gather information from other controls such as sliders, wheels, switches, and pedals. GarageBand can apply the MIDI information to any Software Instrument, effectively turning your Mac into a fully functional music synthesizer.

You can use a MIDI keyboard that connects to your Mac by using a USB connector cable. Two popular models are the M-Audio Keystation 61es, available from the Apple Store, or the Keystation Pro 88, available from M-Audio (www.m-audio.com).

A USB MIDI keyboard is literally plug-and-play: Just plug it in and start GarageBand, and you can play your piano and organ riffs and have them translated into Software Instruments. Just follow the same instructions as though you were using the onscreen music keyboard.

If you don't hear music from your USB MIDI keyboard, try these tricks to troubleshoot the problem:

✔ **Make sure that the keyboard is connected to the USB port and the keyboard is turned on.** When you first start a new song in GarageBand, a Software Instrument track labeled Grand Piano opens automatically — make sure that this track is still selected by clicking the track header.

✔ **Check to see that your system has detected the MIDI device.** If you still don't hear music, choose GarageBand➪Preferences and click the Audio/MIDI button to see the Audio/MIDI pane, shown in Figure 19-2. The MIDI status should indicate that your system detected at least one MIDI input; if it didn't, you may have to troubleshoot your connection by using the Audio MIDI Setup utility. (See the tip on setting up a MIDI instrument in Chapter 23.)

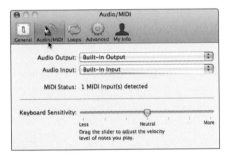

Figure 19-2: The Audio/MIDI pane detects the MIDI keyboard and lets you assign sound input and output.

✔ **See whether your USB MIDI keyboard is playing by watching the LCD display in GarageBand as you play.** The tiny green MIDI status light in the lower left corner of the LCD display should flash every time you play a note. If you still aren't hearing music, make sure that the Volume slider for the track isn't positioned all the way to the left and turn up the output volume for your computer's speakers or your external speakers.

Using Line-In or the Internal Mic

Most Mac models offer a line-in connection that accepts a cable with a ⅛-inch stereo mini-plug, which is common in many music-lover households. You can connect any type of mono or stereo audio source, such as a CD or DVD player, or an electric instrument, such as an electric guitar, or a mono microphone or a stereo set of microphones. Here's how the connections work:

- **For home stereo gear,** all you need to do is find a line-out connection on your stereo system (for line-level output) and connect to it a cable that uses RCA-type left and right (typically marked white and red) stereo plugs or a stereo mini-plug. If you use RCA-type plugs, use an RCA-to-stereo-mini-plug converter or a cable that offers a stereo mini-plug on the other end.

- **For electric instruments such as guitars and microphones,** you can use a phono-to-mini-plug converter such as the Monster Instrument Adapter, which is a short cable that has a mono ¼-inch phono connection on one end and a ⅛-inch mini-plug on the other end to connect to your Mac's line-in connection.

  However, the sound quality isn't at its highest level — an electric guitar or microphone produces a low input signal, resulting in low volume when you record. You want a line-level source of audio — either line-level output from your instrument or your microphone, or from your amplifier or preamp, or via an audio interface, as I describe in the later section "Using an Audio Interface."

If your Mac doesn't offer a line-in connection, you can purchase a USB audio input device, such as the Griffin iMic (www.griffintechnology.com) or the Roland UA-30 (www.roland.com), and use it with the Mac's USB connection.

The Mac's internal microphone can also be useful, especially when recording sound effects or ambient sound on the road with a laptop.

After connecting your gear, you need to assign sound input to your Mac's line-in connection. If you're using the internal microphone, make sure the sound input is assigned to it. See "Setting Inputs and Outputs," later in this chapter.

Using an Audio Interface

An *audio interface* is an adapter or a device that enables you to connect audio sources to your Mac, and they come in several formats, including FireWire, PC card, PCI, and USB.

Many audio interfaces offer both MIDI and connections for other types of audio devices. The Emagic Multichannel Interface 2|6 (www.emagic.com), for example, connects to your Mac's USB port and offers six audio inputs (for line-in music, electric instruments, or microphones), as well as MIDI connections. I use the M-Audio FastTrack guitar and microphone interface (www.m-audio.com), which is small and portable — it draws its power from the USB connection.

To use an audio interface as your input device (so that instruments or microphones connected to it can be used to record), follow these steps:

1. **Connect your instruments, microphones, and sound sources to the audio interface.**

   Follow the connection instructions provided with your audio interface.

2. **Choose GarageBand⇨Preferences; in the Preferences dialog, click the Audio/MIDI Interfaces button.**

   The Audio/MIDI Interfaces pane appears (refer to Figure 19-2).

3. **Choose the audio interface from the Audio Input pop-up menu, and then close the Preferences dialog. (Click the red button in the upper left corner of the window.)**

You can configure the audio interface with more specific controls. The Apple utility Audio MIDI Setup works with audio devices to connect via FireWire, PCI, PCMCIA, or USB. See the tip on setting up a MIDI instrument in Chapter 23 for details.

Setting Inputs and Outputs

To assign sound input to your Mac's built-in microphone, or to its line-in connection for recording from an external microphone or an electric instrument with a line-level output, follow these steps:

1. **For a line-in connection, connect your instrument, microphone, or sound source to the line-in connection on your Mac.**

   If you don't have a line-in connection, you can use a USB audio input device.

2. **Choose System Preferences from the Apple menu in Mac OS X.**

   The System Preferences window appears with icons, separated into sections, for setting preferences.

3. **Click the Sound icon in the Hardware section to open the Sound pane, and click the Input tab.**

   The Sound pane's Input pane appears, as shown in Figure 19-3.

4. **Select Line In or Internal Microphone from the list of sound input devices.**

   The change takes place immediately, by activating the line-in connection or internal microphone.

5. **Quit System Preferences by choosing System Preferences⇨Quit (or click the red Close button in the upper left corner).**

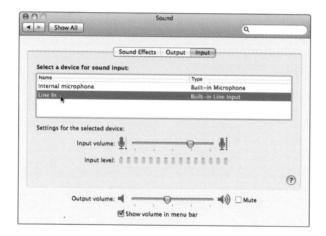

Figure 19-3: Setting up the Mac's line-in connection for recording.

To set the volume level for sound input, follow these steps:

1. **Start playing the instrument you're recording or start singing or talking to the built-in mic.**

   The internal microphone or line-in connection is always on and detecting sound.

2. **Watch the Input Level meter on the Input tab (refer to Figure 19-3).**

   As the volume grows louder, the oblong purple dots are highlighted from left to right. If all dots are highlighted all the time, you're way too hot (too loud). If none of the dots is even highlighted, you're way too low. You want the dots to be highlighted about three-fourths of the way across, from left to right, for optimal input volume.

3. **To adjust the volume, drag the Input Volume slider.**

You can still record from an audio interface, a line-in connection, or an internal mic while your system sound preferences are set differently. Choose GarageBand⇨Preferences and click the Audio/MIDI button to see the Audio/MIDI pane (refer to Figure 19-2). You can then set the audio input to Built-In Microphone, Built-in Line Input, or System Setting (to reflect whatever you set your system sound preferences is set to, as described earlier). You can also set the audio output to Built-in Output or System Settings.

Getting Your Mojo Working

In This Chapter

▶ Creating a new GarageBand project

▶ Setting a song's tempo, time signature, and key

▶ Creating and recording a track

▶ Setting up a track's instrument and sound effects

▶ Changing the amplifier stack and pedal effects for an electric guitar

*T*hough rock music has seen a number of train songs, they have nothing to do with the origins of the word *track* in music. During the phonograph era (late 1870s through the 1980s), a needle tracked its way around a vinyl record disc, following a groove in the record to scratch out the music. The Library of Congress referred to songs as *tracks* way back when Muddy Waters was first recorded on his back porch in Mississippi (in 1941).

As soon as it became possible to record separate performances and join them in a single recording, the idea of a recording track was born. The reason is simple: A sound engineer wants to isolate the sound of one instrument (such as drums) from the sounds of others (such as vocals and guitars) so that one can be made louder or softer than the others. By using multiple tracks, an orchestra or band can record all instrumental parts and the singer can add a vocal track afterward.

This chapter shows you how to create tracks in GarageBand. Just as a professional mixing console does in a recording studio, GarageBand lets you combine separately recorded tracks. This strategy is more than accommodating to musicians who want to record their own instruments — it even simulates various amplifiers that would cost you a fortune to assemble (if you could even find them). And, you can fiddle with the effects and settings until your ears fall off. You can blaze away on your favorite instrument and clean up mistakes in the Track Editor (which I describe in Chapter 22). George Harrison's comments in the mid-1990s were prophetic: He said that musicians in the future would be able to push a button to create the sound that it took the Beatles weeks or months to figure out in the 1960s. And here we are plugging instruments into a Mac and using simulated amplifiers!

Creating a New GarageBand Project

When you first open GarageBand, you see a dialog in which you create a new project, open a recent project, open a song, or do other tasks. (I cover Learn to Play, Lesson Store, and Magic GarageBand in Chapter 18, and I show you how to create an iPhone ringtone in Chapter 21).

To start a new project, follow these steps:

1. **Click New Project, as shown in Figure 20-1.**

2. **Choose an instrument track to start with or a project type.**

Figure 20-1: Click New Project and then choose an instrument to start with.

For example, if you choose Piano, the project starts with a Grand Piano track; for Guitar, the project starts with a guitar track. (If you choose Podcast, the project starts with a set of podcast tracks, which I describe in Chapter 21.)

It doesn't matter which instrument you start with — you can create more tracks for other instruments and delete tracks from within your project or change the instrument for a track.

After you choose an instrument track for your new project, the New Project from Template dialog appears with these default settings, as shown in Figure 20-2:

- *Time signature:* 4/4

- *Tempo:* 120 beats per minute (bpm)

- *Key signature:* C

Figure 20-2: Setting the time, tempo, and key settings.

3. Choose settings for your song.

The default settings are typical for popular songs, so you might want to start with them. You have to set these parameters before adding loops or recording instruments, so that your loops and recordings can fit together and play at the same speed, using the same range of notes. I explain each setting in detail in the following sections.

You can always change a song's parameters later, and all recordings and loops with Software Instruments change automatically to reflect the new settings; however, Real Instrument loops and recordings don't change, so you should set those parameters before recording a live instrument.

Setting the tempo

The *tempo,* measured in beats per minute (bpm), defines the rhythmic pulse of a song. You can set the tempo to any speed between 60 bpm (which is slow — one beat per second) and 240 bpm (a rapid four beats per second). Most pop music selections clock in at 120 bpm. In the New Project dialog (refer to Figure 20-2), you drag the Tempo slider to the left to slow it down and to the right to speed it up.

When you record a live instrument, the recording is fixed in the tempo that's set for the song. You can change the tempo of a Software Instrument recording or loop, but you can't change a Real Instrument recording except by using GarageBand's Flex Time and groove matching tools, which I describe in Chapter 22.

To change the tempo later in your project, click the icon on the left side of the LCD and choose Project. In the LCD, click the tempo and then drag the slider upward to speed up the tempo, or drag downward to slow it down. You can also click the Track Info button (it has the *i* icon) to open the Info pane and then click Master Track and drag the Tempo slider to the new tempo.

Setting the time signature

The *time signature* measures a song's meter with a fraction that indicates the relationship between beats and measures. For example, in a 2/4 time signature, you have two beats in every measure, and each beat has the value of a quarter note (denoted by the *4*). A *measure* is simply a handy metric that separates music into pieces; sometimes, a measure is a *bar* (as in "Beat me, daddy — eight to the bar").

The most common time signature is 4/4, used in such classics as "Hey Jude" and "Let It Be" by The Beatles — but check out the band's "In My Life" for an example of a 2/2 time signature. Their "Norwegian Wood" is in 3/4 time, and you can hear the difference in time signature when "All You Need Is Love" switches from 4/4 time (while John Lennon sings "There's nothing you can do that can't be done") to 3/4 time and then back again (when he sings, "Nothing you can sing that can't be sung").

In the New Project dialog (refer to Figure 20-2), use the Time pop-up menu to set the time signature. You can set the time signature to 2/2, 2/4, 3/4, 4/4, 5/4, 7/4, 6/8, 7/8, 9/8 (try *that,* Frank Zappa wannabes), or even 12/8 (used in The Beatles' "Oh! Darling"). Though other time signatures exist, GarageBand doesn't support them, and generally you can make do with one of these. The time signature defines how the timeline in GarageBand is divided into beats and measures.

To change the time signature later in your project, click the icon on the left side of the LCD and choose Project. In the LCD, click the Signature button, and then choose a time signature from the pop-up menu. You can also click the Track Info button (with the *i* icon) to open the Info pane, click Master Track, and then choose a new time signature from the Signature pop-up menu.

Setting the key

The *key signature* defines the central note around which a song is written, set, and arranged (except, of course, atonal compositions, which GarageBand is perfectly capable of producing, but let's not go there now).

By default, a new song is set to the key of C unless you change it on the Key pop-up menu in the New Project dialog (refer to Figure 20-2). You can choose a major or minor key — select Major or Minor from the pop-up menu next to the Key pop-up menu. Whatever key you use, the Software Instruments you play automatically play in that key.

To change the key later in your project, click the icon on the left side of the LCD and choose Project. In the LCD, click the Key button and then choose a key from the pop-up menu. You can also click the Track Info button (with the *i* icon) to open the Info pane, click Master Track, and then choose a new key from the Key pop-up menu.

Saving the project

To save your project, choose File⇨Save. All projects (even gospel music projects) need to be saved. If you try to close the project without saving, GarageBand prompts you to save it.

After you choose File⇨Save, close your project, or quit GarageBand, a dialog appears, asking whether you want to save your project in an iLife preview. Including a preview lets you place projects in the iLife Media Browser and use them in other iLife applications (without having to transfer them to iTunes first) but takes longer when closing projects. Click Yes to generate an iLife preview or No to close without the preview.

In addition, you can choose File➪Save As to use the following options:

- ✔ **Archive Project:** If your project contains Real Instrument-recorded tracks and loops (or a video podcast track), you may want to save the project as an archive so that the loops and recordings are saved with it. That way, you can move the project to another computer that may not have the same loops installed. Choose File➪Save As and then select the Archive Project option.

- ✔ **Compact Project:** This option reduces the size of the project on your hard drive (making it easier to share) but also reduces audio quality. You choose the audio compression method (such as AAC or MP3) from the pop-up menu. Don't use this option if you plan on using the music in another project (such as a DVD in iDVD) or continuing to edit the music, because it reduces overall sound quality.

Creating a Track

Your performances with instruments, your vocals, and your prerecorded loops are each stored in separate tracks, isolated from other instrument or vocal tracks.

In the 1960s (or the Sixties, if you were there), state-of-the-art recording equipment consisted of four separate tracks. The Beatles had to put their vocals, guitars, bass, and drums on three of the four tracks, reserving the fourth for all the different tape loops. Even more complicated was the task of recording and then playing back all those loops on different tape machines and feeding the result into that fourth track. Studios now have an unlimited number of tracks, with at least one track for each instrument.

In GarageBand, you can use as many tracks as you need (to the limit of your computer's capacity) for both recordings and loops. When you're finished with your song, you can then mix all its tracks into two stereo tracks without losing sound quality.

If you started a project as I describe in "Creating a New GarageBand Project," earlier in this chapter, you probably already have at least one track in the GarageBand window. You can also create more tracks.

To create a track, choose Track➪New Track or click the plus-sign (+) button in the lower left corner of the GarageBand window. A dialog appears, with three types of instruments for the tracks. This list describes what happens when you see each of the three track types:

✐ **Software Instrument:** You see this track if you start a project by choosing Piano, or a set of them by choosing Keyboard Collection. Choose Software Instrument for instrument sounds generated by GarageBand that you can play using the onscreen keyboard, Musical Typing keyboard, or an external USB MIDI instrument. Many prerecorded loops were also created using Software Instruments. (Chapter 21 describes loops.) The notes you play are MIDI instructions, so you can adjust and transpose notes to other keys as much as you want. Even more, you can switch instrument types — if you recorded a drum part into a Software Instrument track, for example, you can change it later to a guitar or piano.

✐ **Real Instrument:** You see a Real Instrument track if you start a project by choosing Voice or Acoustic Instrument. Choose Real Instrument for recording musical instruments and vocals, by way of either a microphone or a line-in connection. Real Instrument tracks are represented as waveforms in the GarageBand window. You can't adjust each note or transpose notes to other keys with excellent results, as you can with Software Instrument tracks, because notes are recorded waveforms. And, although you can tweak the sound of an instrument after recording it, you can't easily make it sound like another instrument (such as making a guitar sound like a drum).

✐ **Electric Guitar:** You see an Electric Guitar track if you start a project by choosing Electric Guitar. Choose Electric Guitar for recording an electric guitar over a line-in connection using simulated amplifiers and foot pedals ("stomp-boxes"). Electric Guitar tracks are just like Real Instrument tracks in that they're represented as waveforms in the GarageBand window. You can't adjust each note or transpose notes to other keys with excellent results.

Defining Track Instruments and Effects

One of the first popular groups to use a synthesizer in live performances was, surprisingly, the Beach Boys. In the late 1960s, the group performed "Riot in Cell Block #9" and used the Moog analog synthesizer to produce the sound of a police siren. Digital synthesizers and GarageBand can now create any type of sound, including real-life instruments and a good number of imaginary ones.

Although you can change the instrument to experiment, a track can have only one instrument for the length of a song. If you want to add more instruments, you need to create a track for each instrument.

Generating a Software Instrument

The advantage you have in using a Software Instrument track is that you can change the note's pitch and length, for example, almost as though you were changing typos with a word processor. (GarageBand offers the Track Editor to make this type of change, which I describe in Chapter 22.) You can therefore record a performance that's less than perfect — even sloppy — and easily fix it.

The following steps walk you through the process of choosing settings for a Software Instrument:

1. **Make sure you have created a track for the instrument you want to define.**

   If you choose Piano to start your project (refer to Figure 20-1), the GarageBand window appears with a single *Grand Piano* track in the time-line.

2. **Click the Info button (look for the *i* icon) to open the Info pane for that track on the lower right side.**

3. **If the Browse tab isn't already selected, click it to browse instruments and settings and change the Software Instrument.**

   Browse the left column of the Info pane to select a type of instrument, such as Organs, and choose a specific instrument in the right column (such Classic Rock Organ). As you pick an instrument, the track name changes to the name of that instrument.

   You can change the instrument for a Software Instrument track at any time, before or after recording performances or adding loops.

4. **(Optional) Play the keyboard to hear what the Software Instrument sounds like.**

   To hear the different instrument settings, choose one and then play the onscreen keyboard, the Musical Typing keyboard, or a MIDI keyboard connected to your Mac (as I describe in Chapter 19).

5. **(Optional) To change the settings for that instrument, click the Edit tab at the top of the Info pane.**

   The settings and effects are different for each instrument — you can see Classic Rock Organ settings and effects in Figure 20-3.

6. **(Optional) To change the Sound Generator preset, click the icon in the Sound Generator section to open the specific settings for that generator, as shown on the left side of Figure 20-4.**

Figure 20-3: Use the Tonewheel Organ sound generator for the Classic Rock Organ.

The instrument's Sound Generator is the code that creates the Software Instrument. The Sound Generator section's pop-up menu (refer to Figure 20-3) is set to Tonewheel Organ; after you click the icon in the Sound Generator section, the Tonewheel Organ settings appear as shown in Figure 20-4 (on the left side).

7. (Optional) Adjust settings for the effects modules.

Effects modules, which appear underneath the Sound Generator section, change depending on which instrument you pick. You can adjust effects as described in this list:

- *Adjust settings:* Click the icon for the Compressor section to open its Settings window and change the settings (refer to the right side of Figure 20-4).

- *Turn an effect on or off:* Click the rectangle to the left of the icon for the effect to turn it on or off. For example, in Figure 20-3, the Visual EQ, Master Echo, and Master Reverb effects are already turned on.

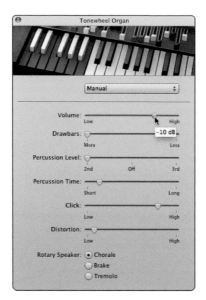 

Figure 20-4: Adjust the Tonewheel Organ settings (left) and Compressor settings (right).

- *Arrange effects to adjust their impact on the sound:* The order in which the effects appear in the Effects section determines how the effects work. For example, in Figure 20-3, the Visual EQ effect is below the Compressor and Chorus effects, so if the Compressor and Chorus effects are turned on, they affect the sound first, *before* the Visual EQ effect. You can rearrange the effects modules and thereby change the way they affect the sound, by dragging them up or down in the list.

Setting up an Electric Guitar track

Rather than spend a fortune on special effects boxes, pedals, and amplifiers to try to discover your unique sound, you can try out effects and amplifier settings in GarageBand. Here's how it works:

1. **Choose Electric Guitar to start your project (refer to Figure 20-1).**

   The GarageBand window appears with a Guitar track, named Clean Combo, in the timeline. This track offers amplifier settings and is ready to record your plugged-in electric guitar.

2. **Click the Info button (it has the *i* icon) to open the Info pane for the Electric Guitar track, as shown in Figure 20-5.**

Figure 20-5: Click the amplifier to change its settings for an Electric Guitar track.

3. **If the Guitar Track tab isn't already selected, click it to see the Guitar Track settings.**

4. **Click the Clean Combo track and pluck some strings on your electric guitar to hear how it sounds.**

5. **(Optional) Experiment with settings that appear when you click the amplifier, the sustain pedal, and the delay pedal.**

   The English Combo amplifier that appears for Clean Combo was a popular amp for British Invasion bands — but you can switch to other amplifiers by clicking the left or right arrows on either side of the amplifier. While your guitar gently weeps, you can also switch your gear (amplifiers, pedals, and effects) by choosing a setting from the pop-up menu in the Info pane for Electric Guitars, such as Classic Crunch, Eighties Alternative, Fat Stack, or Seattle Sound.

6. **(Optional) After you've chosen your gear, click the Edit button to customize the arrangement with pedals for special effects.**

   Your options include a Fuzz Machine, Sustain, Flanger, Chorus, and Delay pedals.

That's all you need to do — GarageBand remembers your settings. However, if you want to save these custom settings so that you can use the identical instrument, sound, and effects settings in *another* song, see "Saving your settings," later in this chapter.

Changing Real Instrument settings

You can choose a Real Instrument and set as many characteristics and effects as you want before recording into a Real Instrument track. On the other hand, if you're unsure what type of sound you want, you can record into the track and then add effects and change the characteristics of the sound later (such as choosing a different amplifier or applying a pedal setting).

If you choose Voice to start your project (refer to Figure 20-1), the GarageBand window appears with two vocal tracks, named Male Basic and Female Basic, in the timeline, as shown in Figure 20-6. These Real Instrument tracks are ready to record over a line-input source or the internal microphone. Follow these steps to choose settings for a Real Instrument track:

Figure 20-6: Change the setting of a Real Instrument track to Vocals.

1. **Click the Info button (look for the *i* icon) to open the Info pane for the Real Instrument.**

2. **Click Browse to choose instrument types in the left column, and settings in the right column, which affect recording in a Real Instrument track.**

Maybe you want *no* effects; or if you want some, you want to apply them later. If all you want is clean, unaffected recording of your instrument or voice, choose Basic Track in the left column and choose No Effects in the right column.

3. **At the bottom of the Info pane, set the input source from the Input Source pop-up menu.**

You can choose stereo or mono for your input source. If you're using an audio interface, choose the appropriate channel or stereo pair of channels. (See Chapter 19 for details on setting your System and GarageBand input connection.)

4. **Turn the monitor on or off from the Monitor pop-up menu.**

Turn on the monitor to hear yourself as you play your instrument or sing — you also hear the other song tracks as you sing or play. You should use headphones if you're monitoring a microphone track.

If you hear a loud shrieking noise, the microphone (or pickup) you're using is picking up the sound from the speakers and causing feedback. You can choose On with Feedback Protection from the Monitor pop-up menu to automatically turn off monitoring if feedback from the input source occurs, or you can choose Off to turn off the monitor and use headphones rather than speakers.

5. **Check and adjust the Recording Level setting, if needed.**

The *recording level* is the input volume over the line-in, microphone, or audio interface connection. The input volume has an upper limit that's set by the Sound preferences pane (as described in Chapter 19). Red dots that appear on the right side of the Master Level meter while recording indicate that the recording volume is too high (technically, the audio input is *clipping*), and you should drag the Recording Level slider to the left to lower the volume.

6. **To change the effects for the Real Instrument track, click the Edit tab at the top of the Info pane.**

The settings and effects are similar to the ones used for Software Instrument tracks — a compressor, an equalizer, echo, and reverb, for example. In addition, blank effects modules appear in the Effects section — click a blank module to add an effect from the pop-up menu that appears. For example, in Figure 20-7, I'm adding the AUBandpass Audio Unit effect (a professional band-pass filter effect) to my list of effects for the selected voice track.

Figure 20-7: Add another effect to the active effects for a Real Instrument track.

Click the rectangle to the left of the icon for the effect to turn it on or off. Just as with Software Instrument effects (see the earlier section "Generating a Software Instrument"), the order in which the effects appear determines how they work, and you can rearrange the effects modules and thereby change the way they affect the sound, by dragging them up or down in the list.

Before recording, make sure that your instrument or microphone is connected and working. After selecting a Real Instrument type and setting, you can hear immediately the sound and any effects that are set up for the instrument by playing it (or by singing, if your track is for vocals).

Saving your settings

As you experiment with settings, every time you make a change, GarageBand shows a dialog that says You have made changes to the current instrument or instrument setting. You can then click Save As to save your changes as a custom instrument or setting, or click Continue to discard the changes and continue working.

Even though the changes you make to instruments and settings are automatically saved with the track in the song, you may want to save these custom settings so that you can use the identical instrument, sound, and effects settings in *another* song. To do so, follow these steps:

1. **Click the Save Instrument button at the bottom of the Info pane for Software Instruments and Real Instruments. Or, click the Save Settings button for Electric Guitar.**

2. **In the Save Instrument dialog that appears, give the instrument or setting a new name and then click OK.**

Recording a Track

The moment of truth has arrived. If you need to summon the courage to perform for your Mac, imagine John Lennon, at age 15, playing to an audience even though he didn't yet know how to tune a guitar. You have to take a chance: If Elvis Presley had not gone to Sun Records on his own initiative to make a recording for his mother's birthday, Sam Phillips never would have helped turn him into a star.

Before recording a track, make sure you've defined the instrument and its settings properly, as I describe earlier in this chapter, in the "Defining Track Instruments and Effects" section. If you're recording a Real Instrument track, pay particular attention to the earlier section "Changing Real Instrument settings," and be sure to set the Input Source, Recording Level, and Monitor settings.

To record into a track, follow these steps:

1. **Select the track for the recording.**

   Click the header of the track to select it. You can record into a new track or into an existing track in a new region or over an existing region.

2. **Drag the playhead to the point in the timeline where you want to start recording (or leave the playhead at the beginning of the timeline).**

3. **(Optional) Turn on the metronome and the Count In option to play one measure before starting to record by choosing Control⇨Metronome and Control⇨Count In (respectively).**

   A more sophisticated metronome is used in professional studios as a *click track* to help keep time while playing an instrument or singing; you can simulate a click track by using the GarageBand metronome: It clicks for each beat of the measure (not recorded with the music). You can turn the metronome on or off by choosing Control⇨Metronome. (A check mark indicates that it's turned on). If you use the metronome, you might also want to turn on the Count In option by choosing Control⇨Count In — just like a bandleader counting 1-2-3-4 to prepare the band to begin a song, GarageBand plays the metronome one full measure before starting to record so that you can get ready to perform along with the beat.

4. **Click the red Record button to start recording, and then start playing (or singing).**

   GarageBand starts to record in the track while playing any other tracks, and it lays down a new region in the track's timeline.

5. **Click the red Record button again to stop recording, and press the spacebar or click the Play button to stop playback.**

To hear your recording, drag the playhead in the timeline back to the beginning or to wherever the new recorded region starts, and then click the Play button or press the spacebar.

As you record each track, you can build up a song. You can overdub a section of a song by simply creating a new track and recording into it at the precise point in the song where you want the section to begin: Click a starting point in a track or otherwise move the playhead to begin recording at that point. You can also correct a mistake this way: Record the correct part in a new track, and edit the other track to delete the mistake.

Arranging Your Tracks

In This Chapter

▶ Adding and extending loops

▶ Moving and copying track regions

▶ Arranging a song with the Arrangement Track

▶ Using cycle regions

▶ Making an audio or video podcast episode

*A*t the time the Beatles and Bob Dylan were recording their first hits, the studios offered only four tracks for recording everything. Somehow the Beatles had to combine — onto only four tracks — all the vocals, guitars, bass, and drum performances, and even a separate harmonica performance (because on songs such as "I Should Have Known Better," John Lennon couldn't play it and sing the chorus at the same time). Tape *overdubbing*, pioneered by Les Paul (who also invented, obviously, the Les Paul guitar), made it possible to erase or record over previous recordings on tape and thus combine tracks in a limited way, even though sound quality is reduced with each re-recording of the tape.

Multitrack recording (still on tape) made *editing* possible — pieces of the recording could be removed, or rearranged, or even recorded over. That sounds much like GarageBand, doesn't it? This chapter shows you how recorded track regions can be rearranged, copied, split into separate regions, joined into one, and even resized. You can record instruments into separate tracks and build up a song by overlaying more tracks to enrich the sound. You can quickly and easily overdub instruments in separate tracks to your heart's content. You can also use cycle regions to record separate takes in the same region.

Track regions can also be repeated in a sequence known as a *loop*. The first tape loops were used in avant-garde recordings during the 1940s and 1950s and in Beatles songs in the 1960s, such as "Tomorrow Never Knows" (the sounds of birds and guitar licks played backward) and "Being for the Benefit of Mr. Kite" on *Sgt. Pepper's Lonely Hearts Club Band* (in which loops of pump organs and circus sounds were literally cut into pieces and thrown into the air and then reassembled at random in the studio). The Beastie Boys paid homage to the Beatles 20 years later by including a loop in "The Sounds of Science" (on *Paul's Boutique*) that repeated part of the Beatles song "The End" (from *Abbey Road*). In this chapter, I show you how to use the high-quality prerecorded loops that are included with GarageBand.

Here We Go Loop-de-Loop

"Yesterday's experiment is tomorrow's cliché," remarked Bob Welch (formerly of Fleetwood Mac, a band that knows a thing or two about clichés). But somewhere in the middle between experiment and cliché is the familiar *riff*, or the sequence of notes in a particular rhythm. Past experiments in guitar licks, keyboard riffs, horn phrases, and drum rolls have become familiar and useful in today's popular songs as samples that repeat over and over. Sequences that repeat are *loops*. You can turn any sequence into a loop as long as it sounds good when it's repeated.

GarageBand is supplied with loops that sound great when repeated, in the Apple Loops format. Okay, Apple Loops sounds like a breakfast cereal, but this cool utility can be used free and clear of any royalties or licenses. GarageBand includes thousands of these prerecorded Apple Loops and a Loop Browser that categorizes them so that you can find the loop you want for a particular mood or genre — everything from Acoustic Noodling 02 (guitar) to Backroads Banjo 19.

You can purchase additional Apple Loops from Apple, and you can use prerecorded loops from other sources in the Apple Loop format, both free and purchased. (Loops from other sources may be royalty-free, but they may have other restrictions — be sure to consult the fine print before you purchase them.)

 You can add loops by dragging and dropping loop files or an entire folder of loop files into the GarageBand Loop Browser. The new loops are copied to the Loops Library and automatically indexed so that they appear in the Loop Browser.

When you drag a loop to the timeline to add a loop region in a track, the loop automatically matches the tempo you've set for the song, and if the loop has a melody, the melodic notes are automatically transposed into the key set for the song. You have no worries about being out of tune or incapable of keeping time — GarageBand takes care of that issue for you.

Searching for the right loop

The Loop Browser lets you browse loops by instrument, and for each instrument, you can narrow the search by genre, mood, or type. Follow these steps to search for and select a loop:

1. **Click the Loop Browser button (the Eye icon) or choose Control⇨Show Loop Browser.**

   The Loop Browser appears on the right side of the GarageBand window.

2. **Click the Musical Notation icon in the center of the row of view icons to the left of the Scale pop-up menu in the upper left corner of the Loop Browser (if it isn't already selected).**

   Loop Browser view shows a grid of buttons, as you can see in Figure 21-1.

Figure 21-1: Choose an instrument type or genre for a loop, and refine your search by clicking more buttons.

3. **Click a keyword button on the grid of buttons at the top of the Loop Browser.**

   When you click an instrument such as All Drums, all drum loops then appear in the scrolling results list below the grid.

4. **Scroll the list of loops and click a loop's name to hear it.**

   The loop repeats until you click the loop again to stop it, or until you click another loop to hear what that loop sounds like.

 You can adjust the volume of playback by dragging the Volume slider in the lower left corner of the Loop Browser.

The grid of keyword buttons helps you refine your search by breaking the loops into categories, reducing the number of loops in the resulting scrolling list. After you click a button for an instrument category, the Loop Browser highlights more buttons in the grid that you can click to narrow your search by genre, mood, or type. For example, you can narrow the search by picking a musical genre (World) and then a mood (Relaxed) or a type (Electric) — or all of them. To reset the grid to show all buttons, click Reset in the upper left corner of the grid.

To browse loops in Column view, click the Columns icon to the left of the Musical Notation icon in the row of view buttons in the upper left corner of the Loop Browser window. After clicking a keyword in the left column, you have a choice of matching categories in the middle column. Click a category in the middle column to show matching keywords in the right column. Click a keyword in the right column to show matching loops in the results list.

Next to the columns icon is the Musical Notation icon, which changes Loop Browser view to a grid of buttons, and the Broadcast icon, which changes it to show sound effects and jingles.

In the list of loops, you can see the loop's tempo, key, and number of beats. The icon to the left of the loop's name is a waveform for Real Instrument loops, or a musical notation symbol for Software Instrument loops.

 If you have already assembled tracks for a song, you can preview a loop along with the rest of your song. The loop automatically plays in the same key and tempo. Click the Rewind button to return the playhead to the beginning, click the Play button to play the song, and click the loop to hear it at the same time. The loop automatically plays along with the beat of the song.

Limiting choices by scale and key

You may want to limit your loop choices to a particular scale or key so that you aren't overwhelmed by choices that make no sense for your song. That way, you don't have to wade through loops such as Orchestra Brass 01 and

Orchestra Brass 02 set in the key of D-sharp, or Medieval Flute 01 through 06 set in the key of E (except, of course, 03, which is set in the key of B) just to find a good horn section for your song in the key of C. You can refine your search for loops by scale (major, minor, neither, or both) and set preferences to show only loops that are relevant for the key of the song.

Most loops (except for drum and percussion loops) are recorded in either a minor or major scale. The Scale pop-up menu at the top of the Loop Browser (refer to Figure 21-1) lets you narrow your results to Any, Major (in a major scale), Minor (in a minor scale), Neither, or Good for Both (loops that can be used in major or minor scales).

Not all loops sound good in certain keys (again, with the exception of drum and percussion loops). Loops recorded in a different key may sound distorted after being automatically transposed — which is what happens when you use the loop in a song set to a different key.

By filtering more relevant options, you can limit the list of loops to those that are relevant to the song's key. Choose GarageBand⇨Preferences, click the Loops tab, and turn on the Filter More Relevant Results option. While this option is selected, the GarageBand Loop Browser displays only loops that are either in the same key as the song or in major or minor scales related to the key of the song.

Adding loop regions

Create a track for one or more loop regions by dragging a loop into an empty space on the timeline. Follow these steps:

1. **Select a loop in the Loop Browser.**

2. **Turn on the Snap to Grid feature (if it isn't already on) by choosing Control⇨Snap to Grid.**

   You know whether the Snap to Grid feature is active because a check mark appears next to it on the Control menu. Though you don't have to use the Snap to Grid feature, it makes it easier to line up regions in the tracks.

3. **Drag the loop to an empty space below the timeline beat ruler, as I do in Figure 21-2.**

   As you drag, you may notice that a vertical line appears and lines up the loop with the beat. The loop snaps to different points in the timeline — points defined by the tempo and time signature (the beat) — if you have the Snap to Grid feature turned on.

Dragging a loop

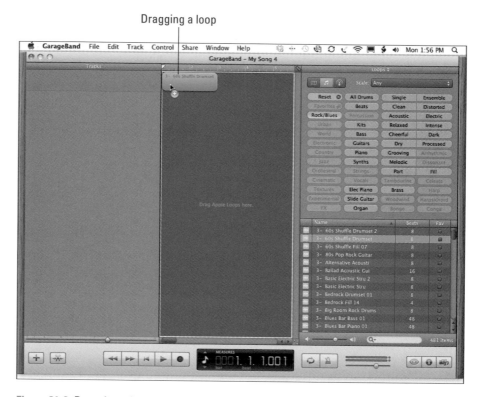

Figure 21-2: Dragging a loop to the timeline.

You can also create a track first, as I describe in Chapter 20. Choose a Software Instrument or Real Instrument for the track, and then drag a loop to the track. This method is useful if you already have in mind an instrument sound that's different from the sound used for the loop.

After you drag a loop to a track, the loop creates a region in the track showing a waveform for a Real Instrument, or a set of dashes that look like notes for a Software Instrument (unless no notes are played, in which case the region is gray). You can drag a Real Instrument loop into a Real Instrument track, and drag a Software Instrument loop into a Software Instrument track. The differences between the types of loops are described in this list:

✔ **Real Instrument:** Although this type of loop is recorded with live instruments in a specific tempo, time signature, and key, the loops are somewhat elastic — you can change the tempo and transpose them into different keys, with mixed results. You can also copy and paste waveform information in the Track Editor, as described in Chapter 22, but you can't change individual notes. Neither can you change the instrument itself, as you can with Software Instrument loops.

> ✔ **Software Instrument:** You can change the tempo and key of this type of loop with no loss in quality. You can even change the type of instrument — change a guitar loop into a drum loop by simply dragging the guitar loop to a track defined as a drum track. Software Instrument loops can also be edited in the Track Editor in detail — you can change the notes, their placement in time, and other attributes, as described in Chapter 22.

Arranging Regions in the Timeline

When you see the Arranged By credit on a song, it doesn't mean that the producer arranged to have the song recorded and distributed or arranged to have the artist paid or arranged the furniture in the recording studio. Someone who *arranges* a song decides exactly *how* the song should be played (and with which instruments) and *when* each part should be played.

An *arrangement* is a written-down description of how to play a song, much like a recipe. Because the arrangement describes notes played over time, it has to show information about the song over time. Arrangers have put together charts, sometimes with meticulous musical scores, to produce arrangements. GarageBand goes a step further and offers a visual depiction of the song using a timeline.

When you drag a loop to the timeline, or record into a track, GarageBand represents the music with a region in the timeline showing graphically what the sound looks like:

> ✔ **Real Instrument regions:** Loops are blue regions showing waveforms, and recordings are red waveforms while recording, and then purple waveforms after you finish recording.

> ✔ **Software Instrument regions:** Both recordings and loops are green regions showing dashes on a musical scale. (Dashes with higher pitch are in the upper part of the region, and dashes with lower pitch are in the lower part.)

As building blocks for your song, regions help you define pieces of music that may change, depending on the arrangement. You might, for example, record into a separate Software Instrument track a guitar part that accompanies a chorus and then copy the region of that single performance to the same places in the timeline as each chorus in the song — so that you need to perform the guitar part only once.

Changing the timeline grid

The timeline beat ruler shows the divisions of time in either beats and measures or minutes and seconds — depending on whether you choose Time or Measures in the LCD at the bottom of the GarageBand window. (See Chapter 18 for a description of the LCD.)

You can use the beat ruler to align musical regions precisely. The timeline offers a grid to snap these segments into place. To turn on the grid, choose Control⇨Snap to Grid.

You can also set the grid to different musical note values, such as quarter notes, eighth notes, sixteenth notes, 30-second notes, quarter note triplets, and eighth note triplets. To set the grid to a different note value, click the grid button in the upper right corner of the timeline, as shown in Figure 21-3, and then choose a note value from the menu. You can set the grid to Automatic so that it becomes more precise as you zoom in or out using the timeline zoom slider under the track names.

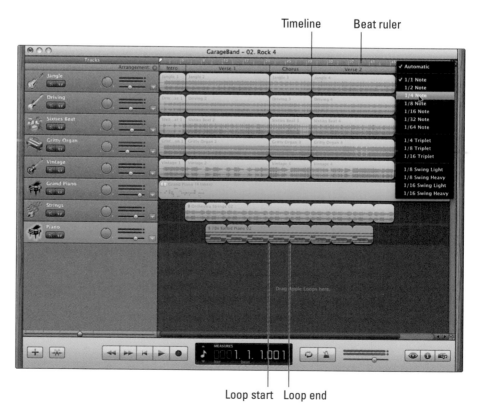

Figure 21-3: Set the timeline grid to a different note value.

Moving and resizing regions

The reason that these pieces of music are organized into regions is so that you can move them easily within tracks. Drag a region within a track (left or right) to change its starting point in the song.

You can even drag a region from one track to another (up or down), if you want the region to take on the characteristics (sounds and effects) of the destination track. When dragging regions, here's what you need to know:

✔ Real Instrument regions can be moved only to other Real Instrument tracks, and Software Instrument regions can be moved only to other Software Instrument tracks.

✔ When you drag a region over another region in the same time slot, the region underneath is shortened to the edge of the region you're dragging over it. If you completely cover a region with another region, the region underneath is deleted.

You also resize regions, making them shorter or longer, as described in this list:

✔ You can shorten a region so that only the visible part of the region plays.

✔ You can also lengthen a Software Instrument region, adding silence — but only to Software Instrument regions; Real Instrument regions can only be shortened or returned to their original lengths.

✔ To resize a region, move the pointer over the lower half of either the right or left edge of the region — the pointer changes to the resize pointer (two arrows pointing sideways). You can then drag the edge of the region to shorten or lengthen it.

Selecting, copying, and pasting regions

Being able to copy and paste regions is useful: You can perform a task once and repeat it thousands of times. You can even copy multiple regions in different tracks at one time. For example, if a set of regions for bass and drum tracks are perfect for a few measures and you want to use them throughout the song, you can select the regions and then copy and paste them. Because you can copy regions from multiple tracks at a time (as in a vertical selection of regions), you can copy entire sections of a song to another place in the song.

Here's how to select, copy, and paste in GarageBand:

- **Selecting regions:** Click a region to select it, and Shift-click to select multiple regions. You can also select multiple regions at a time by dragging an imaginary selection rectangle around all the regions you want to select. As you drag from a point in the timeline, any regions intersecting your imaginary rectangle are highlighted to show that they're selected.

- **Copying regions:** To copy a region, select it and then choose Edit⇨Copy (or press Command+C).

- **Pasting regions:** To paste the copy in the track at a different location in the timeline, move the playhead to the point where you want the copied region to start and then choose Edit⇨Paste (or press Command+V).

To copy and paste multiple regions at a time, select the regions first, and then copy and paste them. If you hold down the Option key while dragging a region, you automatically make a copy of the region; when you drop the copy, it's just like pasting it into the new location.

After you paste one or more regions, the playhead moves to the end of the first pasted region, which is convenient because you can choose Edit⇨Paste again (or press Command+V again) to paste another copy right next to the first one.

- **Cutting and pasting regions:** To delete regions from one location and paste them into another, choose Edit⇨Cut rather than Edit⇨Copy. However, simply dragging the selected regions to the new location in the timeline might be faster.

- **Deleting regions:** You can delete a region by selecting it and pressing the Delete key on the keyboard or by choosing Edit⇨Delete. If you want to move all other regions to the left in the timeline after deleting the region, choose Edit⇨Delete and Move — all regions on the same track move left by the length of the deleted region.

Looping loops and regions

Music is all about repetition, and loops were made to be looped. After you drag a loop to a track, the region occupies only a few measures of the song. Although you can paste a region repeatedly and quickly to repeat a region over time, GarageBand makes this process a lot easier with the loop pointer. When you loop a region, the region plays repeatedly and smoothly without no seams between start and finish. You can loop Real Instrument recordings, Software Instrument recordings, and loops of both types.

To loop a region, move the pointer to the upper right edge of the region — the pointer changes to the loop pointer (a circular arrow). You can then drag the loop pointer to extend the region to the point where you want it to stop looping. The notches at the top and bottom show the beginning and end of the piece of music that loops (refer to Figure 21-3). You can drag to the end or to anywhere in the middle of a looping region.

You can use silence to your advantage. First, extend a Software Instrument region to add silence to a musical phrase, and then loop the region so that the fully extended region, including silence, is repeated. That way, the region can be looped through the rest of the song and play accurately with the same amount of silence between the repeated musical phrases.

To hear the looping region, drag the playhead in the timeline back to the beginning or to wherever the new recorded region starts, and then click the Play button.

Splitting and joining regions

A region can be split into two or more regions. You may want to split a region if you recorded a great performance but you want to use part of it in one place in the song and part of it in another place. You can split the region and then drag one part to another place in the song.

You can also join regions as long as they're already adjacent to one another on the same track, with no space between them. This capability is useful if you recorded an outstanding performance at the beginning and end of a region but made mistakes in the middle. You can split the region into three pieces — the good part, the bad part, and the final good part —and then join the first and last into one region.

- ✔ **To split a musical region into two or more regions,** select the region, move the playhead to the point in the region where you want the split to occur, and choose Edit➪Split. The selected region is split into two regions at the playhead; any notes in a Software Instrument region at the split point are shortened so that they don't extend past the split point.

- ✔ **To join two or more regions,** select the regions to be joined and choose Edit➪Join.

    Software Instrument regions (green) can be joined only to other Software Instrument regions, and Real Instrument recordings (purple) can only be joined to other Real Instrument recordings. Real Instrument loops (blue regions) can't be joined to other regions.

Using the Arrangement Track

GarageBand offers a special Arrangement Track for defining vertical *arrangement regions* in a song, just as an arranger would define sections in a chart, and use labels such as Verse and Chorus for easy identification. You can then drag an arrangement region to move it or Option-drag to copy it to another part of the song. For example, you can define a Chorus arrangement region with multiple tracks and copy the entire arrangement region to another part of the song, without having to select individual track regions.

Follow these steps to use the Arrangement Track:

1. **To show the Arrangement Track (if it isn't already visible), choose Track⇨Show Arrangement Track.**

   A slim track appears above the first track with *Arrangement* as its title, as shown in Figure 21-4. By default, when you start a project, the Arrangement Track is showing.

Typing a region name

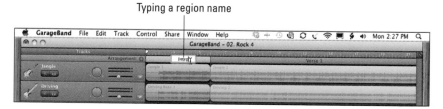

Figure 21-4: Define an arrangement region in the Arrange Track.

2. **Click the Add Region (+) button next to *Arrangement* to add your first arrangement region.**

3. **Click the selected arrangement region (if it isn't selected, double-click it), and after the name is selected, type a new name for the region (refer to Figure 21-4).**

   At first, the arrangement region is eight measures long.

4. **Drag the arrangement region's right edge to adjust it so that it covers the part of the song you want to include.**

   The first vertical region starts at the beginning of the project, and each additional one you add starts at the end of the previous one.

5. **Continue to work your way across the timeline to define the entire song in arrangement regions.**

As you work with an Arrangement Track, the following pointers can help you create the results you want:

- ✓ **Select an arrangement region:** Click the arrangement region name in the Arrangement Track, as shown in Figure 21-5, or Shift-click regions to select multiple ones.

- ✓ **Move regions:** After selecting a region (or regions), you can then drag to move, or Option-drag to copy, the region to a new position in the Arrangement Track, as shown in Figure 21-6. The other regions make room at the point where you want to insert the moved or copied region.

  Moving or copying an arrangement region moves or copies all track regions and other items in the timeline covered by the arrangement region.

Selecting a region

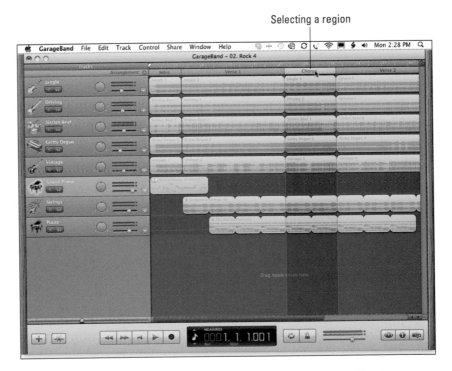

Figure 21-5: Select the Chorus arrangement region in the Arrangement Track.

✔ **Replace an arrangement region:** Simply Command-drag one arrangement region directly over another one.

✔ **Delete an arrangement region:** To delete a region and its music track regions, select the arrangement region and then press Delete to delete the music in the timeline below the arrangement region so that it's empty. Press Delete again to delete the arrangement region itself.

When you move or delete an arrangement region, the rest of the song's track regions to the right move left to fill the deleted section, closing the empty space.

Dragging a region

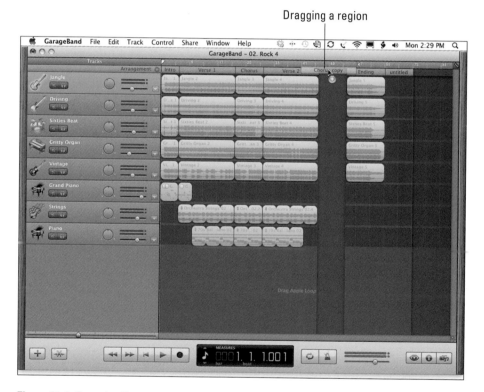

Figure 21-6: Copy the Chorus arrangement region and its music to another part of the song.

Recording into a cycle region

It's nice to know that you can record over any part of a song and correct it with a new version. You can be just like the superstars who make their songs perfect — you can overdub to your heart's content. *Overdubbing* occurs when you record directly over a part of a song, replacing the instrument part with a new part. In GarageBand, you do this by creating a *cycle region,* which restricts the recording to a specific time segment in the selected track.

You can record a performance into a cycle region of a track of the same type (Real Instrument recording into a Real Instrument track, Electric Guitar recording into an Electric Guitar track, or Software Instrument recording into a Software Instrument track).

Each recording in a cycle region is normally stored as a separate take, but you can also use a cycle region to *merge* multiple recorded takes with a Software Instrument to layer the sound (such as multiple drum beats) without having to resort to using multiple tracks. To change the way the cycle region works, choose GarageBand⇨Preferences, click the General tab, and turn on the option labeled Cycle Recording: Automatically Merge Software Instrument Recordings.

To create a cycle region, follow these steps:

1. **Click the Cycle button.**

   The Cycle button, with its revolving arrows, is in the row of transport control buttons. This button opens the cycle ruler, which is a tiny second ruler that appears below the beat ruler.

2. **Drag inside the cycle ruler to define a yellow bar that indicates a cycle region in the timeline, as shown in Figure 21-7.**

   Make sure that the beginning and end of the yellow bar are set accurately in the timeline for the time section.

3. **Select a track and click the Record button to record a performance.**

   With the cycle region defined, you record directly into the cycle region of that track. As you record, the region changes to show a badge showing the number of takes (unless you switched the preferences option to merge recordings, as I explain earlier). You don't have to click to stop and record again — the cycle region loops automatically.

4. **When you finish recording, click the Cycle button to turn off the cycle region.**

After recording multiple takes, you can select different takes or delete takes by clicking the number badge in the recorded region, as shown in Figure 21-8. If you switched the preferences option to merge recordings, you end up with one recording of all merged performances.

Dragging to define a cycle region

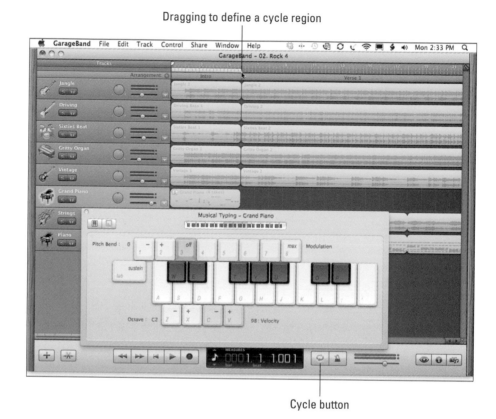

Cycle button

Figure 21-7: Define a cycle region by dragging in the opened cycle ruler.

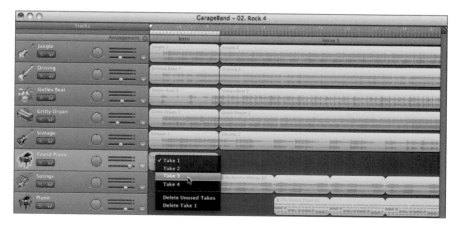

Figure 21-8: Choose a take.

Making a Podcast Episode

GarageBand is the perfect tool for creating audio or video podcast episodes with narration, dialogue, music, sound effects, chapter markers, artwork, and Web addresses (URLs).

To start with the appropriate tracks for a podcast episode, choose New Project from the opening dialog for your new project (see Chapter 20 to find out about creating a new project) and choose Podcast. In a podcast project, the Podcast Track appears above other tracks in the timeline, as shown in Figure 21-9. The Editor underneath the tracks shows the marker list, with columns for the start time, artwork, chapter title, URL title, and URL for each marker.

Podcast Track   Marker   Adding another marker

Marker information

Figure 21-9: A podcast project.

A podcast project includes two Real Instrument tracks — Male Voice and Female Voice — which are optimized for recording spoken narration or dialogue. You set up these tracks and record into them just as you do with any Real Instrument track. (See Chapter 20 for details on Real Instrument tracks.)

A podcast project also provides background tracks — you can add loops for jingles, stingers, and sound effects, as described in this list:

- *Jingles:* You can use these complete background music tracks behind the narration or dialogue. Some jingles are available in long, medium, and short versions.

- *Stingers:* These brief sounds can be used as transitions or audio "punctuation" between speakers or between sections of a podcast.

- *Sound effects:* These effects include the sounds of people, animals, and machines as well as room ambience and other environmental sounds.

To choose any of these tracks, click the Loop Browser button to open the Loop Browser, and click the Podcast Sounds button (with the radiating sound wave) in the upper left corner of the Loops Browser to the left of the Scale pop-up menu (refer to Figure 21-1).

To enhance narration tracks, select the recorded region in the track to edit it in the Editor, which I describe in Chapter 22 — you can adjust the pitch with the Pitch slider (and click the Follow Tempo & Pitch option to keep the audio track on pitch and tempo for the project), enhance tuning with the Enhance Tuning slider (and limit tuning to the set key for the project), and enhance timing to match the set time signature with the Enhance Timing slider.

Including images

You can import media files from other iLife applications, including iTunes and iPhoto, into a podcast project. For example, you can drag artwork or an image from the Photos pane of the Media Browser to the Podcast Track. To find and preview media files, click the Media Browser button in the far right corner of the GarageBand window (or choose Control⇨Show Media Browser). You can even import other GarageBand projects that have been saved in an iLife preview. (See Chapter 20 for details on saving a project.)

To add artwork for the podcast episode (a photo or an image that's visible while the episode plays), drag the image from the Media Browser to the Episode Artwork well in the Editor (refer to Figure 21-9). You can also resize and crop the image: Double-click the image in the Episode Artwork well or the marker list to open the Artwork Editor, and then drag the Size slider in the Artwork Editor to resize the image, and drag the image within the black border to crop it.

Adding and editing markers

Markers are useful for separating sections of a podcast episode. You can add images to each marker region of the Podcast Track so that they appear during that portion of the podcast episode. Follow these basic guidelines to be able to create and add markers:

- **Add a marker:** Click the Podcast Track, move the playhead to the place where you want to add the marker, and click the Add Marker (+) button at the bottom of the GarageBand window. The marker appears in the Editor below the tracks, and the start time for the marker appears in the Time column in the marker's row (refer to Figure 21-9). The marker also appears as a marker region in the Podcast Track: To resize the marker region, drag either edge of the marker region; to move it, drag it to a new position in the Podcast Track.

- **Add an image to a marker region:** Drag the image from the Media Browser to the Artwork box in the marker's row in the Editor. You can also drag the image directly to the Podcast Track, as I do in Figure 21-9, which adds a new marker region including the image.

- **Add a chapter title to a marker, turning it into a chapter marker:** When people play a podcast episode in iTunes, they can easily move to a specific chapter in the episode. To add a chapter title to a marker, select the placeholder text in the Chapter Title column of the marker's row and then type a title.

Adding episode information

Podcasts require information such as the episode title, author, and description. An episode may also have a parental advisory, which appears when someone plays the podcast in iTunes.

To edit the podcast episode's information, select the Podcast Track and click the Track Info (look for the *i*) button (or choose Track⇨Show Track Info) to see the Episode Info pane. Click the Title field to type a title, and click the Artist field to add artist information. You can choose None, Clean, or Explicit from the Parental Advisory pop-up menu and include a description of the podcast episode in the Description field.

Learning to duck

You may want to *duck,* or lower the volume of, the backing tracks for a podcast episode in order to better hear spoken narration or dialogue. (When you duck, you lower your head quickly to avoid something, right? You also learn about ducking with iMovie in Chapter 9.) The ducking controls appear in the track header for a podcast project (refer to Figure 21-9) with arrows pointing up and down. (If the arrows aren't visible, choose Control⇨Ducking to turn them on.)

First you make a track the lead track by clicking the upper part of its ducking control (the arrow pointing upward). Then you make other tracks backing tracks by clicking the lower part of the track's ducking control (the arrow pointing downward). As a result, whenever sound appears on a lead track, the backing tracks are lowered and the volume of the lead track stays the same.

Making a video podcast

Creating a video podcast episode is similar to creating an audio podcast episode, except that a Movie Track (with video clips) is substituted for the Podcast Track and doesn't include artwork. You can drag an iMovie project or another QuickTime-compatible video file from the Media Browser to the project, view the video as you add more audio, and add and edit markers as you would do for an audio podcast episode.

A project can have either a Podcast Track or a Movie Track, but not both. As you drag a video from the Movies pane of the Media Browser, GarageBand asks whether you want to replace the Podcast Track with a Movie Track. Click Replace to turn the episode into a video episode. (You lose any existing markers and artwork.)

A podcast project holds only one video file. If you drag another video into a project that already has one, a dialog appears, asking whether you want to replace the existing one with the new one. If you want to combine multiple videos in a single video podcast episode, combine them in an iMovie project first, as I describe in Chapter 10.

After you drag a video to the project, the Movie Track appears at the top of the timeline, showing still frames from the video. To preview the video, click the Preview button (the large, square button showing a movie frame) in the header of the Movie Track.

If the video includes an audio track, a new Real Instrument track named Movie Sound appears below the Movie Track for the video's audio. You can adjust settings and edit the Movie Sound track exactly as you would edit any Real Instrument track. You can also record narration exactly the same way as in an audio podcast episode, add sound loops, and record into Real Instrument and Software Instrument tracks.

22

Getting the Best Mix

In This Chapter

▶ Setting the volume and pan position for each track

▶ Using the Track Editor

▶ Adjusting the timing of real instruments

▶ Matching all tracks to the groove

▶ Using the master track controls

▶ Making a final mix

▶ Exporting your song or podcast

*M*ixing is an art form unto itself: It's the process of controlling and balancing the volume of all tracks and adding track effects while combining all tracks into a final song. You've probably bought CD versions of older vinyl record (LP) albums that were "remixed" as well as remastered for CD. These terms simply mean that the song tracks were recombined in such a way as to bring out subtleties in the music.

Mixing engineers know how to make a performance of nine instruments sound good when you hear it on two stereo channels, balancing the loud and soft instruments. Bands have been known to split up over the handling of their album mixes — Paul McCartney cited Phil Spector's mix of the *Let It Be* album as a major reason for the arguments that led to the demise of the Beatles. Skip Spence of Moby Grape got so mad about the mix that he sunk a hatchet into the door of the expensive studio they were using and had to be escorted off the premises.

Nothing like that is likely to happen, because this chapter shows you how to mix your tracks into a song quickly and easily. In this chapter, you can find out all about mixing and shaping the sound to create an excellent stereo result.

Mixing Tracks

Sir George Martin, arguably one of the most influential music producers of his time as the producer of the Beatles, described making a record as painting a picture in sound. Stereo was designed to give listeners a broader auditory experience; hearing sounds coming from both the left and right speakers adds a spatial dimension. The picture Sir George Martin is talking about is more like a *panorama*. A common studio technique — used explicitly by Pink Floyd, Jimi Hendrix, the Moody Blues, and other bands — was to *pan* the sound across this dimension so that the sound seems to travel from the left to the right (or vice versa).

Consequently, in GarageBand, you can "place" each track of the sound in this panorama and control the volume of each track.

Creating a mix of the song isn't always complicated. You may simply need to raise or lower the volume of the individual tracks by using the track volume sliders. If it sounds good after doing so, you're well on your way to finishing the mix. However, you may need to refine the volume for each track to create a good mix by setting the pan position for each track and setting automation curves for settings, as I explain in the following sections.

Setting the volume and pan position

The volume for each track can be raised or lowered so that you can achieve a balance of sound across all tracks. You can drag the track's Volume slider in the track header to the left to lower the track's volume, and to the right to raise it.

In addition, you can place the sound for each track in the stereo field with the pan wheel in the track header. Drag counterclockwise to pan to the left channel, or clockwise to pan to the right — the wheel's white dot indicates the position. Option-click the pan wheel to return it to the center position.

Drum and bass tracks are typically set to the middle (balanced between the left and right stereo fields), and vocals, lead instruments, and supporting instruments and vocals can be put in either channel.

Setting automation curves for settings

Sound is fluid, and by controlling the ebb and flow of the volume and other settings for a track, you can work wonders to improve a song. GarageBand provides an *automation curve* for controlling the track volume, track pan, and automated mixing settings over the duration of a song. You can raise or lower the volume of a track at specific points to simulate a crescendo or decrescendo, to make specific tracks fade in or out, or even to hide a bad note by lowering the volume in the track at that moment.

To set an automation curve for Track Volume, follow these steps:

1. **Click the Curves (triangle) button in the track header, and choose Track Volume from the pop-up menu.**

2. **Click the rectangle next to Track Volume to turn it on or off.**

   After you turn it on, a horizontal volume line appears in the row underneath the track, as shown in Figure 22-1.

3. **Click the line to create several points, and then drag each point to define a curve.**

   A setting of 0 indicates even volume, dragging up into positive numbers increases volume, and dragging down into negative numbers decreases volume. The volume changes evenly between points on the volume curve, providing smoother volume control for the track.

Figure 22-1: Click and then drag a point on the automation curve for Track Volume.

Setting an automation curve for Track Pan works in the same way as the Track Volume curve works. Just choose Track Pan from the pop-up menu. As you drag the curve, the 0 setting is the middle, dragging up into positive numbers pans to the right channel, and dragging down into negative numbers pans to the left channel. The pan changes evenly between points on the curve, providing smoother pan control for the track.

Choose Add Automation from the pop-up menu to add automation curves for Visual EQ and Echo & Reverb settings.

Tightening Up the Groove

Music producers sometimes "put down" the drum and bass tracks first, before building the rest of a song, so that the other musicians have a good rhythm to play against. Still, at times, tracks just don't fit the rhythm of the drumbeat, or the drums don't match up to the bass. Somewhere in the mix, however, is a track that defines "the groove" of the song.

I don't have to define the groove — you know that perfect rhythm when you hear it (or feel it). After you have identified the track that makes the groove happen (usually a drum track), you can tell GarageBand to adjust all other tracks to match the groove of the groove track. This *groove matching* can automatically turn an amateur-sounding project into a professional production.

After identifying the track that has the groove, click the far left side of the track header. When the gray star appears, click it to mark the track as the groove track. A dialog appears and explains that GarageBand needs to take a few moments to analyze the audio for groove tracks. Click Continue to analyze the audio (or Cancel to cancel).

GarageBand spends a few moments analyzing the audio and then displays the tracks with check marks next to them, as shown in Figure 22-2, to note that they're now adjusted for the groove.

You can change the groove track to another track by dragging the star, and you can click the star to turn the groove track into a regular track.

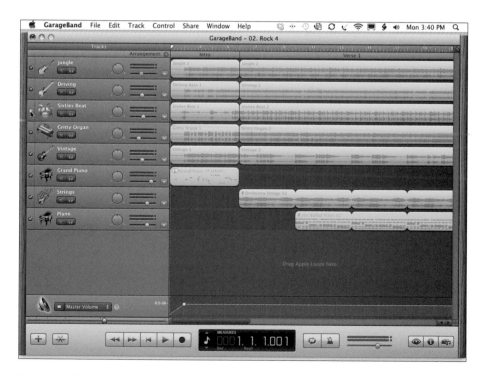

Figure 22-2: Tracks are now adjusted to the match the Groove Track (note the star).

Using the Track Editor

Play a bum note? Can't get that bass line to match up with the drumbeat? Or, maybe you just want to tweak the notes of a particular loop you like. Using the Track Editor, you can view the music in a region as though you're seeing it in a microscope, viewing either the actual notes in a Software Instrument track or the waveform of a Real Instrument track.

To open the Track Editor, select the track to edit and click the Editor button (the one with the scissors) in the lower left corner of the GarageBand window (or choose Control⇨Show Editor). The Track Editor appears below the timeline and Transport buttons and has its own Zoom slider. Depending on the type of track, you see either a note-by-note representation of a Software Instrument or the waveform of a Real Instrument.

With both kinds of tracks, you can move the region forward (to the right) or backward (to the left) in the timeline. You can zoom in to see larger notes or a more detailed waveform by dragging the Track Editor's zoom slider in the lower left corner.

Editing Real Instrument tracks

Your performance with a Real Instrument may be slightly off the beat, but you can use the Track Editor to edit the track in one of these ways:

- **Move a region to adjust its location in the song.** You can move a region precisely in order to line it up with the beat.

- **Adjust the timing with flex time.** You can drag any part of the waveform to change the timing of a note or beat — move, stretch, or shorten individual notes without changing the rest of the recording. As you drag the Flex Time marker (shown in Figure 22-3), the waveform stretches or shortens. You can use this trick to extend guitar riffs or fix a rhythm part that is slightly off.

- **Select, and then cut or copy, a section of a region and paste it into one or more locations in the song.** You can cut or copy part of a Real Instrument region and paste it over another part of a region or in another place in the track. Select a section by dragging a selection rectangle from the center of the Track Editor screen with the crosshair pointer so that it draws a dark gray screen over the waveform.

To copy and paste sections of a Real Instrument region in the Track Editor, select a section and choose Edit⇨Copy to copy the section, Edit⇨Cut to cut it, or Edit⇨Delete to delete it. If you cut or delete a section, it disappears, leaving the rest of the track locked to the timeline at the same point — so that you can delete small sections and not disturb the rest of the performance. To paste a copied or cut section, move the playhead to the new location in the Track Editor and choose Edit⇨Paste.

Dragging the Flex Time marker

Figure 22-3: Stretch or shorten the timing of a Real Instrument performance by using flex time.

Editing Software Instrument tracks

Software Instruments were made for the kind of editing the Track Editor enables you to do. Using the Track Editor, you can change the *actual notes* of a Software Instrument track (performance or loop), including the note's duration, pitch, velocity, and location in the timeline. You can also adjust the pitch and fix the timing of notes automatically.

When you open a Software Instrument region in the Track Editor, it starts out in Piano Roll view, which looks like an old-style piano roll with holes that served as instructions to a player piano. The holes, or notes, are rectangular and precise. The left edge of each note indicates where the note starts in the timeline, and the right edge indicates where it stops. If you use a MIDI keyboard with velocity-sensitive keys, GarageBand also shows each note's *velocity,* which is how hard you pressed the key. Notes played lightly (softly) are light gray, and notes played more forcefully (loudly) are darker.

The following list describes the different ways you can edit the notes in the Track Editor's Piano Roll view:

- **Shorten or lengthen the duration of a note:** Drag the lower right corner of the note to resize it. As you drag, the note's edges snap to the lines in the beat ruler.

- **Change a note's starting point:** Drag the note itself to the left or right, using the timeline grid as a guide.

- **Change a note's pitch:** Drag the note up or down. The vertical position of the note in the grid shows the note's pitch, as it would appear on the simulated piano keyboard displayed along the left edge.

- **Change the note's velocity (from soft to hard):** Drag the Velocity slider from left to right. (You may have to click the triangle to the left of the Track Editor's beat ruler to open the Advanced section of the Track Editor, which offers the Velocity slider.) The note becomes lighter or darker as you drag the slider. Hold down the Shift key while dragging to change it by finer increments.

To change your view of a Software Instrument track to a score, click Score in the upper left corner of the Track Editor pane next to Piano Roll. You can then drag the musical notation itself to edit the track region. You can move notes to adjust their pitch and where they start playing, and change how long they play. For example, you can drag a note left or right to change its position, or up or down to change its pitch.

Using the Master Track Controls

Using a separate track for each instrument and vocal performance is necessary in order to create the best results with your sound. However, controlling all these tracks at once is also necessary. As in the military, you must follow the chain of command for volume controls, and the General is the *master track,* which has controls that define the uppermost volume of all tracks, and turns on the crucial reverb and echo effects for all tracks. You can also control the volume for all tracks with a master track volume curve, and turn on other useful effects that work across all tracks. Every song has a master track — usually hidden, until you explicitly show it.

Controlling the master volume

To control the volume of the overall song and to add effects to the entire song, show the master track by choosing Track➪Show Master Track, which appears at the bottom on the timeline as the last track, with the heading *Master Volume.*

The master Volume slider (to the right of the LCD at the bottom of the GarageBand window) controls the volume for the entire song. To adjust the master volume, setting the upper limit for all tracks, drag the slider to the right to raise it or to the left to lower it.

As the song plays, watch the level meters above the master Volume slider. The level meters show green (see Figure 22-4 in the following section), and then orange, and then red, as the volume grows louder. The red part at the far right end appears only when the volume is at its highest. If the red dots to the right of the meters appear, the volume is way too high — these *clipping indicators* stay on to remind you that clipping occurred in the song (so that you can go back and change the volume). You can reset these indicators by clicking them.

Setting the master volume curve

The master track gives you the opportunity to control the volume with an automation curve for all tracks in a song so that you can be precise and set fade-ins and fade-outs affecting all tracks.

The master volume curve overrides the track volume curve to establish an upper limit for the volume of the individual track. Your settings in each track can still control the volume at levels lower than the limit set the by the master volume curve, but volume can't increase above the master limit.

To define the master track volume curve, follow these steps:

1. **Turn on the Master Volume option by clicking the rectangle next to** *Master Volume* **in the track header.**

2. **Click the horizontal line to establish points in the line, and then drag each point to define a curve, as shown in Figure 22-4.**

    In the figure, the curve is set to fade the volume up from the beginning for all tracks at the same time.

You can set effects for the master track that work on the entire song — including echo, reverb, equalizer, and compressor. Select the master track and click the Track Info (look for the *i*) button to open the Info pane for the master track. The Browse tab in the Info pane offers presets for master track effects — you can choose Rock in the left column, for example, and then choose Live Gig, Rock Hi Fi, or LA Rock.

Click the Edit tab at the top of the Info pane for effects modules such as Echo, Reverb, and Visual EQ. You can set these effects for the master track the same way as you set them for a Real Instrument track. (See Chapter 20 for details on setting effects for tracks.) However, the master track settings establish the upper limit for the same effects used in individual tracks.

Figure 22-4: Set the volume curve for the master track.

Sharing Your Song or Podcast

The multiple-track display of your finished song or podcast episode in GarageBand is impressive, and now that you have the volume just right for all tracks — and you've mixed your tracks to the pan positions you want, you've switched on the effects you want, and mixed all elements properly — you're ready to share your creation with the rest of the world.

If you saved your song project using an iLife preview, as I describe in Chapter 20, your song is already available to other iLife applications, such as iMovie and iDVD. You can transfer a podcast episode project directly to iWeb by choosing Share⇨Send Podcast to iWeb. (For ringtones, see Chapter 21.)

You can transfer your great work of musical genius to iTunes. Follow these steps:

1. Choose Share⇨Send Song to iTunes.

After choosing Share⇨Send Song to iTunes, you have a chance to set the name of an iTunes playlist as well as the artist and composer.

2. **Enter the iTunes playlist name, artist and composer names, and album title, as shown in Figure 22-5.**

   iTunes automatically places the song in its library according to the playlist and album titles you specified. After your song shows up in your vast iTunes library, you can find it with this information or select the playlist.

   You can set all this song information in advance in the My Info pane of the GarageBand Preferences window. Choose GarageBand⇨Preferences and click the My Info tab.

Figure 22-5: Set the song information and compression (if any).

3. **(Optional) Turn on the Compress option (shown in Figure 22-5) to select options for a compressed file.**

   You can choose AAC Encoder or MP3 Encoder from the Compress Using pop-up menu and a quality setting from the Audio Settings pop-up menu. You can turn off the Compress option to export the song at its highest quality (the AIFF format).

4. **Click Share to begin the transfer to iTunes.**

   GarageBand mixes all your tracks automatically, according to the settings you selected, and exports the song as a two-track stereo audio file to iTunes. After your song is in iTunes, you can play it on your Mac and on your iPod or iPhone, and burn a CD with it as well as use it with projects in iPhoto, iMovie, and iDVD.

You can also export a song or podcast episode to a file on your hard drive: Choose Share⇨Export Song to Disk. You can then click the Compress option and choose AAC Encoder or MP3 Encoder from the Compress Using pop-up menu and a quality setting from the Audio Settings pop-up menu, or turn off the Compress option to export the song as an AIFF file.

To export only a piece of a song, such as a sample or a loop, you can set a cycle region first as described in Chapter 21. Normally, GarageBand exports the song from the first measure to the end of the last region in the song, unless a cycle region is turned on. A cycle region can also be useful for extending a song past the last region, so that GarageBand exports the silence at the end. This information is useful if you used any effects that cause reverberations, echoes, or remnants of the "trail off" period that occurs at the end of a song.

Part VI
The Part of Tens

ou've reached the last part, the part you've come to expect in every *For Dummies* book that neatly encapsulates just about all the interesting aspects of this book's topic. Like the compilers of other important lists — David Letterman's Top Ten, the FBI's Ten Most Wanted, the Seven Steps to Heaven, the 12 Gates to the City, the 12 Steps to Recovery, The 13 Question Method, and the Billboard Hot 100 — I take seriously this ritual of putting together the *For Dummies* Part of Tens.

✔ In Chapter 23, I offer the top ten tips not found elsewhere in this book — such as sharing an iPhoto library over a network, adding chapter markers to a video in iMovie, and setting up a MIDI instrument with GarageBand.

✔ Chapter 24 presents ten Web sources for more information about iLife, including where to find answers to typical support questions.

23

Ten iLife Tips

*T*hough this book is filled with tips, I've put in this chapter ten truly handy ones that didn't fit in elsewhere — but can help make your iLife experience a more satisfying one.

Installing the iLife Applications

All Macs come with the iLife applications preinstalled. But if something nasty happens to your hard drive and you need to reinstall them, or if you have older versions of the iLife applications and you want to replace them with the newest versions, you can purchase the iLife package directly from the Apple Store (either online or in the building).

The single-user version of the entire iLife package is $49, and the family pack is $79. The family pack lets you install one copy of the iLife applications on a maximum of five Apple computers at a time, as long as those computers are located in the same household.

The iLife package offers a DVD with the iLife Installer, which — you guessed it — installs iLife for you. The package also includes iPhoto '11, iMovie '11, GarageBand '11, iWeb, and iDVD, along with printed and electronic documentation. The Installer replaces older versions of these applications on the hard drive on which you choose to install. The following steps walk you through the installation:

1. **Slip the DVD into your Mac's SuperDrive, read the introduction, and click Continue.**

   The installer displays more information about the latest release; you can click Print to print this information, Save to save it on your hard drive, Go Back to go back to the introduction, or Continue to continue.

2. **Click Continue and the software licensing agreement appears. Click Agree to go on with the installation.**

   The installer then displays a dialog, shown in Figure 23-1, that you use to select a destination hard drive for the iLife applications. Your hard drives appear as icons along the top. (Only one appears if you have only one drive.)

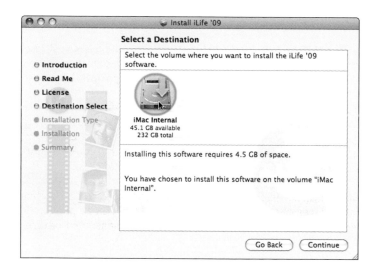

Figure 23-1: Select a destination drive for the iLife applications.

3. **Select a hard drive and click Continue.**

   The Installer displays both the Install and Customize buttons for the standard and custom installations.

4. **Click Install to perform the standard install; if you want to install only some of the iLife applications, click Customize, select which applications to install, and then click Install.**

If you click Customize, you can install, in advance, the iDVD extras — themes from the first five versions of iDVD. You don't have to do it now; when using iDVD, you can select older themes from the Theme Browser's pop-up menu, and iDVD prompts you to download the older themes.

After installing the applications, the Installer opens the Apple registration screen.

5. **Register your iLife applications to get the full benefit of Apple support.**

Updating the iLife Applications

If you enabled the Software Update option in your Mac OS X System Preferences, the system automatically informs you of updates to your Apple software for the Mac, including all iLife applications. All you need to do is select which updates to download and then click the Install button to download them.

To enable the Software Update option, choose System Preferences from the Apple menu, click Software Update, and then click the Check for Updates option and choose Daily, Weekly, or Monthly from the pop-up menu.

Mac OS X can automatically run software update checks in the background and let you know when an update is available; simply click the Download Important Updates Automatically option. iLife updates are considered important! With this option, the system automatically notifies you of an update and gives you the option to install it immediately.

When an update appears, you can choose to install it or click Cancel to install it later. After choosing to install the update, you're prompted for your login password, so make sure that you know the password before trying to install the update.

You can also check for an update of each application from within the application: In iPhoto, choose iPhoto⇨Check for Updates; in iMovie, choose iMovie⇨Check for Updates; in iDVD, choose iDVD⇨Check for Updates; in iWeb, choose iWeb⇨Check for Updates; and in GarageBand, choose GarageBand⇨Check for Updates.

Grouping iPhoto Albums into Folders

If you have diligently read Chapter 3 and created a bunch of photo albums in iPhoto, you might find it helpful to group them into folders. I created a Work folder for all my work-related photo albums, and another, named Band, for all band-related albums.

To create a folder in iPhoto, choose File⇨New Folder. The new folder appears in the Albums section of the iPhoto Source pane; double-click the folder to type over its name with a new one. You can then drag photo albums in the Source pane directly to the folder name to include the albums in the folder. Click the triangle next to the folder name to see the albums in the folder.

You can also drag slideshows and keepsakes such as books, calendars, and cards into folders. All folders, regardless of their contents, appear below the word *Albums* in the Source pane.

Sharing an iPhoto Library on a Network

If you live like *The Jetsons* — with a Mac in every room connected by a wireless or wired network — you can share your iPhoto library, including all photo albums and keepsakes, with other computers in the same network.

To share your iPhoto library with other Macs on a network that are also running the current version of iPhoto, follow these steps:

1. **Choose iPhoto⇨Preferences and then click the Sharing tab.**

   The Sharing pane of preferences appears, offering options for sharing your iPhoto library.

2. **Select the Share My Photos check box.**

3. **Select the Share Entire Library option to include everything (including all albums and keepsakes), or select the Share Selected Albums option and then choose albums and keepsakes to share.**

4. **Enter the name of the iPhoto library in the Shared Name field.**

   Use a name such as Tony Bove's Photos to identify the library. The shared library appears with this name in the Shares section of the iPhoto Source pane on other Macs on the network.

5. **Add a password if you want to restrict access to the shared library.**

Pick a password that you *don't* mind sharing with other users; for example, your name is a good password because you want to share it with people you know. Your ATM PIN is *not* a good password because you should keep it secure. The password restricts access to only those people who know it.

6. **Click the OK button.**

To turn off sharing your iPhoto library, deselect the Share My Photos check box in the Sharing pane.

Before turning off sharing for your library, first notify anyone sharing the library to eject the shared library. Otherwise, iPhoto displays a warning dialog that allows you to continue (and break off the connection to the shared library) or to leave sharing turned on for the moment.

You can access the shared library from other Macs on the network that are running the current version of iPhoto by following these steps:

1. **Choose iPhoto⇨Preferences and then click the Sharing tab.**

   The Sharing pane appears and offers options for sharing content.

2. **Select the Look for Shared Photos check box.**

   The shared libraries appear in the Shares section of the Source pane. After the shared library loads, you can browse its contents. You can also click the triangle next to the shared library in the Source pane to see albums in the shared library.

3. **To unload the shared library, click the tiny Eject button that appears to the right of the shared library name in the Source pane.**

Making Colors Brighter in Photos with iPhoto

You can make the colors in your photos pop without affecting skin tones so that that faces and bodies don't look like they spent too much time on a beach in Cabo San Lucas. To adjust colors without affecting skin tones, select the picture's thumbnail in the iPhoto Viewer pane, click the Edit tool, and then click the Adjust tool on the toolbar. The Adjust window appears on top of the Viewer pane (see Chapter 4). Click the Avoid Saturating Skin Tones option.

You can then adjust the Saturation slider without affecting skin tones. In fact, you can adjust the color level, exposure, contrast, saturation, and other settings. Drag the sliders left or right gradually to make changes, or click anywhere along the slider bar to jump directly to a setting. To improve clarity and enhance detail, experiment with the Definition slider.

If you don't like all the changes you made, you can click the Reset button at the bottom of the Adjust window to reset the sliders to their original settings.

Adding Chapter Markers to a Video in iMovie

You can add chapter markers to a video in iMovie — first choose iMovie➪Preferences and select the Show Advanced Tools option. A set of tiny orange rectangular markers with white arrows shows up in the upper right corner of the Project Browser (refer to Chapter 10). The left marker is for adding comments, and the right marker (with the white arrow) is for adding chapter markers.

To add a chapter marker, drag the marker to any place in the video sequence in the Project Browser. After you drag the marker, an orange-brown label appears above the project clip with a number in it (starting with 1). You can type over the number if you prefer another chapter designation. If you drag the clip elsewhere in your project, the marker moves with the clip.

Drag a chapter marker to the start of your video if you're going to use it with iDVD, in order to avoid the automatic *Beginning* marker that iDVD automatically creates. Placing your own chapter marker in iMovie prevents iDVD from adding one.

Changing iDVD Disc Preferences

iDVD displays an Apple watermark on your disc's video menus, but you can remove the watermark by choosing iDVD➪Preferences, clicking General, and deselecting the Show Apple Logo Watermark option. You can also fade out the audio volume at the end of a menu loop so that it starts the loop with sound again (a good idea if your loop starts with a definitive sound) by selecting the Fade Volume Out at End of Menu Loop option.

To always add the original photos of a slideshow to the DVD-ROM portion of a disc when burning the disc, choose iDVD➪Preferences, click Slideshow, and then select the Always Add Original Photos to DVD-ROM Contents option. (See Chapter 14 for details on burning a disc and adding files to the DVD-ROM portion.) You can also fade out the audio volume at the end of a slideshow by selecting the Fade Volume Out at End of Slideshow option. To show titles and comments in the slideshow, select the Show Titles and Comments option.

Adding an Email Me Button in iWeb

If you need people to e-mail you directly from your Web site, you can add an Email Me button to any page of your Web site in iWeb. When a visitor clicks the button, a new e-mail message appears so that the visitor can type a message and send it.

If you publish your site to MobileMe, the message is addressed, by default, to your MobileMe Mail account. If you publish your site to a different hosting service, the message is addressed using the address on your Me contact card in the OS X Address Book application. (To mark your Address Book contact card as Me, select the name in Address Book and choose Card⇨Make This My Card.)

To modify the Email Me button, follow these steps:

1. **To change the Email Me button to send to another e-mail address, click the name of the Web site in the Sidebar, and in the Site Publishing Settings window that appears, type the address in the Contact Email field.**

2. **To add the Email Me button to a Web page, select the Web page in the Sidebar and choose Insert⇨Button⇨Email Me.**

   The button appears on the page, and you can drag the button to a new location on the page. Blue alignment guides appear as you drag to help you align the button with other page elements.

Setting Up a MIDI Instrument with GarageBand

You don't have to use a USB keyboard for MIDI input to GarageBand, as I describe in Chapter 20 — any MIDI instrument or device can be connected by using an *audio interface,* which is a box that has many ports for connecting various types of audio equipment. The Emagic Multichannel Interface A62m is a good example — it connects to your Mac's USB port and offers six audio inputs (for line-in music, electric instruments, or microphones), two audio outputs (for speakers or preamps), and MIDI input/output (for connecting MIDI devices). Apple provides the Audio MIDI Setup utility, which works with audio devices connected by FireWire, USB, PCMCIA, or PCI.

To use an audio interface with one or more MIDI devices, you must first install the software that comes with the interface. (Follow the manufacturer's instructions.) You can then use Audio MIDI Setup (in Applications/Utilities) to select audio channel input and output devices for your Mac and control volume levels and other characteristics. Follow these steps:

1. **Connect the audio interface to your Mac and connect the MIDI devices to the interface.**

2. **Double-click the Audio MIDI Setup application (in Applications/ Utilities) to open the Audio MIDI Setup window, and then click the MIDI Devices tab.**

   The MIDI devices connected to your computer appear in the Audio MIDI Setup window. If your MIDI devices don't appear, click the Rescan MIDI button on the toolbar along the top of the Audio MIDI Setup window.

3. **Choose New Configuration from the Configuration pop-up menu; in the dialog that appears, name the new configuration and then click OK.**

4. **Double-click the icon for your MIDI interface device and name the device or change its settings.**

   The Properties dialog for your device appears, enabling you to name the device. You can change settings for the MIDI properties and ports for the device.

5. **Click the OK button to finish making changes.**

6. **To add another MIDI device to your new configuration, click Add Device.**

   The Add Device button is on the toolbar along the top of the Audio MIDI Setup window. For each MIDI device connected to your MIDI interface device that you want to include in the configuration, repeat Steps 4 through 6.

7. **When you're finished, choose Audio MIDI Setup➪Quit Audio MIDI Setup.**

Your MIDI device should now be working with GarageBand. To check, choose GarageBand➪Preferences and click the Audio/MIDI button to see the Audio/ MIDI pane, as I describe in Chapter 19.

Video Shooting Techniques

A professional video looks, well, *professional* for many reasons. But you can use iMovie to make a video look as professional as broadcast TV, if you have the skills required to set up shots properly. I can't teach you those skills in this book. However, a lot of books discuss the topic of shooting video properly, and techniques haven't changed with the advent of digital video.

Keep these few tips in mind when shooting video:

✏ **Get the shot.** Quality matters, but nothing matters more than being at the right place at the right time with the lens cap off and your video camera ready to record. Whether you cover important news events or document your baby's first steps, worry about quality later.

✏ **Shoot more than you need.** Before digital, shooting less and frequently using the Pause button was the conventional wisdom. Editing video was hard and expensive, if not impossible, and the audience ended up seeing everything — even the lousy footage. Digital video reverses this logic: Shoot more than you need and cut the video you don't need.

✏ **The sound is better with a carefully placed microphone.** Camcorders have microphones built into them, but because you're holding the camcorder, what you hear is mostly what is right around you (including your own heavy breathing, if you're not careful). That faraway sound you hear in a home video interview sounds amateurish — and it happens whenever the subject is too far away from the microphone. Use a separate microphone (even a clip-on lavaliere microphone works well with interview subjects) and place it appropriately to hear what you want to hear in the video. Many camcorder models allow you to connect external microphones for audio recording.

✏ **Don't pan or zoom too much while shooting.** Camcorders have wonderful pan and zoom features, but refrain from using them except before a shot. Zooming into a scene during a shot can make viewers uncomfortable, even nauseous (unless, of course, you're trying to create that effect).

✏ **Keep the camcorder steady while shooting.** An unsteady image is probably the most distinguishing characteristic that separates home videos from professional ones. iMovie can stabilize scenes but is somewhat limited when it comes to fixing scenes with movement. The trick is to keep the camcorder steady; using a tripod, if possible, helps avoid the problem. Some camcorders offer image stabilization, which smoothes out the shakes and jiggles that show up when your camcorder is unsteady. If you can't use a tripod, use anything — a table, a window ledge, a tree stump, a body part — or at least lean against something solid to steady yourself.

✏ **Try to use the best lighting conditions.** You've heard about directors canceling movie shots because the camera operator complained that the lighting wasn't right. Good lighting is extremely important, as with still-image photography. Video captures an even smaller range of light and darkness than film, and images sometimes lack depth. (Film, of course, is much higher in resolution.) Videographers and cinematographers spend years developing lighting skills, but you can read books to learn the basic techniques.

Ten (Plus) Online Resources

*T*he Internet offers a ton of information related to the iLife applications. I was told to limit this chapter to ten (because it's a chapter in The Part of Tens), but I couldn't stop — so I give you a few more than ten sites. From any of these sites you can follow links to even more information.

Apple

Apple has a lot of information and support for iLife users and Mac developers. Because they're all under the Apple roof, I list the Apple sites as just one resource.

✔ **The iLife Web site (**www.apple.com/ilife**):** The Apple iLife minisite provides a wealth of information about the iLife applications. You can follow links to the individual product pages that are miniature Web sites of their own, with video tutorials, instruction manuals, and extras and add-ons for downloading.

✔ **The Apple support site (**www.apple.com/support**):** To solve problems with any Apple product, visit the Apple support site. You can browse the support sections for all Apple products, read popular discussions and the latest support news, post queries on bulletin boards to get help from others, and connect to the software download server. You can even find and print manuals for Apple products (as if you need a manual now that you have this book!).

- **Apple Photo Services** (www.apple.com/support/photoservices): If you order photo books, calendars, or cards using iPhoto (as I describe in Chapter 7), you can check your order status and view delivery times, as well as change or cancel orders, at the Photo Services minisite. All your payment options and account details are explained there. You can even watch video tutorials on preparing photo books with iPhoto.

- **Apple training and certification** (http://training.apple.com/certification/associate?cmp): Apple Certified Associate certifications are designed for professionals, educators, and students to validate their skills in iLife (and iWork, the Apple application for documents, spreadsheets, and presentations). As an Apple Certified Associate, you can differentiate yourself to schools, potential employers, and prospective clients and gain a competitive edge in the ever-changing job market.

- **Apple Developer connection** (http://developer.apple.com): The Apple Developer connection site is for anyone who feels the need to push the envelope by developing products that work with other Apple products. You can join the iOS Developer Program to develop applications for the iPad, iPhone, and iPod touch, and join the Mac Developer Program to develop applications for Mac OS X.

Version Tracker

http://download.cnet.com/mac

You can get loads of free and low-price commercial software by visiting Version Tracker, an accurate and up-to-date source of software updates. Looking for video or sound converters? Widgets for iWeb? Camera controllers? This site is a helpful place to start.

Hardcore iLife Users

www.myapplespace.com/group/hardcoreilifeusers

This group within AppleSpace (a social network) is for hardcore iLife users — people who use the iLife applications every day or make a living with them. Join to discuss issues and share experiences.

Pro Studio Supply

www.prostudiousa.com

Pro Studio Supply is the world's oldest and largest supplier of photographic items for the professional and advanced amateur iPhoto photographer. The site includes many types of cameras and lighting equipment, in addition to backgrounds, backdrops, and props.

B&H Photo: The Professional's Source

www.bhphotovideo.com

B&H offers professional and consumer video cameras, including used equipment. You can find excellent deals on camcorders of all types to use with iMovie.

DVDThemePak

www.dvdthemepak.com

DVDThemePak offers both free and commercial themes for iDVD. All themes are available in widescreen and standard formats.

The List: The Definitive Internet Services Buyer's Guide

http://isp.thelist.com

Need a place to host your iWeb site? The List is a resource for people looking for an Internet service provider (ISP). You can search by location or check out ISP deals.

GarageBand and Musician Resources

When you need help or hardware for your GarageBand project, or just want to explore music-making, check out the following resources:

- **The Garage Door** (www.thegaragedoor.com): The Garage Door offers all things GarageBand — tips, tricks, video tutorials, and descriptions of the best JamPacks (loops).

- **Musician's Friend** (www.musiciansfriend.com): This site may well be the largest online music-gear shop in the world, and you can find good deals on instruments and equipment.

- **GarageBand.com** (www.garageband.com): The site that licensed its name to Apple for GarageBand is now operated by iLike, a social music-discovery service and the dominant music application on the Bebo, Facebook, Google, hi5, and Orkut platforms. The site offers a range of free and paid services to musicians, such as gig promotion and advice from industry experts.

- **iCompositions** (www.icompositions.com): Do you have some grooves to share? This site hosts GarageBand music submitted by members who join the community, as well as discussion groups about GarageBand.

- **Rockument** (www.rockument.com): The Rockument Channel, hosted by me (Tony Bove), offers podcasts that explore the roots of rock music with licensed rare and historical tunes and performances. Rockument also hosts the *Flying Other Brothers* podcast of live shows. (It goes without saying that I used GarageBand to create these podcasts.) You can find both Rockument and the *Flying Other Brothers* in the podcast section of the iTunes Store.

TonyBove.com

www.tonybove.com

At my own site, I offer a free tips section loaded with tips and techniques for readers, including bonus material from this book and links to other books and to a variety of Web sites and blogs. I also offer the *Tony's Tips for iPhone Users Manual* app for your iPhone, and *Bove's Blips,* a blog about innovation and future personal technologies. The *Tony's Accessories* online shop offers a convenient way for you to buy the items I write about.

Index